Literature for Little Learners

Table of Contents

Books About the Basics

Books About People

Books About Places

My Grandma Is Wonderful

A tree grows strong and tall
to give gifts to one and all.

shade
wood
fruit
leaves to play in
paper   pretty colors

About This Book

Get your youngsters involved in the reading process with the fun and educational activities in *Literature for Little Learners!* We've created one comprehensive resource combining the best of the five previously published books from the Booktime! series (*Basics, Animals, Feelings, People,* and *Places*). In this literature-rich book, you'll find 90 units that each feature a favorite picture book for reading aloud and your choice of activities that tie to the book, ranging from math and science to art and cooking.

Engaging Activities

The 450 activities in *Literature for Little Learners* include related songs, curriculum ideas, art projects, movement suggestions, and recipes.

Storytime Song

Invite your little ones to storytime with a catchy tune that gives a clue about the book you are about to share. Now skip to my Lou, and I'll share a book with you!

Learning Links

Each Learning Links activity ties to one of your curriculum areas. The title gives you the skill that's covered and the art will help you see what the product will be! Math, science, social studies, and language arts—Learning Links has it all!

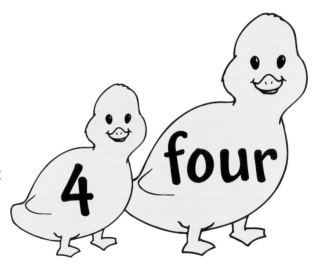

Art Smarts

Art and literature? You bet! Youngsters love showing what they know about a story—especially when it involves drawing, coloring, painting, and other fun art activities. Whether it's making alliterative circus performers in *Star of the Circus* or thumbprint frogs in *Jump, Frog, Jump!,* Art Smarts is the place to release your children's creative energy!

Purposeful Play

Play has never been so fun and educational than with Purposeful Play! The activities in this section involve fine- and/or gross-motor movement. So get students ready to "chicka chicka bounce bounce" the alphabet after hearing *Chicka Chicka Boom Boom* or play a gorilla game after hearing *Good Night, Gorilla!*

Storybook Café

Recipes for yummy treats—that's what you'll find in Storybook Café! Make them in advance for a tasty storytime snack or to prompt prior knowledge, or allow your little ones to help make their own. Any way you stack it, connecting a good book with a savory snack has never been so tasty!

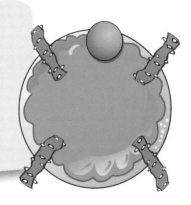

Theme Sections

Literature for Little Learners is divided into five sections based on early childhood themes. Each section is color coded and has a unique icon so you can find the sections you need quickly and easily! The sections are as follows:

 The Basics

 Animals

 Feelings

 **People**

Places

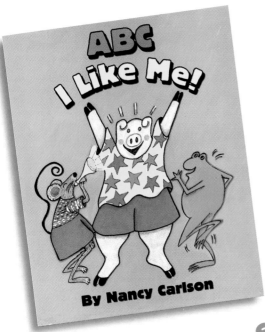

By Nancy Carlson

ABC: I Like Me!

Written and illustrated by Nancy Carlson

Join a cast of cheerful characters as they share ways in which they feel good about themselves.

Storytime Song

Your little ones will feel good when you invite them to storytime with this song sung to the tune of "This Old Man."

A, B, C, I like me.
I'm the best that I can be.
I am unique, from *A* to *Z*.
Come and hear all about me!

A, B, C, I like me.
I'm sure you will all agree
That reading's fun from *A* to *Z*.
Come and read this book with me!

(Repeat this likable tune until all your youngsters have joined together.)

Once your little letter lovers are gathered together, read aloud *ABC: I Like Me!*

Learning Links

Beginning-Letter Link

Boost students' self-esteem with this A+ idea. Have each child write the first letter of her name on a sheet of construction paper. Then have her dictate words or phrases with the same beginning letter to describe herself—her personality, looks, and likes. (A more advanced child might write her first name vertically on her paper and then list a word/phrase for each letter.) Invite her to decorate her paper using a variety of art supplies. During group time, ask each child to share her special picture with the class. Then set the papers aside to use with "All-About-Me T-Shirt" on page 7.

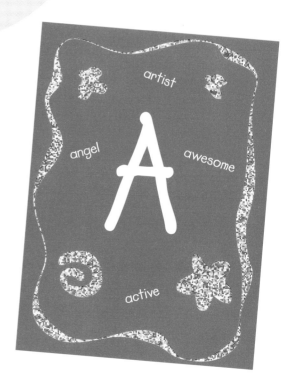

Art Smarts

All-About-Me T-Shirt

Each child can model his great qualities with this boast-about-me T-shirt! To make a sleeveless paper T-shirt, cut out a neck hole and armholes from a large paper bag as shown. Paint the shirt with tempera paint. After the paint dries, cut the shirt open along the back seam to make it easier to put on and remove. Have each child glue his art from "Beginning-Letter Link" (page 6) onto the front of his T-shirt. Invite him to embellish his shirt with additional craft items and

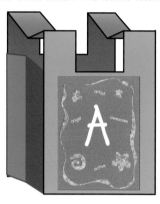

designs as desired. Later divide your class into small groups; then have students in each group model their shirts in a class fashion show. During the show, photograph each child in his designer T-shirt; then display the photos collage-style with the title "I Like Me!"

Purposeful Play

Daily Dressup

Set up this I Like Me vanity in your dramatic-play center. Place a table with dress-up props next to a full-length mirror. (Refer to the book for prop ideas.) Also provide a box of assorted dress-up clothes nearby. Place the book near the mirror. Each day mount a letter cutout (or several cutouts) onto the mirror. To use, the child finds the page in the book that corresponds to the displayed letter. Then she dresses up and/or uses props to role-play different characteristics, qualities, or talents beginning with that letter. Afterward, invite her to illustrate herself in one of her dress-up roles.

Storybook Café

Uniquely Me Letter Cookie

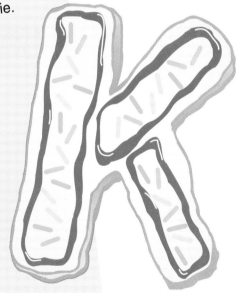

Invite each child to celebrate his uniqueness with a personalized cookie. Mmm! It's "ME-licious!"

Supplies:
letter-shaped cookie cutters
cookie sheet
oven
plastic knives
napkins

Ingredients:
refrigerated cookie dough
assorted tubes of decorating gel
assorted cookie decorations, such as sprinkles, confetti stars, and colored sugar
chocolate and butterscotch chips
M&M's mini baking bits

To make one letter cookie:
1. Cut a cookie dough letter that matches the first letter of your first name.
2. Bake cookie according to package directions. Allow cookie to cool.
3. Use choice of items to decorate cookie with personal flair.
4. Enjoy!

Brown Rabbit's Shape Book

Written and illustrated by Alan Baker

Brown Rabbit receives a triangle-covered package with a rectangular card attached. And so his adventure begins as he discovers one shape surprise after another.

Storytime Song

Sing this song to the tune of "Pop! Goes the Weasel" to introduce your class to the story.

Circles, squares, and rectangles,
Ovals, and triangles
Came in Rabbit's special gift
Wrapped in red triangles.

Oh, won't you join me as we read
About a little rabbit
Who opened up a special box.
Out came shape presents!

(Repeat until all your little ones have hopped into a huddle.)

Once your little bunnies have joined together, share this shape-filled tale.

Learning Links

Shape Surprises

Brown Rabbit's shape surprises will prompt youngsters to discover shapes all around. To prepare, collect a set of identical lidded gift boxes. Or cover a set of same-size boxes with identical gift wrap. Place a different shape cutout into each box and put the lid on it. Seat children in a circle; then give each box to a different child. Have the children pass the boxes around the circle while you play music. When you stop the music, instruct the children to stop passing the boxes. In turn, ask each child with a box to open it and remove the shape. Have her name the shape and then find an item in the classroom that corresponds to her shape. After all the shapes have been identified, return each one to its box, replace the lid, and start the music for another round of play.

Shape Prints

Invite youngsters to make these surprise gifts to show off their shape knowledge. To prepare, provide several trays of paint colors and an assortment of shape cutters, small gift box lids, plastic lids, and lids from canisters (such as oval or hexagonal tin canisters). Invite each child to use the lids provided to print colorful shapes onto a 9" x 12" piece of black construction paper. After the paint dries, have him place a 9" x 12" piece of gift wrap atop the black paper and staple the two sheets together along the top edge to create a lid that opens and closes. Invite him to attach a label and a bow to the gift wrap. Then have him present his surprise gift to a family member. Encourage him to name each shape inside his gift when the recipient opens the lid. It's a shape surprise!

Listen to Rabbit

With a twitch of your whiskers and a twist on the words, the game of Duck, Duck, Goose is easily converted into this listening game. To begin, seat students in a circle; then choose one child to be Rabbit. To play, Rabbit circles the seated children. He gently taps each child on the head on passing and says a color word. When he says a shape word, the tapped child jumps up and quickly follows Rabbit around the circle. If Rabbit reaches the space without getting caught, he is safe! Then the child takes on the role of Rabbit and the game continues in the same manner. If Rabbit gets caught, he must continue his role.

Brown Bunny Bites

How children love Brown Rabbit and his curiosity! But they'll also love these bunnies—oh, so chocolatey!

Supplies:
plastic knives
napkin

Ingredients for one child:
1 oval cookie (such as a Pepperidge Farm Milano cookie)
chocolate frosting
chocolate sprinkles
2 chocolate graham sticks
2 brown M&M's minis candies
tube of black decorating gel

To make a brown bunny bite:
1. Spread chocolate frosting on the cookie.
2. Sprinkle chocolate sprinkles onto the frosting to represent bunny fur.
3. Put on graham stick ears and M&M's minis candies eyes, and add black gel dot pupils.
4. Add nose, mouth, and whiskers using decorating gel.
5. Nibble, nibble, nibble.

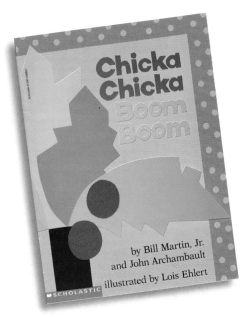

Chicka Chicka Boom Boom

By Bill Martin Jr. and John Archambault
Illustrated by Lois Ehlert

To the cadence of skip-hopping rhymes, all the playful lowercase letters race to the top of a coconut tree. But at the top, the tree flops, the letters drop, and the worried uppercase letters rush to dust them off!

Storytime Song

Challenge youngsters' listening skills as you call them to story-time with this song sung to the tune of "The Farmer in the Dell."

The letters raced up a tree.
The letters raced up a tree.
They reached the top,
And then, ker-plop!
What happened to the [*D*]?

(Repeat the song, replacing the letter D *with a different rhyming letter each time—such as* E, G, P, T, V, *or* Z—*until all your little ones have joined together.)*

Once your little listeners are ready, read aloud *Chicka Chicka Boom Boom.*

Learning Links

A to Z Matchup

Youngsters will find *A* through *Z* on this coconut tree. To create this interactive display, attach a large paper coconut tree to a bulletin board. Insert 26 pushpins along the trunk and in the top of the tree. Then die-cut an uppercase and lowercase set of laminated letters. Punch a hole near the top of each letter and insert an ornament hanger. Hang each lowercase letter from a separate pushpin. Then distribute the uppercase letters to students. In turn, have each child hang her letter with the corre-sponding lowercase letter. Or have her remove the corresponding letter from the tree. Later, invite students to the display to practice letter matching and sequencing skills and to create their own alphabet activities.

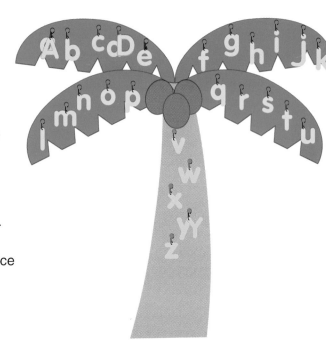

Art Smarts

Nutty Memory Game

Reinforce letter skills and enhance memory with this "coco-nutty" game! Invite students to help you make a complete set of upper- and lowercase coconut letters. To make a set of coconut letters, a child traces a large circle on brown construction paper twice. Then he traces a smaller circle twice onto white paper. He cuts out the circles; then stamps an uppercase letter on one white circle and the corresponding lowercase letter on the other. Next, he glues each white circle onto a brown circle (letter side up) so that it resembles the inside of a coconut half. Once students complete their letters, divide them into small groups to use their coconut creations in a memory game. To play, students randomly place their coconut halves facedown. Then each player takes a turn to try to match a set of letters. The game ends when all the coconut halves are matched. Keep these coconut creations in a center for more letter-matching fun, or staple the matching halves together along one edge and display them on a classroom wall.

Purposeful Play

Bouncing Beginning Sounds

Chicka chicka bounce bounce your little ones into letter skills practice. Cut a set of all 26 letters from tagboard; back each letter with the hook side of a Velcro sticky dot. Put a tennis ball in a center along with the letters. During group time, examine a coconut with your class. Then tell students that the ball in this game will represent a coconut. To play, invite two children to the center. One child sticks a letter on a "coconut" and then bounces it to his partner across the playing area. That child removes and names the letter. He sticks it on a flannelboard and then names an item beginning with the letter. After all the letters are on the flannelboard, the partners switch roles to continue play.

Storybook Café

ABC Coconut Tree

"Chicka chicka boom boom! Will there be enough room?" This filling coconut tree snack is created from an interesting blend of children's "flavor-ites."

Supplies:
waxed paper
plastic knives

Ingredients for each child:
pretzel rod
cream cheese
Alpha-Bits cereal
4 pear wedges
3 pieces of Cocoa Puffs cereal

To make one coconut tree:
1. Spread cream cheese on pretzel rod tree trunk.
2. On waxed paper, position pear wedges at top of trunk to represent tree fronds.
3. Add Cocoa Puffs cereal coconuts.
4. Put several letters on tree trunk.
5. Eat tree piece by piece from top to bottom.

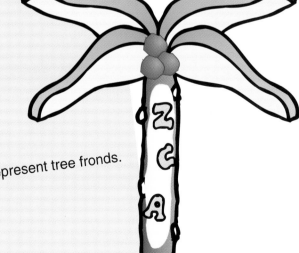

11

Clap Your Hands

Written and illustrated by Lorinda Bryan Cauley

Rhythmic lyrics and energetic illustrations invite readers to clap, hop, count, and fly right along with the lively characters in this high-spirited book.

Storytime Song

Move your class into storytime with this action-packed song sung to the tune of "Head and Shoulders."

Shake your shoulders.	Blink your eyelids.	Let's jump up and down.
Stretch your arms.	Bend your knees.	Spin around and round and round.
Tap your toes.	Touch your nose.	It's storytime now!
		Everyone, please sit down.

Once your youngsters have settled in, read aloud *Clap Your Hands*—but don't expect students to sit still for long! After several readings, challenge their rhyming skills by omitting the last word on each two-page spread and inviting students to fill in the missing rhyme before they perform the actions.

Rhyming Action

Set youngsters' rhyming skills into action with this movement activity. To begin, collect a class quantity of objects or pictures to create several rhyming sets. For example, you might gather items or pictures for a block, sock, and rock. Give each child an item. Explain that you will name an item from a rhyme set. The child with that item calls out an action, such as, "Jump around," or, "Flap your arms." Each child with a corresponding rhyming item performs the action. Periodically signal students to exchange their items; then continue play. Let's get moving!

Handy Rhyming Prints

Get ready to rhyme with this creative handprint art. Spread a length of bulletin board paper on the floor; then spread newspaper around its perimeter. Place cookie sheets with different paint colors on the newspaper. To create handprints, ask each child to press her palms into a paint tray; then have her make a pair of handprints on the paper. When she finishes, have her wash and dry her hands. After the paint dries, have each student dictate a pair of rhyming words. Use a marker to write the rhyme pair on the student's handprints. Hang this colorful rhyme art on a classroom wall for some "hand-y" reinforcement.

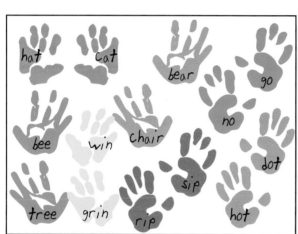

Books About the Basics

Copycat Parade

Your little ones will clap their hands for this dress-up, copycat parade! Stock your dramatic-play center with a wide assortment of wacky dress-up clothes and accessories. To begin, point out the colorful costumes worn by the book characters. Then invite one small group at a time to visit the center. Have each child create his own funny ensemble to wear. Then line youngsters up for a copycat parade. Invite the line leader to model a walk style or movement for the group to imitate as it parades around the classroom. Lead the rest of the class in a rhythmic hand-clapping accompaniment. Then appoint a different leader and send the group around again. Repeat this procedure until each child has had a turn to lead the group; then send another group to the center for some dress-up fun.

Tummy Ticklers

Here's a tongue-tingling, tummy-tickling snack that all your youngsters will enjoy.

Supplies:
snack-size zippered plastic bags
small scoops

Ingredients:
chocolate chips
small crackers
M&M's Minis candies
mini pretzels
Froot Loops cereal

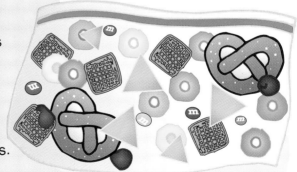

To make one tummy tickler:
1. Put a scoop of each desired ingredient in a bag.
2. Zip the bag and shake it up to mix the ingredients.
3. Munch. Crunch. Giggle, giggle, giggle!

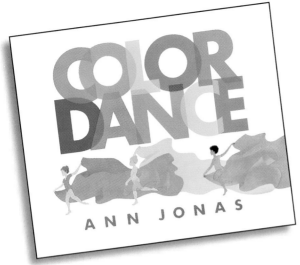

Color Dance

Written and illustrated by Ann Jonas

A delightful mix of movement and color dances off the pages of this book as four performers create a rainbow of colors with their scarves. Encore!

Storytime Song

Sing this colorful song to the tune of "London Bridge" as you invite youngsters to storytime.

> Mix blue and yellow to make green,
> To make green, to make green.
> Mix blue and yellow to make green,
> In our color dance.
>
> *(Repeat the song, replacing the color words each time with combinations that create different colors, such as "Mix red and yellow to make orange.")*

Once your colorful little ones have joined together, ask them to listen to the story to discover new colors that can be created from different color combinations.

Learning Links

Combining Colors

Invite youngsters to create their own color combinations with this experiment. To prepare, fill each of three quart-size freezer bags one-third full of water. Add red, blue, or yellow food coloring to each bag. Zip the bag, squeezing out as much air as possible; then seal the top of each bag with clear packaging tape. Lay the bags flat on a large sheet of white paper. Ask each child in a small group to predict which new color can be created by combining two of the color bags. After he guesses, invite him to overlap the two color bags to check his answer. Then sing the song from "Storytime Song," filling in the appropriate colors in the song and changing the last line to "With our color bags." Afterward, have each child use primary crayon colors to illustrate the results of his experiment. Encourage him to share his discoveries with his family.

Art Smarts

Drip Drop Scarf

Create colorful dance scarves with this crafty idea. Half-fill three clear plastic cups with water. Add red, blue, or yellow food coloring to each cup. (The more drops you add, the darker the water color.) Put an eyedropper in each cup. To make a scarf, a child drops different water colors onto a thick white paper towel to mix and create new colors. After the towel dries, cut it in half lengthwise and tape the halves together to make a long, narrow scarf. Invite students to use their color scarves with "Color Dance Chant."

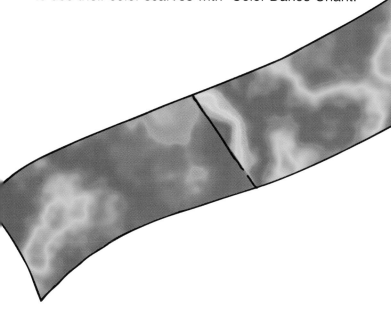

Purposeful Play

Color Dance Chant

Books About the Basics

Everyone's a star in this special color dance. To prepare, cut out a class supply of large circles from red, blue, yellow, green, orange, and purple construction paper. Tape the colors onto the floor to form a large ring. Give each child the scarf she made from "Drip Drop Scarf." Then have her stand on a color. To begin, chant "[Red and yellow], here's your chance. Step inside and do a color dance!" The children standing on the named colors step inside the ring and wave their scarves as they dance to a selection of lively music. The remaining children circle around the colors while the music plays. When you stop the music, repeat the chant using two different colors. The children on the named colors then enter the ring while the former dancers move to a color circle. Continue the dance rounds in this fashion as student interest and energy dictates.

Storybook Café

Tango Toast

It takes two to do the tango toast—two colors, that is! When youngsters practice their color-combination skills on this snack, they'll dance with delight over the tasty results.

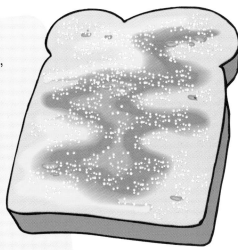

Supplies:
3 basting brushes
paper plates
toaster oven

Ingredients:
white bread
3 cups of milk, each tinted with either red, blue, or yellow food coloring
sugar

To make one slice of tango toast:
1. Paint a design with two milk colors on a slice of bread.
2. Sprinkle sugar onto bread.
3. Toast bread in oven.
4. Enjoy tasty tango toast!

Color Zoo

Written and illustrated by Lois Ehlert

Vivid colors and an assortment of shapes combine to create a zoo full of interesting creatures and features.

Storytime Song

Sing this song to the tune of "Going to the Zoo" to gather youngsters for a group sharing of this colorful book.

Let's all go to a zoo full of colors,
A zoo full of colors,
A zoo full of colors.
Let's all go to a zoo full of colors
And learn all about our shapes.

(Repeat until all your little zoo lovers are ready to listen.)

Once everyone has settled down, read aloud *Color Zoo*.

 Learning Links

I Spy Shapes

Shape up your youngsters' views of their world with these shape viewers. To make the viewers, draw a number of large shapes on poster board. Cut out the shapes. Next, cut out a smaller window of the same shape from each large cutout to create a shape viewer. Discard the small cutouts. Give a viewer to each child in a small group. Have one child at a time peer through the opening in her viewer to search for a shape that matches her viewer. Then instruct her to describe her discovery without actually naming it. For example, a child using a rectangle viewer might describe a book by saying, "I spy a rectangle that I like to read." Encourage the other group members to try to guess the child's discovery. Then have youngsters switch viewers for the next round of play.

Art Smarts

"Grrreat" Animal Mask!

Bring the color zoo to life with these shapely animal masks. To begin, give each child a paper plate. Have him draw or trace a shape in the center of his plate. Then help the child cut out the shape to create a mask opening. Instruct him to glue colorful shape cutouts onto his mask to make an animal. Encourage him to refer to the book for inspiration. Attach a wide craft stick to each child's mask. Then line up and parade your little zoo creatures around the school for other classes to enjoy. Later invite youngsters to use their masks in their dramatic-play activities.

Purposeful Play

Animal Action

Give students' color and shape skills a spin with this zany zoo game. To prepare, cut out each of four different shapes from three construction paper colors and laminate them. Then cut out small versions of the same color shapes to use on a spinner board. To make the board, glue the shapes onto a poster board square; then loosely attach a paper clip spinner to the board with a brad. Arrange the laminated shapes on the floor; then place a toy zoo animal (or picture of a zoo animal) on each one. To play, a child spins a color shape on the board. He moves to the corresponding shape on the floor and then pantomimes the actions and sounds of the animal on the shape. Periodically move the animals to different shapes; then continue play. My, my, it's a zoo in here!

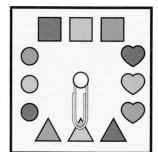

Books About the Basics

Storybook Café

Tasty Shapes

These cookie shapes will help reinforce youngsters' shape knowledge—and they make tasty snacks, too!

Supplies:
waxed paper
shape cutters
cookie sheet
oven
napkins

Ingredients:
refrigerated sugar cookie dough
tube of icing

To make a tasty shape:
1. Form a cookie dough patty on waxed paper and then cut a shape from the patty.
2. Bake the cookie according to the package directions; then allow it to cool.
3. Trace the edge of the cookie shape with icing. Draw consecutively smaller icing shapes inside the large one.
4. Get ready. Get set. Eat!

Eating the Alphabet:
Fruits and Vegetables From A to Z

By Lois Ehlert

Brilliant illustrations invite readers to eat their way through the fresh and healthful foods in this alphabet book.

Storytime Song

Gather youngsters to storytime with this song sung to the tune of "Twinkle, Twinkle, Little Star."

A, B, C, D, E, F, G,
Share this yummy book with me.
Take a look. You will see
Fruits and veggies—A to Z.
A, B, C, D, E, F, G,
Share this yummy book with me!

(Repeat until your youngsters have gathered to listen.)

Once your little fruit and veggie lovers are settled, read aloud *Eating the Alphabet: Fruits and Vegetables From A to Z.*

Learning Links
Letter Formation Fun

Let produce made from play dough lead students to practicing letter formation. Place several copies of the book in the play dough center along with rolling pins and plastic knives. Provide page protectors or pieces of laminating film. Invite a few children to the center at a time. Encourage them to create play dough foods, referring to the book for examples. If desired, cover a page with a page protector; then have the child create an identical play dough model right on top of the food picture. For each food creation, have the child form a corresponding play dough letter. If desired, allow the play dough foods to dry thoroughly; then use them in the housekeeping area for dramatic-play activities.

Printed Placemats

Make these placemats to use at snacktime during your book-study unit. Provide an assortment of produce to use for fruit and vegetable prints. For instance, you might include potato, apple, pear, and bell pepper halves; cucumbers and carrots cut in half lengthwise; corn on the cob; broccoli florets; and beans. Also provide a set of alphabet sponge painters. To make a placemat, a child decorates a large sheet of construction paper with paint prints of the produce of

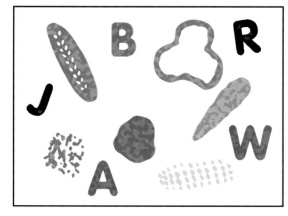

her choice. Then, using the alphabet sponge painters, she adds letters at random. Laminate each child's placemat for durability. At the end of your book study, send each child home with her placemat to tell her family how she created each print.

Beginning Sound Servers

Fresh and wholesome produce are the menu items at the Alphabet Café! To set up, gather an assortment of real and play produce; then label each of several trays with a different letter (as dictated by the available foods). To use, a student waiter places each food item on the tray labeled with the corresponding beginning letter. The waiter then serves the customers—other students—their food choices from the different trays, each time announcing the food being served and its beginning letter. At the end of the pretend meal, a new waiter prepares the trays for the next meal.

Veggie Letter Delights

With eye appeal and flavor too, these veggie delights are good for you!

Supplies:
letter-shaped cookie cutters
napkins

Ingredients for each child:
slice of bread
cream cheese spread
diced vegetables, such as cucumbers, yellow squash, red cabbage, carrots, tomatoes, and green peppers

To make one veggie letter delight:
1. Spread a layer of cream cheese on slice of bread.
2. Select letter cutter; then press onto bread to make a letter imprint.
3. Sprinkle choice of diced vegetables onto letter shape.
4. A, B, C! Good for me!

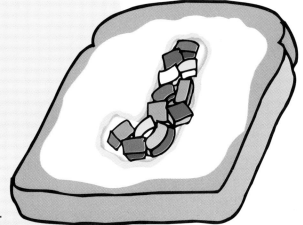

Every Buddy Counts

By Stuart J. Murphy
Illustrated by Fiona Dunbar

When a young girl feels lonely and sad, she counts on her buddies to make her cheery and glad.

Storytime Song

Gather youngsters for storytime with this song sung to the tune of "Twinkle, Twinkle, Little Star."

I have buddies here and there.
I have buddies everywhere.
At home, at school, where e'er I go,
My pets, my toys, in books I know,
I have buddies here and there.
I have buddies everywhere!

(Repeat until all your little ones have joined together.)

Read aloud *Every Buddy Counts,* and then invite each child to tell one thing about his own buddies.

Counting Buddies

This story is sure to prompt warm thoughts of buddies near and far. Invite each child to illustrate her favorite buddies on a large sheet of paper. Students might draw pictures of friends, family members, pets, or toy animals. Write each child's dictation about her drawing; then help her count her buddies and label her paper with the corresponding numeral. During group time, ask each child to share her picture with the class. Display the pictures on a wall or bulletin board titled after the book.

Art Smarts
Shining Stars

When students make this starry scene, they'll discover just how sweet it is to have stargazing buddies! To prepare, cut out several tagboard star tracers in different sizes. Invite each child to trace and cut out a tagboard star. Instruct him to paint his cutout and then sprinkle the wet paint with glitter. After the paint dries, hang the stars overhead. At the beginning of naptime, encourage some stargazing with this idea. Shine a flashlight on one child at a time. Ask the child to recite the first two lines of "Twinkle, Twinkle, Little Star"; then hand him the flashlight and invite him to shine it on one star in the classroom sky. Ask him to describe the star; for instance, he might describe a big red star or a little shiny star. After several of your youngsters have had a turn to stargaze, encourage your little ones to continue their stargazing silently as they drift into peaceful rest.

Purposeful Play
Buddy Hoop

Round up some giggling buddy groups with this game. To play, three students are each given a large plastic hoop. On a signal, each child "captures" a buddy with her hoop. Then students sing the song below. Afterward, the captured child calls a buddy to join her in the hoop. The song is repeated, using the plural of "buddy." The children in the hoop cooperatively agree on which buddy to call next. Continue the game until the hoops are too full of giggling, ticklish buddies to hold any more. Count the number of buddies in each hoop; then give the hoops to three different children to play again.

(sung to the tune of "The Farmer in the Dell")

I have my buddy here.
I have my buddy here.
Heigh-ho! The derry-o!
I have my buddy here.

Storybook Café
Buddy Bear Biscuits

Count on this "bear-y" delicious buddy to give youngsters a tasty treat.

Supplies:
paper plates
plastic knives
toaster oven

Ingredients for each child:
refrigerator biscuit
chocolate chips
cinnamon sugar
black cake-decorating gel

To make one buddy bear biscuit:
1. Cut the biscuit in half; then cut one biscuit half in half again.
2. Shape each biscuit section into a patty. Put the patties together in the shape of a bear's head.
3. Sprinkle cinnamon sugar on the bear.
4. Press chocolate chip eyes and nose onto the bear's face.
5. Bake according to the directions on the biscuit package.
6. Allow biscuits to cool; then add gel mouth.

Exactly the Opposite

Written and photo-illustrated by Tana Hoban

Imaginative photo-illustrations of outdoor scenes prompt readers to explore their opposites knowledge.

Storytime Song

Interest your class in the book with this song sung to the tune of "Ring Around the Rosie."

Let's look at the opposite—
Exactly the opposite.
[Hot and cold]
Are opposites.
Yes, they are!

(Using the book as a reference, name a different opposites pair, such as empty-full or left-right, each time you repeat the song.)

After sharing each two-page spread in the book, encourage students to generate as many opposites labels as possible for each picture pair.

Learning Links

Opposite Pairs Booklet

Picture plenty of learning opportunities for youngsters as they create this photo-illustrated class book about opposites! To begin, divide your class into student pairs and then assign each pair different opposites, such as in-out, hot-cold, or empty-full. Ask the partners to find and arrange items to represent their assigned opposites. For example, they might place a teddy bear *in* a box and then position it *out* of the box. Take a picture of each arrangement for the opposites concept. Then glue each photo pair onto a separate sheet of construction paper. Label the page with the opposites represented by the pictures; then bind all the pages between two construction paper covers. Title the front cover "Exactly the Opposite."

in   out

Art Smarts — Animal Flips

Heads or tails? When students create these animal pictures, they won't need to make a choice—they'll get both! Have each child select a toy animal to use as a model for her drawing. Instruct her to illustrate the front of the animal on a sheet of paper. Then have her flip her paper over (and turn the animal around) and draw the back of the animal. Invite the child to decorate both of her drawings with assorted craft items, such as wiggle eye stickers, pom-poms, and yarn; then label both sides of her animal pictures. Hang all of the opposites drawings on a line strung beneath the classroom ceiling so that both sides can be enjoyed.

Horse fr[ont]

Horse back

Purposeful Play — Opposing Poses

Give youngsters' visual skills a spin with this game of Opposites Spin the Bottle. Seat youngsters in a circle; then place an empty plastic soda bottle in the middle of the circle. To play, a child spins the bottle. When the bottle stops, the child to whom it is pointing stands up and faces the bottle spinner. The bottle spinner then strikes a pose and challenges the other child to do the opposite. If the child has difficulty positioning himself in an opposite pose, appoint a volunteer to help him. Then invite the imitator to spin the bottle for the next round of play.

Storybook Café — Separate Shoes

Lace the concept of opposites into the preparation of this tasty snack.

Supplies:
plastic knives
napkins

Ingredients for each child:
2 oval cookies (such as Keebler Vienna Fingers cookies)
vanilla frosting
eight 1" lengths of licorice lace
two 2" lengths of licorice lace
one 4" length of licorice lace

To make a pair of opposites shoes:
1. Spread a layer of frosting on each cookie.
2. Use the one-inch licorice laces to make two Xs on each cookie to resemble laced shoes.
3. On one cookie, loop and position the four-inch licorice lace to look like tied shoelaces.
4. On the other cookie, position the two-inch laces to look like untied shoelaces.
5. Nibble, nibble, nibble.

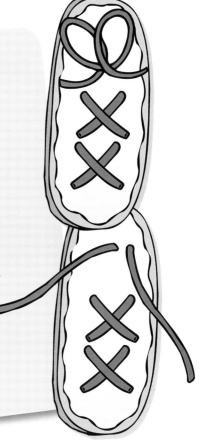

23

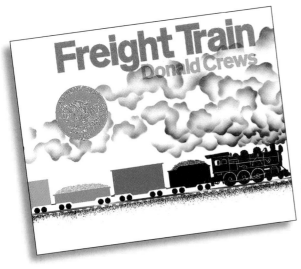

Freight Train

Written and illustrated by Donald Crews

All aboard! A black engine pulls a line of colored train cars through tunnels, past cities, and across trestles. Brief text and bold illustrations blend to create a colorful and exciting cross-country journey.

Storytime Song

Use this choo-choo chant to steer youngsters to storytime.

Red caboose moves down the track,
Clickety-clack, clickety-clack.

[Orange] train car moves down the track,
Clickety-clack, clickety-clack.

Big engine moves down the track,
Shiny and black, shiny and black.
Toot! Toot!

(Repeat the second verse for each car color in the book—yellow, green, blue, purple, and black. Then sing the last verse.)

After your little ones have clickety-clacked together, invite them to take an imaginary ride on the freight train as you read this story.

Learning Links — On Track Color Match

Set your students on the right track when it comes to color recognition. To make train cars, cover each of seven shoeboxes with a different color featured in *Freight Train*. Working with groups of seven students at a time, give each child a box; then sequence students according to the color sequence in the book. Instruct the child with the black train car to lead the student train around the room to find an item matching his car color. Have him put the item in his box and then move to the back of the train. Invite the new train leader (the purple car) to follow suit. Once the black car returns to the front of the train, reassign the color cars; then send the train down the track for another round of color collecting.

Art Smarts
Colorful Choo-Choo

Your little engineers can choose colors for their own color trains with this creative choo-choo art. To begin, make several tagboard rectangle tracers. Then fill a separate shallow tray with a paint color for each train car: red, orange, yellow, green, blue, purple, and black. Have each child trace a row of rectangles onto a long strip of paper. To make a train engine, have the child overlap and trace two rectangles as shown. Have him paint each car a different color and then paint color streaks between the adjoining cars to give the appearance of a speeding train. Have him complete the train by painting black wheels on the cars. Once their color trains have dried, encourage your little ones to take them home and share them with family members as they invent new stories about where freight trains go.

Books About the Basics

Purposeful Play
Calling All Colors

Youngsters can toot their own horns in this color-recognition activity. Appoint a child to be the train engine. Ask him to call out a color in his own clothing. Have the other children check their clothes for the named color. Instruct all the children wearing that color to connect hands to form a train behind the engine. Then invite the engine to pull his color-coordinated train cars around a designated train track. When the train chugs back to the station, appoint a different child to be the engine; then invite youngsters to play again.

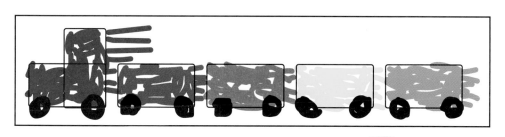

Storybook Café

Fruity Freight Train

Give youngsters a nutritious sampling of some "tooty-fruity" flavors with this snack. Toot! Toot!

Supplies:
large napkins
plastic knives

Ingredients for each child:
6 graham cracker sections
whipped topping
watermelon cube
small chunk of orange
banana slice
peeled green grape quarters
blueberry
peeled purple grape quarters
12 pieces of Cheerios cereal

To make one fruity freight train:
1. Spread whipped topping on each cracker train car.
2. Line up cars; then put a different fruit on each one.
3. Add two cereal wheels to each car.
4. Roll train down the track and into tummy. Chug-a-chug-a-yum-yum!

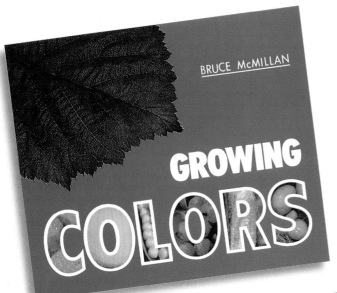

Growing Colors

Written and photographed by Bruce McMillan

Take a peek through Bruce McMillan's camera to view a cornucopia of colors growing in the garden.

Storytime Song

Call your class to storytime with this song sung to the tune of "London Bridge."

Red and yellow, orange and green,
Purple and brown, black and blue,
Colors grow for me and you,
Good and tasty!

(Repeat until all of your little ones have joined together.)

After youngsters gather together, share the sights and colors of *Growing Colors.*

Colorful Mural

What colors does your garden grow? To learn more about colors that grow in the garden, invite students to create a garden mural. To prepare, visually divide a length of white bulletin board paper into eight equal sections. Label each section with a different color: red, orange, yellow, green, blue, purple, brown, or black. Then assign each child a section of the paper on which to draw. Instruct her to draw a plant that grows food of her given color. Refer students to the book for ideas, but also encourage them to brainstorm plant foods not pictured in the book, such as apples, lettuce, and eggplant. Label each child's drawing with the plant name. Then display the garden mural with a leafy border. Title the display "Growing Colors."

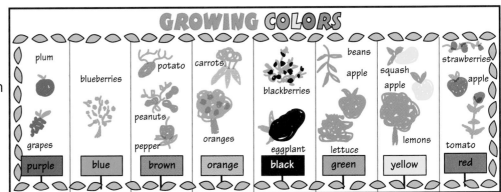

GROWING COLORS

plum	blueberries	potato	carrots	blackberries	beans apple	squash apple	strawberries apple
grapes		peanuts pepper	oranges	eggplant	lettuce	lemons	tomato
purple	blue	brown	orange	black	green	yellow	red

Carrot Painting

Art Smarts

When youngsters make these carrot drawings, they'll discover that some garden foods are good for more than just eating! Invite each child to spread fingerpaint on a large sheet of fingerpaint paper. Have her use a carrot like a pencil to draw designs, pictures, or letters in the paint. To erase the drawing, have her simply smooth out the paint and then begin drawing again. When each child creates a drawing she wants to keep, have her set it aside to dry. Later, invite each child to share her drawing with the class. Then encourage her to take her carrot art home to share with her family.

Purposeful Play

Color Wheel Game

Challenge youngsters' categorizing skills with this Wheel of Color game. To prepare, cut a large circle out of bulletin board paper for every six to eight students. Visually divide each circle into eight segments. Color only the tip of each segment with a different color from an eight-count box of crayons. Then place the crayons in a bag. To play, a group of six to eight students sits around the color wheel and passes the bag from child to child. When a signal is given, the child holding the bag removes a crayon. The group identifies the crayon color and then rotates the wheel so that the corresponding segment is in front of the player with the crayon. On the segment, she draws an item that is commonly that color, such as a yellow banana or a red fire truck. Afterward, she returns the crayon to the bag and passes it for the next round of play. When these wheels go round and round, students will create a collection of color categories to display for the enjoyment of classmates and class visitors.

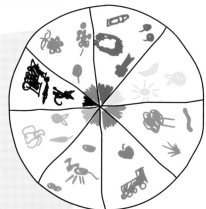

Storybook Café

Garden Goodies

Combine these common garden foods to create a cup of colors with a crunch!

Supplies:
clear plastic cups
plastic spoons

Ingredients:
carrot shavings
squash cubes
diced red peppers
celery slices
ranch salad dressing

To make one serving of garden goodies:
1. Layer vegetables in a cup.
2. Top with dressing.
3. Crunch! Crunch! Crunch!

27

Handsigns:
A Sign Language Alphabet

Written and illustrated by Kathleen Fain

This book treats readers to a beautifully illustrated menagerie of animals along with the handsign for the beginning letter of each one.

Storytime Song

Call youngsters to storytime with this song sung to the tune of "If You're Happy and You Know It."

We're going to learn the handsign ABCs.
We're going to learn the handsign ABCs.
We'll sign the letter *A,*
And all the letters up through *Z.*
We're going to learn the handsign ABCs!

(Repeat the song until your youngsters have all gathered together. As you sing, make the handsigns for the letters mentioned.)

Read aloud *Handsigns,* challenging students to form the sign for each featured letter when you show them the corresponding illustration.

Learning Links Making Handsigns

The signs are all here for Handsigns Walkabout. To prepare, make enlarged construction paper copies of the handsign cards on pages 186 and 187. Cut the cards apart and put them in a basket. Then tape a set of alphabet cards to the floor, creating a large circle. Instruct students to move around the circle to some lively music. When the music stops, have each child stand behind the nearest letter. Draw a card from the basket and show it to students. Ask the child on the corresponding letter to name the letter and then make the sign for it. Invite that child to draw the card for the next round of play.

Handy Fingerpainting

Art Smarts

Use this fingerpaint finger-spelling activity to provide youngsters with fine-motor letter learning. To make handsign posters, enlarge and copy the handsign cards on pages 186 and 187 onto tagboard; then laminate the posters. Display them in the art center for this activity. Have each center visitor fingerpaint an animal on fingerpaint paper. Ask her to handsign the first letter of the animal's name, referring to the posters as necessary. To conclude, instruct each child to write her name in the fingerpaint and then create a border on her paper. Send each child home with a copy of the handsigns and her fingerpainting. Encourage her to finger-spell her name for her family and then challenge family members to spell their names as well as items around the home.

Silent Talking

Purposeful Play

Give youngsters an opportunity to communicate with handsigns with this idea. During an appointed week, designate several short periods of silent play. During this time, encourage students to communicate their thoughts and needs with each other using only handsigns and gestures. Afterward, have them discuss their experiences and feelings about communicating without their voices. Although their attempts to handsign and pantomime may end in silly pandemonium, youngsters will learn to appreciate the challenges facing those who rely on handsigning. And they'll also refine their fine-motor and problem-solving skills in the process!

Books About A! the Basics

Storybook Café

Letter-Perfect Punch

Pack this punch with some cool letter-learning opportunities for your students. During preparation, have each child make the handsign for her ice letter. Then, while students enjoy their drinks, lead them in a whole-class alphabet handsigning session.

Supplies:
plastic letter molds
punch bowl
ladle
clear plastic cups

Ingredients:
lemon-lime soda
orange juice
whipped topping
optional: letter-related snacks such as Alpha-Bits cereal
 or Haribo alphabet letters

Preparation:
1. Fill a set of letter molds with orange juice; then freeze overnight.
2. Half-fill the punch bowl with soda.
3. Have each child pop a letter from its mold into the punch bowl.
4. Add more soda as desired.

To make one serving of letter-perfect punch:
1. Ladle punch into a cup.
2. Top drink with a dollop of whipped topping.
3. Serve with snack.

Have You Seen My Duckling?

Written and illustrated by Nancy Tafuri

A carefree duckling leaves its nest to chase a butterfly. Meanwhile, Mother Duck searches for her missing duckling with the rest of her brood in tow. Can the pond residents help Mother Duck?

Storytime Song

Entice your little ducklings to listen to this old favorite by singing the verse below to the tune of "Oh Where, Oh Where Has My Little Dog Gone?"

Oh where, oh where
Has my duckling gone?
Oh where, oh where
Can it be?
It left the nest
To wander alone.
Oh where, oh where can it be?

(Repeat until your little ones have waddled over to join you.)

Once students are nestled in your circle, ask them to be on the look-out for the duckling as you read aloud *Have You Seen My Duckling?*

Memory Match

Your students will become "quacker-jack" pros at basic skills with this memory game. To prepare, copy a supply of large and small duckling pairs (page 188) on yellow construction paper; then cut them out. Label the front of each cutout pair with a matching basic skill. For instance, a large duckling might be labeled with a number word or an uppercase letter and the small duckling with the corresponding numeral or lower-case letter. Laminate if desired. To play, a pair of students places the cards facedown on a large blue pond cutout. Each player turns over a large duckling and "swims" it around the pond to choose a small duckling. He checks to see if the small duckling matches. If the cards match, the child keeps them. If not, the child returns them to the pond and play moves to the next player. Continue in this manner until all the duckling matches are found.

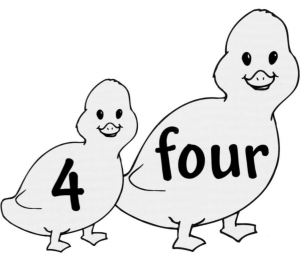

Art Smarts

Just Ducky

These adorable ducks will make great props for dramatic play or a beautiful classroom display. For each child, duplicate the duck head and foot patterns (page 188) on tagboard. To make a duck, a child folds a paper plate in half and staples the edges together. He glues craft feathers onto both sides of the plate to create a duck body. While the glue dries, he colors and cuts out the patterns. He attaches a wiggle eye sticker to each side of the duck's head and then staples the cutouts onto the duck body as shown.

Purposeful Play

Quack-and-Seek

Invite youngsters to role-play the story with this Hide-and-Seek game. Divide your class into several small groups. Appoint one child in a group to be Mother Duck. Ask Mother Duck to cover her eyes while the other group members—her ducklings— hide a toy duck. Then have Mother Duck ask each of her ducklings in turn, "Have you seen my duckling?" Prompt each duckling to give Mother Duck a clue to help her locate the hidden duckling. For example, one duckling might say, "Look near the blocks." Then the next duckling gives an additional clue, such as, "It's under something blue." Encourage the duck-lings to continue giving clues until Mother Duck finds her lost duckling. Then reassign roles and invite the group to play again.

Books About A the Basics

Storybook Café

Quacker Crackers

It's no secret—your little ones will go "quackers" over these delicious snacks!

Supplies:
toaster oven
aluminum foil
pastry brush
duck cookie cutter

Ingredients:
pita rounds
olive oil
Parmesan cheese in a shaker can

To make quacker crackers:
1. Use the cookie cutter to cut out as many duck shapes as possible from one pita round.
2. Brush each duck shape with olive oil.
3. Sprinkle each duck with cheese.
4. Place the ducks on a sheet of aluminum foil.
5. Toast until golden brown.
6. Cool and enjoy!

Hot, Cold, Shy, Bold: Looking at Opposites

Written & photographed by Pamela Harris

A delightfully diverse collection of photographed faces illustrates a number of opposites concepts.

Storytime Song

Smiling faces will gather around when you invite youngsters to storytime by singing the verse below to the tune of "It's Raining, It's Pouring."

Faces, faces,
Opposite kinds of faces.
There's hot and cold,
And shy and bold
In many different places.

(Repeat until all your smiling youngsters have joined your circle.)

Once those sweet, shining faces are circled around you, read aloud *Hot Cold Shy Bold.*

Musical Opposite March

Invite youngsters to face the opposites challenge with this musical game for large or small groups. To prepare, duplicate the opposites pictures on page 189. Laminate and then cut out the pictures. Next, tape sheets of construction paper on the floor to form a large circle. Randomly place each picture on one of the construction paper sheets. To play, students walk around the outside of the circle while you play music. When you stop the music, each child picks up the nearest picture and then searches for its opposite, checking the pictures remaining on the floor and those held by other children. After each student finds the match to his picture, ask him to name the opposites concepts in his picture pair. Randomly replace the pictures before beginning the next round of play.

hot

cold

Different Dough

What expressions will show on your youngsters' faces during this sensory activity? Prepare several batches of this play dough and find out. Make one batch in advance and refrigerate it. Just before the activity, make a fresh batch so that it will be warm while youngsters use it. (Or microwave a batch made in advance to warm it up.) Give each child a portion of the warm and the cold play dough. Encourage him to create faces and other shapes from both portions. Invite him to comment on the temperature contrast between the two portions. Which temperature is most favored by each child? Why?

Play Dough
4 c. flour
1 c. salt
1 3/4 c. warm water

Combine flour and salt. Add water; then knead the dough for about ten minutes.

Purposeful Play

Opposite Bingo

Play this three-in-a-row bingo game with small groups of students to reinforce opposites concepts. Make a supply of the opposites pictures on page 189 and the desired number of bingo cards from page 190. Cut out the pictures; then sort them into opposites pairs. Set one of each picture pair aside to use as caller cards. Use the remaining pictures to create several different bingo cards (see example). Make sure you glue only one picture from an opposite pair onto each card. To play, each player covers the "Smile!" space with a marker.

Then the caller picks a card. She names and shows the card to the players and directs them to find the opposite of the card. If they have the corresponding picture on their cards, players cover it with a marker. When a child covers three pictures in a row, she calls out "Three-in-a-row bingo!" Then she names all of the opposites represented on her card.

Storybook Café

Round Face, Square Face

Faces square. Faces round. These are the tastiest treats in town!

Supplies:
plastic knives
paper plates

Ingredients for one child:
round cracker (such as a Ritz cracker)
square saltine cracker
cream cheese
Cheerios cereal
Chex cereal

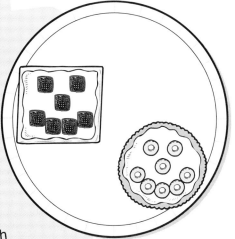

To make one of each face shape:
1. Spread cream cheese on both crackers.
2. Use the corresponding cereal shape to create a face on each cracker shape.
3. Put on a happy face and eat these shape treats.

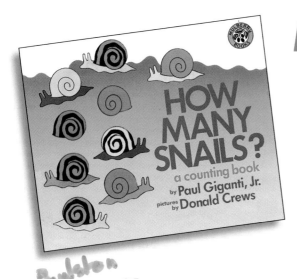

How Many Snails?
A Counting Book

By Paul Giganti Jr.
Illustrated by Donald Crews

A walking journey highlights the wonders of things seen along the way and leads readers to wonder about the quantities and characteristics of those things.

Storytime Song

To attract youngsters to storytime, display the two-page spread in the book picturing the snails; then sing this song to the tune of "Did You Ever See a Lassie?"

How many snails are in this picture,
This picture, this picture?
How many snails are in this picture?
How many snails do you see?

(Continue singing until your little ones have gathered around.)

Encourage students to silently count the snails on the two-page spread you displayed. Invite them to share their answers before you read the story.

Learning Links

Attribute Sort

Reinforce sorting by attributes with this small-group idea. To begin, cut out three different-size construction paper rings. Then gather sets of items that can be sorted by different attributes. (You might collect counters, toy vehicles, plastic animals, paper shapes, and blocks.) Nest the rings as shown; then give students a set of items, such as the plastic animals. Ask them to put all the animals in the open space of the large ring. Then instruct them to place the farm animals in the medium-size ring. Finally, have students sort the farm animals by a specific characteristic, such as leg count. Direct them to put those animals in the small ring. Then use the book's questioning technique to guide youngsters in counting the items with each attribute. For example, you might ask, "How many animals are there?", "How many animals are farm animals?", and, "How many animals are farm animals with four legs?" Encourage a volunteer to lead the group as it chorally counts the response to each question.

Textured Snails

Youngsters will get lots of counting practice when they count these colorful snails. In advance, cut a quantity of two-inch-wide lengths of tissue paper in a variety of colors. Then cut out a class supply of simple bubble wrap snail bodies. To make a snail, invite each child to twist two tissue paper colors together into a long rope. Have him glue a snail body onto a five-inch black square and then spread a circle of glue above the snail. Next, have him roll the rope into a spiral and then press the spiral onto the glue to create the snail shell. After the glue dries, display the snails on a black background with the title "How Many Snails?"

Books About the Basics

Attribute Action

Challenge youngsters' listening and observation skills with this game. To begin, seat students in a circle. Then give a command involving a personal attribute and an action, such as, "If you are wearing red, stand up and turn around." If this criteria applies to a child, she follows the given directions. Otherwise, she remains seated. Continue calling out different commands, varying the attributes and actions. Include attributes such as hair and eye color, beginning letters of student names, and types of clothing. Later, you might combine two attributes with an action. For instance, you might say, "If you are a brown-haired girl, clap your hands." As an additional challenge, invite volunteers to give the commands.

Yummy Cupcakes

Label a chart with the different frostings and toppings available for decorating these cupcakes. Then have each youngster mark the appropriate chart columns for his cupcake before he eats his yummy snack. Compare the results with the class.

Supplies:
plastic knives
paper plates

Ingredients for each child:
cupcake
choice of vanilla or chocolate frosting
choice of colored sprinkles or star toppings

To make a yummy cupcake:
1. Spread frosting on the cupcake.
2. Add your topping choice.
3. Enjoy!

	chocolate	vanilla	sprinkles	stars
Amber	✓		✓	
Alan	✓			✓
Jamie		✓		✓
Chelsea		✓	✓	
Vince		✓		✓

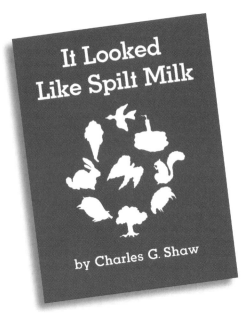

It Looked Like Spilt Milk

Written & illustrated by Charles G. Shaw

With each turn of the page, a shape that looks like one thing begins to look like something else. But what are those white shapes on blue backgrounds? Only clouds in the sky.

Storytime Song

Call youngsters to storytime with this song about clouds, sung to the tune of "Pawpaw Patch."

The first time I looked, it looked like ice cream.
The second time I looked, it looked like a flower.
The third time I looked, it looked like a mitten.
But it was just a cloud puff in the sky.

(Continue singing until your youngsters have gathered.)

Once your students have floated together, read aloud *It Looked Like Spilt Milk*.

Descriptive Dictating

This class scroll book will perfectly demonstrate the changing nature of clouds in the sky. Obtain two 12" x 18" sheets of blue construction paper to serve as the book covers. Cut an 8" x 10" window out of the front cover as shown. Use a correction pen to label the cover as shown. Laminate the covers; then glue them together along the top, bottom, and lower side edges using craft glue. (Do not glue the edges beside the window cutout.) Invite each child to pencil a shape outline onto a 9" x 12" sheet of blue construction paper. Have him cotton-paint the shape to make a white cloud. After the paint dries, use a correction pen to outline the shape and label his picture with his dictated description. Tape all the pictures end to end to create a long scroll, adding an extra sheet of paper to each end. Tape one end of the scroll to a paper towel tube and roll it onto the tube. Slide the other end of the scroll between the book covers so that the pictures show through the front opening. Attach that end to another paper towel tube. To use, a student pair scrolls the pictures through the covers as they read the book. To keep the scrolls rolled when the book is not in use, punch a hole on each side of the cover and near the top of each tube; then insert ribbons through the holes and tie the tubes in place.

It looked like a duck but it was just a cloud in the sky.

Milky Painting

Mix up a batch of blue milk paint to make these cloudy creations. To make the paint, dissolve one-fourth cup of powdered milk into one-half cup of water. Stir in about 15 drops of blue food coloring. Then add a few more drops at a time until the paint reaches the desired shade. To paint a cloud, a child lightly traces a shape on white construction paper with a pencil. Then she paints around the outside of the shape with the blue paint and sets the painting aside to dry. Once all of your students have completed their milky visions, display their work in patchwork-quilt fashion to create a cloudy sky scene. Title the display "Shapes in the Sky."

Shape Guessing Game

Whether it's sunny or cloudy, the sky's the limit in this imagination game! To play, gather a small group of students into a circle. Invite one child at a time to whisper a cloud shape into your ear; then have her pantomime clues to help the other students guess the shape. Continue play as student interest dictates. Then invite another group of youngsters to drift over for a few rounds of cloud play. Hmmm, that imaginary cloud looks like a snowman...an icicle...an ice-cream cone!

Cloud Puffs

These puffy clouds look good enough to eat—and they are!

Ingredients for each child:
¹/₄ c. marshmallow cream
¹/₄ c. powdered milk

Supplies:
measuring cups
bowls
plastic forks
waxed paper

To make one cloud puff:
1. Mix marshmallow cream and powdered milk in a bowl. Use a fork to work the ingredients together to form a soft dough.
2. Make different cloud shapes with the puffy dough on waxed paper.
3. Eat your favorite cloud puff shape.

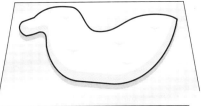

Jump, Frog, Jump!

Written by Robert Kalan
Illustrated by Byron Barton

A frog jumps all around the pond as he avoids being caught by one animal after another. Jump into this cumulative tale to find out if the frog gets away!

Storytime Song

Display a large toy frog with the book. Then call youngsters to storytime with this song sung to the tune of "Skip to My Lou."

Fish wants to catch him, what'll frog do?
Snake wants to catch him, what'll frog do?
Turtle wants to catch him, what'll frog do?
Jump, frog, jump, little froggy!

(Repeat until your froggies are ready to jump into reading.)

Once your little ones have gathered around, read aloud *Jump, Frog, Jump!*

Learning Links

Action Word Game

How did the frog get away? He jumped, of course! Jump into learning about action words with this imaginative game. To prepare, gather toy animals corresponding to the characters in the book, as well as a variety of other animals. Put the animals into a box. To use, remove two animals from the box, such as the snake and fish. Then say, "This is the snake that chased the fish. How did the fish get away?" Ask a volunteer to respond in a pattern similar to the story. For example, he might answer, "Swim, swim!" Then have students demonstrate the animal's action. Invite each child, in turn, to select two animals and then phrase a similar problem for the class. Youngsters are sure to jump into some silly sentences and even sillier solutions!

Art Smarts

Froggy Prints

Youngsters will get lots of counting practice when they capture these thumbprint frogs. To make the frogs, a child uses a green stamp pad to create thumbprints all over a large sheet of paper. Then she draws frog features onto each thumbprint with a marker. To make a net, she dips a strawberry basket bottom into a shallow tray of yellow paint, and then stamps the basket over groups of frogs so that it looks like they are captured in nets. After the paint dries, have each child count and label the frogs in each net on her paper. Thumbs up for counting!

Purposeful Play

Wet-n-Wild Storytelling

Jump right into some creative storytelling with this play activity. Put a small plastic pool or a large tub atop a sheet of plastic in your discovery center. Fill the pool bottom with water. Then add plastic or rubber pond animals, such as frogs, fish, snakes, turtles, and insects. Float craft foam lily pad cutouts on the water. Complete the pond scene with plastic plants. Then invite small groups of children to visit the pond. Encourage them to use the items to act out the story. Or have them create their own pond tales to share with the class later.

Storybook Café

Froggy Fritters

Youngsters will be "hoppy" to make these froggy marshmallow treats.

Supplies:
pan
measuring cup and spoon
stirring paddle
waxed paper

Ingredients (for 12–15 servings):
35 marshmallows
1 stick margarine
1 tsp. vanilla flavoring
4 c. cornflakes
1 tsp. green food coloring
24–30 brown or blue mini M&M's candies
licorice laces

Preparation:
1. Melt margarine and marshmallows in a pan over low heat.
2. Stir in vanilla, cornflakes, and food coloring.
3. Let mixture cool slightly; then give a portion to each child.

To make one froggy fritter:
1. Form mixture into a frog shape on waxed paper.
2. Add M&M's eyeballs.
3. Use licorice laces to make a mouth and legs.

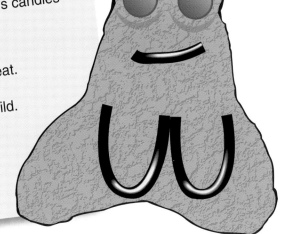

Look Out, Bird!

Written and illustrated by Marilyn Janovitz

Snail slips and starts a chain of events involving a menagerie of unsuspecting animals. The clever blend of alliteration, art, and an amusing plot keep the reader engaged from the first slip of the snail to the last.

Storytime Song

Gather your class for storytime by singing this song to the tune of "Three Blind Mice."

Look out, bird!
Look out, bird!
Snail's falling down.
Snail's falling down.
Snail bumped into bird, who frightened frog.
Then frog toppled turtle right into the bog.
Soon all were bothered, or bumped, or jogged.
So look out, bird!

Once your little birds have flown together, invite students to listen to the story to discover which animals were bothered, bumped, and jogged.

Alliteration Action Game

Guide small student groups in active alliteration with this round-robin-style game. To begin, the first player names an animal (or person) and an alliterative action, such as, "Worm wiggles." The next player names an animal beginning with a different letter and then adds a different action word to create a similar phrase. Continue in this manner, creating a chain reaction of alliteration, until each child has had a turn.

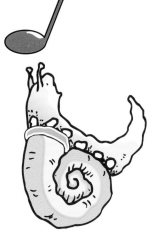

Salt Dough Critters

Here's a creative idea inspired by the art in the book. Make a batch of salt dough using the recipe below. Invite each child to shape a portion of the dough into an animal of her choice. (She might refer to the book for ideas.) After the dough animal hardens, have her paint her creation in simple, bold colors. Then label her animal with her dictated alliterative description of it, such as "funny, frightened frog" or "silly, slithering snake." Display all the critters in a classroom art gallery.

Animal Actions

Salt Dough
2 c. flour
1 c. salt
1 c. cold water

Mix the ingredients in a bowl. Knead the mixture to form a smooth dough. Add more flour or water to achieve the desired consistency.

funny, frightened frog

Hopping horses and galloping geese? It *could* happen in this action-packed alliteration game! To play, name an animal. Call on a volunteer to name an action with the same beginning sound as the animal name. Then have all the students act out that animal performing the action. After a short period of time, signal students to stop. Then ask another volunteer to name a different action with the same beginning sound. Continue in this manner until students have named as many actions as they can imagine. Then call out a different animal and start the game over.

Spiral Snail Snack

These chocolatey snail snacks are fun to make and even more fun to eat.

Supplies:
paper plate

Ingredients for each child:
½ Little Debbie Swiss Cake Roll
tube of blue icing
banana (sliced lengthwise)

To make one spiral snail snack:
1. Trace the spiral design of the cake roll with the icing to make a colorful snail shell.
2. Lay the banana under the cake to resemble a snail.
3. Add two icing dot eyes.
4. Look out, snail!

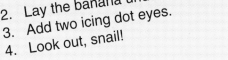

Lunch

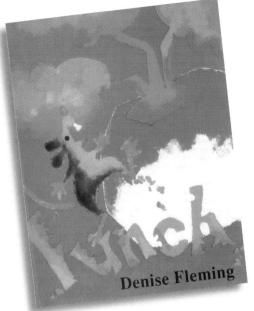

Written and illustrated by Denise Fleming

A very hungry mouse frolics across the table, lunching on a feast of colorful fruits and vegetables. With a festive flair, this tale leaves readers eager for Mouse to return for his dinnertime eating excursion.

Storytime Song

Assemble your class for storytime with a rollicking version of this song, sung to the tune of "Mary Had a Little Lamb."

Sniffle, sniffle.
Crunch, crunch, crunch.
Munch, munch, munch.
Crunch, crunch, crunch.

Sniffle, sniffle.
Crunch, crunch, crunch.
This little mouse is having lunch!

(Repeat until all of your little mice have joined together.)

Once your munchy mice have joined you, ask them to listen to the story to discover all the different food colors eaten by Mouse.

Learning Links

Lunchtime Color Words

Youngsters will develop an appetite for reading with these mini versions of the story. To prepare, make a class supply of page 191. Then make a class supply of the mouse patterns (page 192) on gray construction paper. Give a copy of the booklet pages and the mouse patterns to each child. Invite each child to illustrate his booklet pages and personalize the cover. Then have him cut apart the pages and stack them in order. Hole-punch at the dot, through the entire stack. Insert one end of a half-length pipe cleaner through the holes, bend the end toward the stem, and then twist together to secure. Next, have him cut out the mouse patterns and glue the cutouts together back-to-back. Punch a hole in the mouse on the dot. Insert the loose end of the pipe cleaner through the hole and twist closed. To use, a child "feeds" his mouse the food as he reads each page. When he reaches the last page, he turns the mouse over and puts him down for his nap. Sweet dreams!

Lunch
for
MacKie
Mouse

Mouse Print Count

Use these multicolored mouse prints to combine counting and color skills into a multicurricular treat. To begin, cut out a supply of sponges in the shape of the mouse pattern on page 192. Put one sponge in a separate tray of tempera paint for each desired color. Give each child a large sheet of white paper and invite her to print colored mouse shapes all over it. After the paint dries, have her create thumbprint ears for her mice. Then have her use her pinky tip to print a nose and eyes for each mouse. Help her draw a tail and whiskers for each of her mice with a black marker. During small-group instruction, ask each child to share her picture. Ask her to lead the other students in counting the number of mice for each color and the total number of mice.

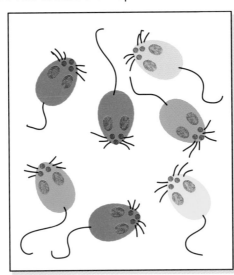

A Colorful Sort

Get out your checkered tablecloth and set the table to serve up some color-matching practice. First, collect a colorful assortment of real or plastic fruits and vegetables and place them in a large basket. Next, label a different paper plate with each color represented by the foods. Finally, set the table by inverting the plates so that the color labels are not visible. To use, each child in a small group turns over a plate to discover the color it represents. Then he removes all the corresponding foods from the basket and places them on the plate. Continue in this fashion until each food is served on a plate. Then invite students to have an imaginary feast on their favorite colors before returning the foods to the basket for the next group.

Cheesy Mouse Morsels

For lunchtime, dinnertime, or anytime, these mouse morsels will please youngsters of all ages.

Supplies:
heart-shaped cookie cutter
napkins

Ingredients for one:
slice of bread
slice of cheese
3 baby carrot slivers
2 shelled sunflower seeds
dried chow mein noodle

To make one cheesy mouse morsel:
1. Fold bread and cheese in half separately.
2. Cut a mouse shape from each using one side of a cookie cutter.
3. Separate cheese.
4. Put one cheese shape inside the folded bread. Top the bread with the other cheese shape.
5. Press on sunflower eyes and carrot ears and nose.
6. Insert noodle tail.

More Than One

Written by Miriam Schlein
Illustrated by Donald Crews

Is one always one? Not when you have one pair of two shoes or one team of nine baseball players. Simple text and bold illustrations explore how one can be more.

Storytime Song

Display a pair of shoes in a shoebox as you sing this song to the tune of "This Old Man"; then tell students that two shoes make one pair.

> I have one
> Pair of shoes.
> Two shoes make
> One pair of shoes.
> Oh, one is one,
> But sometimes one is more—
> One pair is one plus one more.

(Continue singing until all your little ones have joined together.)

Ask students to listen for other ways in which one is more than just one as you read the story.

Learning Links — Count On Family

A family can be two people, or even three, but there's only one me in my family. Promote self-awareness with this idea that helps each child take a head count of his family. Provide several tracers shaped like people. Have each child trace one shape for each family member—including himself—onto a large sheet of paper. Then have him decorate the shapes to represent family members. Label each child's picture with "1 family, ____ people." Have the child write the numeral for the people in his family. During group time, ask each child to share his picture and to tell about each family member.

1 family, 3 people

Estimation Mural

How many students are in your school? Share this information with students; then explain that the students in your school can be counted, but it's nearly impossible to count the fish in a school of fish! Then have youngsters help create this mural. Provide an assortment of fish-shaped sponges and trays of different paint colors. Invite a few students at a time to sponge-paint fish on a length of blue bulletin board paper until it is covered. Then display the mural, bordering it with construction paper coral cut-outs. Ask each child to estimate the number of fish in the mural; then have her label a sticky note with her name and estimate. Post the esti-mates near the mural. Then, on several different occa-sions, chorally count the fish with your class. Which child has the closest estimate? Did you get the same results each time? Hey, are those fish moving?

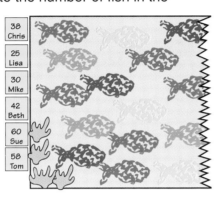

| 38 Chris |
| 25 Lisa |
| 30 Mike |
| 42 Beth |
| 60 Sue |
| 58 Tom |

Color-Sorting Game

Team up color skills, counting, and movement with this fun and simple game. First, put a supply of colored counters in a bag. Then ask each child to remove one counter from the bag. Next, signal students to sort themselves into groups according to their counter colors. Then instruct each group to count its members and report the results. Finally, assign each color group a movement to perform, such as hopping in circles or running in place. Afterward, have students return their counters to the bag; then pass the bag for another round of play.

Chocolate Nest

One nest is just one, but a nest of eggs can be much more. How much more? Invite youngsters to fill these nests with eggs to find out.

Supplies:
pan
measuring cup
stirring paddle
muffin tins
paper plates
butter knife

Ingredients (for six nests):
2 c. mini marshmallows
¼ c. margarine
¼ c. chocolate chips
2 c. Frosted Flakes cereal
Corn Pops cereal

Preparation:
1. Melt mini marshmallows, margarine, and chocolate chips in the pan.
2. Stir in Frosted Flakes cereal.
3. Allow to cool slightly; then form six balls with mixture.

To make one nest:
1. Press chocolate-cereal ball into a muffin cup to form a nest.
2. Allow nest to cool completely at room temperature, or quick-cool the nest in the refrigerator for ten minutes.
3. Loosen nest with a butter knife; then remove it from the muffin tin.
4. Fill with Corn Pops cereal.
5. Count the eggs. Count the nest. Count this snack the very best!

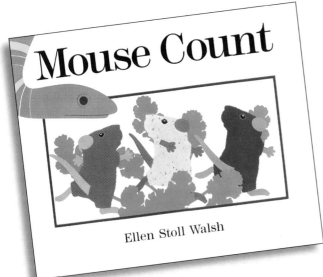

Mouse Count

Written by Ellen Stoll Walsh

A hungry snake collects ten little mice in a jar for his dinner. But will ten mice be enough? Not when there's still one big mouse to be caught! Readers will applaud the ingenuity of the captured mice as they "uncount" themselves to safety.

Storytime Song

S-s-sing this song with a snaky voice to the tune of "Ten Little Indians" as you invite students to storytime.

One little, two little, three little mousies-s-s,
Four little, five little, six little mousies-s-s,
Seven little, eight little, nine little mousies-s-s.
Ten mousies-s-s in my jar!

(Repeat until your little mice have all scampered together.)

Challenge your students to be as quiet as mousies-s-s while you read the story.

Colorful Estimation

Count on these mice to give youngsters practice in making estimates. To begin, gather several baby food jars and a collection of small rubber mice. Put a different number of mice in each jar; then label the bottom of each jar with the corresponding numeral. Attach a different sticky-dot color to each jar lid. Place the jars in a center along with a chart labeled with your students' names and the colors corresponding to those on the jar lids. To use, each child estimates the number of mice in each jar and then writes that numeral in the row beside her name on the chart. After all the estimates are recorded, have your class chorally count the mice in each jar. Which child made the closest estimate for each jar?

	⚪	⚫	⚫	⚪
Dustin	9	13	3	10
Danelle	7	20	3	16
Leigh	10	14	3	21
Jannah	8	16	3	18
Vince			3	19
Amber	3	10	3	20
Russell	2	9	3	15
Lee			3	17

Art Smarts

Mouse Count Collage

Show youngsters the first two-page spread in the book picturing the mice in the meadow. Explain that the illustration is a collage made from different paper shapes; then invite each child to create her own mouse-in-the-meadow collage. Have her tear mouse shapes from brown, natural, and gray shades of construction paper. Then glue the shapes onto a large sheet of white paper. Next, have her cut out ears, feet, and a tail for each mouse in a contrasting paper color, and then glue the features onto the mouse. Have her add black paper circles for eyes and use a correction pen to add a little white to the mouse eyes. Invite her to complete the collage with torn or cut green paper grass. Ask her to label her paper with the number of mice in the meadow. Then display all of your students' artful collages on a bulletin board titled "Count Our Mice!"

Purposeful Play

Snakes in the Grass Game

It's time to head outdoors to play Mouse Count! To set up, arrange three large rope circles—to represent jars—at the edge of a field. Appoint three children to be snakes; then assign each snake to a rope jar. Tell the rest of the class that they are mice. Secretly give each of several mice a rock, instructing him to keep his rock hidden. Then have all the mice quietly curl up in the field as if napping. On a signal, the snakes begin to gather mice for their dinners. To do this, each snake taps a mouse to awaken him. Then he escorts the mouse to his jar. But if the mouse has a rock, he places it in front of him and stays put—safely in the meadow. After all the mice have been awakened, each snake counts the mice in his jar. Then students chorally count the mice with rocks. Afterward, reassign roles, pass out a different number of rocks, and invite students to play again.

Storybook Café

Striped Snakes

For goodness' sake! These snacks are snakes! Youngsters are sure to enjoy these striped bread stick treats.

Supplies:
napkins

Ingredients for each child:
bread stick
small tubes of green, blue, and yellow icing
2 chocolate chips

To make a striped snake:
1. Squeeze color stripes onto the bread stick with tubes of icing.
2. Put chocolate chip eyes on icing dots at one end of the bread stick.
3. It's s-s-snacktime!

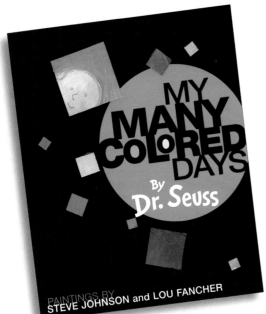

My Many Colored Days

Written by Dr. Seuss
Illustrated by Steve Johnson and Lou Fancher

Playful text, moody characters, and bold colors express the ever-changing nature of emotions. Readers readily identify with the many colored days depicted in this book.

Storytime Song

Set the mood for storytime with this song sung to the tune of "Pop! Goes the Weasel."

I have so many colored days.
The colors match my feelings.
I'm mad, I'm glad, I'm lonely, and sad—
So many colored feelings!

(Repeat until all your little ones have joined together.)

Once your youngsters have gathered around, share the story. Afterward, invite student comments on the many different sensations evoked by the book.

Learning Links

Handy Color Identification

Here's a handy small-group game to reinforce color skills. To prepare, make two copies of the hand pattern on page 192 for each child; then make two additional copies. To make a spinner board, cut out and color the additional pair of hand patterns, as shown. If desired, label each color. Glue the cutouts onto a sheet of tagboard to create a modified color wheel. Use a brad to attach a paper-clip spinner to the center of the wheel. Then have each child cut out and glue together his own hand patterns in similar fashion. Provide a crayon for each color on the spinner board. To play, each child spins the spinner and then colors a finger on his pattern the corresponding color. Each time he spins a different color, he colors a finger on his pattern. If he spins a color already used on his pattern, he must pass. When a player completes his wheel with the ten colors on the spinner board, he performs a mixed-up moods dance. Afterward, encourage each child to share his handy color guide with his family.

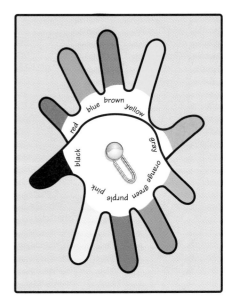

Sponge Paint Prints

A red square, a blue square. Everywhere, a color square! That's what youngsters will be seeing when they create these colorful pictures similar to the book cover. To begin, cut out a supply of sponge squares of various sizes; then provide trays of different paint colors. Invite each child to use the sponges to stamp different square colors all over a large sheet of paper. After the paint dries, have her trace people shape cutters over the colored squares. Invite each child to share her art with the class as she describes the mood(s) of one of her colorful characters.

Mood Motion Game

Emotions and moods change from day to day and sometimes all in one day! Encourage children to demonstrate their mood changes with this game of Wham! In advance, cut out a color card corresponding to each color in the book and put the cards in a basket. To play the first few rounds, display a two-page spread in the book representing a color-related mood. Students pantomime the mood until you close the book—*wham!* At this time, they freeze until you display a different two-page spread for them to pantomime. Later, put the book aside; then randomly select a color card. Have students act out the mood associated with that color. Wham two blocks together to signal students to freeze and wait for the next color cue.

Cool 'n' Crunchy Colors

This multicolored treat will create some brightly colored moods in your youngsters.

Supplies:
clear plastic cups
plastic spoons

Ingredients:
red, green, yellow, orange, and blue Jell-O gelatin cubes
whipped topping
Fruity Pebbles cereal

To make one serving of cool 'n' crunchy colors:
1. Layer several cubes of each Jell-O gelatin color into a cup.
2. Add whipped topping.
3. Top with cereal.

Old Black Fly

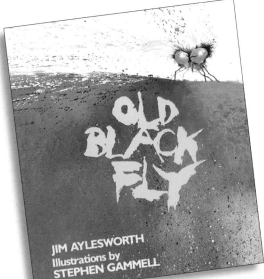

Boylston

Written by Jim Aylesworth
Illustrated by Stephen Gammell

"Shoo fly! Shoo fly! Shooo." Old Black Fly's alphabetical antics create quite a commotion in this clever comedy.

Storytime Song

Invite youngsters to buzz over to storytime with this song sung to the tune of "The Wheels on the Bus."

A busy, bad fly went buzzin' around, buzzin' around, buzzin' around.
A busy, bad fly went buzzin' around—all around the house.

That fly made a mess from ceiling to floor, ceiling to floor, ceiling to floor.
That fly made a mess from ceiling to floor. But *not* anymore!

(Repeat the first verse several times. After your fluttering friends land, sing the last verse, clapping your hands together loudly on not.*)*

Once your little ones have flown together, read all about Old Black Fly's mischievous adventures.

Learning Links

Beginning Letter Class Book

Entice students to take a fly's-eye view of household items with this idea. To prepare, label a large sheet of construction paper for each letter. Sequence the papers in a large area of your room. Then prompt each youngster to imagine that he is a fly in a house. What might he see as he flies around? Have him find and cut out magazine pictures of several household items that a fly might see. Then have him glue each cutout onto the paper corresponding to the initial letter of his picture. (If a picture cannot be found for a letter, ask a volunteer to illustrate an item for that letter.) Afterward, bind the sequenced letters between two construction paper covers to create a class book. Title the book "ABCs All Around the House."

Fly Print Tracers

Land these busy, bad flies on letter outlines to create some interesting artwork. For each child, label a large sheet of paper with the letter that begins her name. Attach a short length of string to a plastic fly. Have the child dip the fly's legs into paint and then land the fly at random all over her letter. Or have her trace her letter by dragging the fly over it. To complete her picture, ask the child to make fly prints around the border of her paper with different paint colors. Display the pictures with the title "My, Oh My! A Fly Went By!"

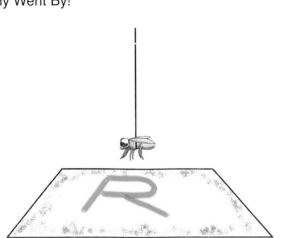

Alphabet Swat

Youngsters will be abuzz with letter-sequencing practice when they play this alphabetical fly-swatting game. To prepare, use a white paint pen to label each of 26 large plastic flies with a letter. Scatter the flies around a designated area. Then give a fly swatter to each child in a student pair. To play, one child finds and swats fly *A*. He calls out the letter and then puts the fly in a basket. His partner follows the same procedure when he locates fly *B*. Then play returns to the first child to locate fly *C*. Have the partners alternate turns in this manner until they have swatted all the flies. Then scatter the flies again and appoint another student pair to play.

Swat-Fly Pie

This pie is a fun-to-make treat and it's just fine to eat—the flies are only chocolate chips!

Supplies:
plastic spoons
napkins

Ingredients for each child:
mini pie shell
whipped cream
chocolate chips
Chex cereal
short pretzel sticks

To make one swat-fly pie:
1. Fill pie shell with whipped cream.
2. Place chocolate chip flies on top of whipped cream.
3. Position one piece of cereal partially over each chocolate chip fly.
4. Insert a pretzel stick beneath each cereal piece to create fly swatters.
5. Shoo fly! This is my swat-fly pie!

Pigs Aplenty, Pigs Galore!

Written and illustrated by David McPhail

Join these lovable, playful pigs as they revel, romp, and rollick through the home of a surprised host.

Storytime Song

Invite students to gather for storytime with this song sung to the tune of "Here We Are Together."

Let's gather here together, together, together.
Let's gather here together to read this fun book,
With pigs here and there
And pigs everywhere.
Let's gather here together to read this fun book.

(Repeat until your little ones have gathered together.)

Read aloud *Pigs Aplenty, Pigs Galore!* Then ask youngsters to imagine that their homes are suddenly filled with pigs like these. What would they do?

Learning Links

Rhyming Piggy Tails

Reinforce rhyming skills with this small-group game of Pin the Tail on the Pig. To prepare, enlarge the pig and tail patterns on page 193. Trace one pig and a supply of tails onto pink construction paper; then cut them out. Label each tail cutout with a word or picture for which youngsters might easily think of more than one rhyme, such as *hat, block,* or *cake.* Laminate for durability. Mount the pig on a wall; then attach rolled tape to the back of each tail. To play, a child closes her eyes and tries to stick a tail on the appropriate end of the pig. Then she reads the word or identifies the picture on the tail and calls out as many words as she can that rhyme with the word. After she exhausts her rhyming repertoire, the next player takes a turn.

Potato Print Snorts

Display these adorable potato print pigs on a bulletin board titled "Pigs Aplenty!" To begin, cut several potatoes in half. Carve out two narrow grooves from each potato half so that it resembles a pig snout. Put the potatoes in the art center with a tray of black paint. Have each child draw several large pig heads—without the snouts—on a large sheet of construction paper. Have him stamp a potato print snout onto each pig's face and then add wacky hair, hats, and other features similar to those in the book. Encourage the child to name his pigs with real or made-up rhyming names; then label each pig with its name.

Piggy Jig

Round up some rhyming skills with this small-group game. Place the pig from "Rhyming Piggy Tails" on page 52 on the floor. Randomly put objects from rhyming pairs on the pig. Have the students join hands and circle around the pig while reciting this chant. Fill in the blank with a child's name; then have her find a rhyming pair of objects on the pig.

Ring around the piggy,
Jig-a-jig-a-jiggy,
[Child's name, child's name], find a rhyme.

Piggy Pizza Pie

Youngsters will be happy to pig out on these piggy pizza pies. Perfect!

Supplies:
paper plates
cookie sheet
toaster oven
spoon

Ingredients for one:
English muffin
1 tsp. spaghetti sauce
grated cheese
4 olive slices
pepperoni slice
green pepper strip
2 Tostitos bite-size tortilla chips

To make one piggy pizza pie:
1. Spread spaghetti sauce on the muffin.
2. Sprinkle cheese on top of the sauce.
3. Create a piggy face with olive eyes, a pepperoni and olive nose, and a green pepper mouth.
4. Bake at 350°F until the cheese melts and the muffin is toasted (about eight minutes).
5. After the pizza cools, add tortilla chip ears.

The Shape of Me and Other Stuff

Written and illustrated by Dr. Seuss

Readers explore their world of shapes with inventive rhymes and detailed silhouettes created by Dr. Seuss.

Storytime Song

Pique youngsters' interest in shapes by singing this song to the tune of "Twinkle, Twinkle, Little Star."

Where can all the shapes be found?
Shapes can be found all around—
In the water, in the air,
High and low, most everywhere.
When you need a shape or two,
Just take a look—they're all round you.

After your class assembles for storytime, read aloud *The Shape of Me and Other Stuff* to discover a variety of shapes.

Storytelling Shapes

Spin a yarn or two—or even more—with this storytelling activity designed to sharpen youngsters' knowledge of shapes *and* their listening skills. Give each child a two-foot-long piece of yarn. Then tell a simple story. Each time you name a character or item in your story, pause to allow students to create a corresponding yarn shape. For example, your story might begin like this: "A large *circle* was very sad. He wished more than anything that he were a *flower*. One day his wish came true, but soon a big *dog* came along and stepped on him...." (During the story students will make shapes for each italicized word.) Tell additional stories as student interest dictates. Or invite volunteers to add to your story or to make up their own tales. Afterward, have each child shape his yarn as he desires and then glue it onto a sheet of paper. Encourage him to use his shape as a story starter with his family.

Art Smarts

Silly Creations

These silly silhouettes are actually made from the shapes of real things. Invite each child to choose three small objects from the classroom. Have him use chalk to outline each object twice on black paper. Then have him cut out all of the resulting shapes. Instruct him to glue one of each shape on the left side of a large sheet of white paper. Then have him glue the remaining cutouts on the right side of the paper, combining them to form a silly silhouette creature. Label each child's dictation for the object shapes on the left and his own shape creation on the right. Then invite him to share his silly silhouette with the class.

scissors
heart shape
crayon
a flying bug

Purposeful Play

Touchable Guessing Game

Put students' shape feelers to the test with this large- or small-group game. To begin, collect an assortment of common items and put them in a box. Then seat youngsters in a circle and have them hold their hands behind them and close their eyes. To play, a volunteer secretly selects an item from the box. He walks around the seated children with the item until you signal him to stop. Then he places the item from the box into the hands of the nearest child. That child tries to guess the identity of the item without looking at it. If necessary, the first child gives him clues about the item. After the second child makes a correct guess, the first child returns the item to the box. Then the two children switch places and play continues.

Storybook Café

Silhouette Sandwiches

Sandwich these silhouettes together to create a simply scrumptious snack.

Supplies:
shape cutters
toaster oven
paper plates

Ingredients for each child:
2 slices of bread
1 slice of ham
1 slice of cheese

To make a silhouette sandwich:
1. Use a shape cutter to cut identical shapes from the ham, the cheese, and both bread slices.
2. Toast the bread shapes; then allow the toast to cool.
3. Sandwich the ham and cheese shapes between the toast shapes.
4. Enjoy your scrumptious silhouette sandwich.

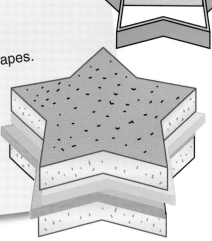

Sheep in a Shop

Written by Nancy Shaw
Illustrated by Margot Apple

A group of sheep create comical chaos as they shop in a general store.

Storytime Song

Herd your little lambs to storytime with this song sung to the tune of "Baa, Baa, Black Sheep."

Little sheep, little sheep,
Have you any wool?

Yes sir, yes ma'am.
Three bags full—
To buy a red ribbon
And a beach ball
To give as a present
From us all!

Little sheep, little sheep,
Have you any wool?

Yes sir, yes ma'am.
Three bags full!

(Repeat until all your little lambs have joined together.)

Once you've shepherded your youngsters into the reading area, read aloud *Sheep in a Shop*.

Learning Links

Memory Shapes

Challenge your young lambs' visual memory skills with this sheep shopping game. To begin, put three or four common objects on a table for a small group of children. Appoint one child at a time to be the sheep shopper. (If desired, have her put on her headband from "Woolly Headband" on page 57.) Tell her that she will take an imaginary shopping trip to purchase the items on the table. Encourage the child to memorize the items. Then send her on a quick trip around the room while you mix several more items in with those already on the table. When the shopper returns, challenge her to pick out her purchases—those items that were originally displayed. After she makes her choices, invite the other students to correct any wrong choices. Then repeat the procedure for each child, adjusting the difficulty of the task to the child's ability level.

Woolly Headband

Add to the fun of "Memory Shapes" on page 56, "Rhyming Pair Purchases" on this page, and youngsters' dramatic-play activities with these woolly sheep headbands. To make one, a child cuts out and staples two tagboard sheep ears onto a sentence strip headband. Then he glues white crinkle paper strips onto the sheep headband. After the glue dries, he folds the ears slightly forward and glues crinkle strips to them. When these dry, fit each child's headband to his head and staple the ends together.

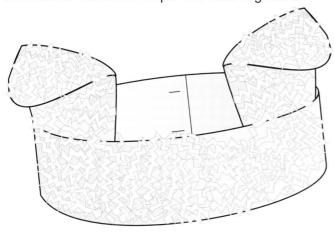

Books About the Basics

Purposeful Play

Rhyming Pair Purchases

Send students on a rhyming shopping spree at this shopping center. Set up a toy cash register with toy shopping baskets, a few paper bags, and a box filled with items (or pictures) for which students might find corresponding rhyming objects in the classroom. Appoint a sheep shopkeeper; then invite a few sheep shoppers to go on a shopping spree. (Have all the players wear their headbands from "Woolly Headband.") To begin, a sheep picks an item from the box. She shops the room to gather items that rhyme with her choice. Then she takes her purchases to the shopkeeper. Together, the two sheep check out the rhyming objects in the basket. All the rhyming items are bagged and the nonrhyming items are put aside to be reshelved. Then the next shopper takes an item from the box and goes on a spree. To close the shopping center, simply have the sheep return all the items to the proper locations.

Storybook Café

Sheep Snackers

Little ones will come "baa-ack" for second helpings of this sheep-shaped snack.

Supplies:
plastic knives
paper plates

Ingredients:
2 oval crackers, such as Town House crackers
1 smaller oval cracker, such as Nabisco Flavor Crisps bacon-flavored crackers
cream cheese spread
2 shelled sunflower seeds
2 almond slices
4 short pretzel sticks

To make one sheep snacker:
1. Spread cream cheese on one side of each oval cracker.
2. Partially sandwich the small cracker between the large crackers to make a sheep head and body.
3. Insert pretzel legs.
4. Add sunflower seed eyes and almond ears.

Some Smug Slug

Written by Pamela Duncan Edwards
Illustrated by Henry Cole

A slug—as smug as smug can be—slithers up a slope, ignoring the warning signals of his animal friends.

Storytime Song

Sing this slippery tongue twister to the tune of "The Bear Went Over the Mountain" to summon students to storytime.

A slug slithered up a slope.
A slug slithered up a slope.
A slug slithered up a slope,
As smug as he could be.

The slope slurped up the slug.
The slope slurped up the slug.
The slope slurped up the slug
For a snack—oh, so tasty!

(Repeat until your youngsters slide into your reading area.)

She sells seashells by the seashore.

Beginning Letter Twist

It's time to play twister—tongue twister, that is! Challenge youngsters to say well-known tongue twisters such as "Peter Piper," "She Sells Seashells," and "How Much Wood Could a Woodchuck Chuck?" Write some of these twisters on chart paper. Then discuss why they are so difficult to say. Have volunteers find and circle the repeating beginning letters in the chants. If desired, teach youngsters the song from "Storytime Song." Then invite each child to make up a simple tongue twister using his own name, such as "Michael makes milk shakes in the middle of the morning." Write his dictation on a paper strip; then encourage him to recite his tongue twister to his family.

Snail Trails

When slugs (or snails) slither along, they leave sparkly trails that create interesting designs. Invite each child to design her own slug trail with this idea. To begin, use glue to draw a design—such as a letter, number, shape, or random figure—on black construction paper. Then sprinkle iridescent glitter over the slug trail design. After the glue dries, glue a play dough slug at one end of the trail. Display the pictures with the title "Happy Trails."

Sand Slugs

Send youngsters to the sensory center for this "sand-sational" slug activity. To prepare, put plastic worm halves into the sand table to represent slugs. Invite each center visitor to slide a slug along the sand to create a trail. (She might make trails in the form of letters, shapes, or other designs.) Then have the child trace the trail with several more slugs. Afterward, instruct her to smooth out the sand with her hand and then send a slithery, slimy slug on its way to blaze a new trail.

Storybook Café

Banana Slug Slurper

Students will slurp up this savory, sweet drink in seconds. And don't be surprised if they ask for seconds!

Supplies:
9" clear plastic cups
straws
ice-cream scoop
measuring cup

Ingredients for each child:
½ c. root beer
scoop of ice cream
whipped topping
½ banana
colored cake decorating gel

To make one banana slug slurper:
1. Put ice cream in cup.
2. Add root beer.
3. Top with whipped topping.
4. Put banana in cup with narrow end sticking out.
5. Add icing dot eyes to tip of banana.
6. Slurp it up!

59

To Market, To Market

Written by Anne Miranda
Illustrated by Janet Stevens

To market, to market for a shopping cart full of surprises! Join this shopper as she adds one animal after another to her chaotic collection of purchases.

Storytime Song

Call youngsters to join storytime with this market-bound ditty sung to the tune of "The Mulberry Bush."

Come with me to the supermarket,
The supermarket, the supermarket.
Come with me to the supermarket
To buy a [fat pig].

(Each time you repeat the song, replace the underlined words with one of the following: red hen, plump goose, live trout, spring lamb, milk cow, white duck, *or* stubborn goat.*)*

Challenge students to listen for what happens to each animal in the story after the lady gets it home as you read aloud *To Market, To Market.*

Learning Links

Rhyme Time

Send little ones shopping for rhyming skills with this wordplay game. Copy, color, and cut out each animal pattern on pages 194–195. Then tape each animal to a different child. Label a sheet of chart paper with each animal name; then list student-generated rhyming words for each animal. To play, ask the children to line up as if they were on a supermarket shelf. Then pretend to be a shopper and select one of the animals to come "home" with you. Recite, "To market, to market, to buy a [fat pig]. Home again, home again…" Ask the child to finish the chant with a rhyming phrase, such as "the pig wore a wig." (If needed, refer him to the chart for rhyming ideas.) Then invite him to become the shopper. Continue in this manner until all the animals are home.

pig	hen	goose	trout	lamb	cow	duck	goat
jig	ten	loose	out	ham	now	truck	coat
wig	men	moose	about	slam	wow	stuck	boat
dig			shout		how	luck	

Art Smarts

Shopping Scenes

Examine the illustrations in the book; then invite youngsters to make similar grocery store scenes. To begin, have each child create a black-and-white background of a grocery store on a large sheet of white construction paper. Then ask her to illustrate—on another sheet of paper—colored items that she might find in a grocery store, such as produce, canned foods, cereal, candy, and meats. Have her cut out and glue her colored pictures onto the grocery store background. Title her scene "To market, to market, to buy…"; then write her dictation for each colored item. Invite each child to share her picture with the class.

Purposeful Play

Minimarket

Books About the Basics

Ready, set, shop! Arrange a minimarket in your dramatic-play center to promote your students' shopping savvy. Supply the market with an assortment of play foods, toy shopping baskets, cash registers, and grocery bags. Also provide dress-up clothes, play money, and toy animals representing those in the story. Then invite student groups to visit the center to create their own grocery store scenarios.

To market, to market, to buy...
cereal · cereal · pizza · ham · milk · doughnut

Storybook Café

Market Fresh Salad

Invite youngsters to make these hassle-free, healthy salads for a hearty snack.

Supplies:
plastic bowls
plastic forks

Ingredients for 15 servings:
1 head torn lettuce
20 cherry tomatoes, quartered
grated carrots
large diced cucumber
2 stalks diced celery
ranch dressing

To make one market fresh salad:
1. Put lettuce in bowl.
2. Add tomatoes, carrots, cucumbers, and celery.
3. Top with dressing.
4. Healthy eating!

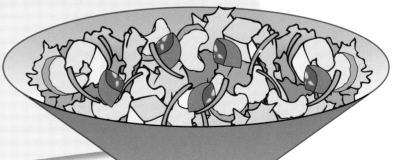

61

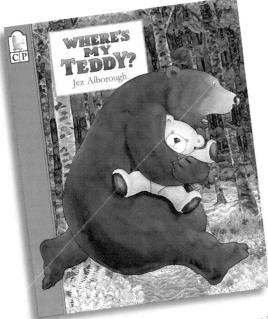

Where's My Teddy?

Written and illustrated by Jez Alborough

When Eddie searches the woods for his lost teddy bear, he stumbles upon a larger-than-life teddy instead.

Storytime Song

Secretly hide a teddy bear in the reading area, leaving a small part of its body exposed, such as a foot or an ear. Then sing this song to the tune of "Where Is Thumbkin?" to invite youngsters to storytime.

Where's my teddy?
Where's my teddy?
Hidden away,
Hidden away.
Tell me, do you see him.
Tell me, do you see him
Here today,
Here today?

(Repeat until your little ones have gathered.)

Once your little bears have joined together, ask them to visually scan the area to locate the hidden teddy bear. After the bear is found, read aloud this delightful story.

Learning Links

Rhyming Class Book

Reinforce rhyming skills and positional concepts with this class flip book. To create the book backing, copy, color, and cut out the bear pattern on page 196; then glue the cutout onto the right side of a large sheet of tagboard. Write "Teddy says…" across the top of the tagboard. Then gather rhyming sets of objects or pictures, such as *corn* and *horn,* and *coat* and *goat.* Have each child choose a rhyming pair from the collection. Ask her to illustrate one item from the pair on a nine-inch construction paper square. Help her label her drawing with "Where's my [coat]?" Have her write or dictate and illustrate the rhyming answer, such as "The coat is on a goat," on the back of her paper. Stack all the pages along the lower left edge of the backing. Hole-punch the pages and the tagboard backing and attach them with metal rings. During group sharing, invite each child to read her page to the class. Then make this book a traveling book to share with families.

62

Art Smarts

Remember Teddy?

Boost memory skills and challenge youngsters to identify their own work with these anonymous teddies. To begin, label the back corner of a sheet of art paper with a child's name. On the front of his paper, have the child paint a teddy bear similar to his favorite teddy. After the paint dries, display the paintings at random around the room. Then ask children to try to locate their own paintings, but to keep their discoveries secret. During group time, chant to each child, "[Child's name], ready? Show us your teddy!" Invite the named child to point out his teddy art to the class. Later, move the pictures to new locations; then repeat the activity.

Purposeful Play

Bear Hide-n-Seek

It's time to play teddy bear hide-and-seek! On an appointed day, have youngsters bring their favorite teddy bears from home. (Provide extras for those without teddies.) Label each child's bear with her name. Then divide your class into small groups. Assign one child in the group to be It. Have the other children cover their eyes while It hides each of their teddy bears. On a signal, send each child on a search for her own teddy. Invite the first child to find her teddy to take the role of It during the next round of play. Now, where's my teddy?

Storybook Café

Snuggle Bears

Students will find that these toasted teddies make terrific treats.

Supplies:
bear-shaped cookie cutter
pastry brush
toaster oven

Ingredients for one:
slice of bread
melted margarine
cinnamon-sugar mixture
black decorating gel
teddy bear cracker

To make one snuggle bear snack:
1. Brush melted margarine onto bread.
2. Sprinkle cinnamon mixture on butter.
3. Toast in oven. Allow toast to cool.
4. Cut out a bear shape from the toast.
5. Use decorating gel to create a face on the bear toast.
6. "Glue" a teddy bear cracker onto the bear toast with a gel dot.

Around the Pond: Who's Been Here?

Written and illustrated by Lindsay Barrett George

Two youngsters discover that there's lots of life around their pond when they find and decipher the clues left behind by an interesting collection of critters.

Storytime Song

Your youngsters will be eager to discover the book of the day when you invite them to storytime with this song sung to the tune of "London Bridge."

Who's been here around the pond,
Round the pond, round the pond?
Who's been here around the pond?
Let's discover!

Has a **duck** been round the pond,
Round the pond, round the pond?
Has a **duck** been round the pond?
Let's discover!

(Repeat the second verse several more times, replacing the animal name with a new animal from the story each time.)

When your little ones are seated, read the story aloud.

Story Recall Clues

Once they've heard this nature detective tale, your little ones will be intrigued by the chance to gather around a classroom pond to answer the question "Who's been here?" Prior to reading the book, prepare a discovery mat to use with your youngsters in a post-story activity. To prepare the discovery mat, cut an 18-inch circle from blue bulletin board paper and a 36-inch circle from brown bulletin board paper. Glue the blue circle in the center of the brown circle to simulate a pond and its shoreline. Make a hand- or footprint on the brown paper with brown paint to provide the first clue on the discovery mat. Next, gather some common items similar to those in the story—such as a feather, a broken chicken eggshell, a small pet collar, and an apple core—to be used on the mat as additional clues. Hide the mat and clue objects in a box or bag. After you've read and discussed the story, ask your youngsters to close their eyes while you lay the discovery mat in the center of the reading circle and place the clue objects around the paper pond. After directing your youngsters to open their eyes, say, "Let's look around the pond in the center of our circle. Who's been here?" Invite each child to recall what she learned in the story, and then use her knowledge to figure out what kind of creature left the clues around your pond mock-up. Later, place the mat and accompanying items in a discovery center, adding more clue objects to the collection as desired.

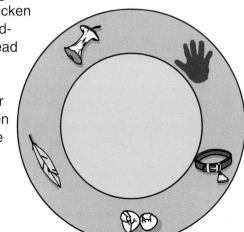

Pond Mural

Art Smarts

This bulletin board mural project will have all of your youngsters as busy as beavers. To prepare, back a bulletin board with brown paper. Cut a large pond shape from blue paper to fit the board; then lay the paper on a newspaper-covered floor or table. Divide your students into three groups. Direct the first group to sponge-paint the pond shape with dark blue paint. When the blue paint is dry, have the second group apply a sponged layer of purple paint. To complete the pond, ask the third group to sponge it with a light layer of white paint. Post the pond in the center of the bulletin board. Next, review *Around the Pond* with your youngsters, prompting them to pay attention to the animals and plants that are illustrated. Invite each child to draw and color an animal to cut out and display around the pond mural. Encourage your students to fill out the mural with their own illustrated cutouts of plants and trees.

Berry-Gathering Game

Purposeful Play

Though your youngsters may not be able to go berry picking like the children in the story, they'll enjoy playing this berry-gathering game. To prepare, make a berry pail like those in the story from a milk carton and a length of twine. Fill the pail with a collection of pom-poms, one for each child in the class. Include one blue pom-pom to represent a blueberry. To play, ask your students to stand in a circle. Then go around the circle to each child in turn. Direct each child to close her eyes, reach into the pail, and pick a berry. Urge her to conceal the pom-pom in her hand so that no one can see it, then have her peek into her hand to see what color berry she has. Next, say, "Blueberry, blueberry! Who has the blueberry?" Invite each child in turn to respond by saying either, "Not me, I have the [color] berry," or, "Me! I have the blueberry!" Invite the child who has picked the blueberry to pass the berry pail for the next round.

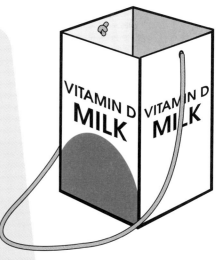

Blueberry Buckets

Storybook Café

The storybook's adventure begins when the children take their blueberry pails to the pond to pick a sweet snack. Your youngsters will love making and snacking on these edible berry bucket treats!

Supplies:
spoons

Ingredients:
12-ounce can of blueberries, drained
half gallon of vanilla ice cream, slightly softened
cake-style ice-cream cone (1 per child)
6" piece of red shoestring licorice per child

To make one blueberry bucket treat:
1. Fill a cone with ice cream to within a half-inch of the rim.
2. Top the ice cream with a spoonful of blueberries.
3. Bend the licorice to resemble a bucket handle; push the ends into the ice cream.

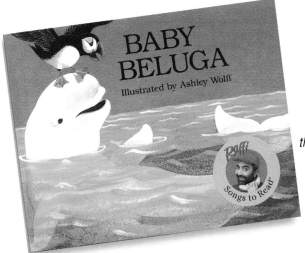

Baby Beluga

Written by Raffi
Illustrated by Ashley Wolff

Your youngsters will love getting to know a baby beluga whale as they follow its doings in the deep blue sea.

Storytime Song

When you sing this song to the tune of "I'm a Little Teapot," you'll bring your youngsters to storytime right away!

What is a **beluga?** Do you know?
Where does a **beluga** like to go?
What does a **beluga** like to do?
You'll know when I read this book to you.

Who is this **beluga?** Do you know?
Where does this **beluga** like to go?
What does this **beluga** like to do?
You'll know when I read this book to you.

(Display the cover of the book as you sing this verse.)

(Repeat until all your curious kiddies have joined together.)

When all of your youngsters are ready, read aloud *Baby Beluga*.

Learning Links

Whale Action Words

This whale's tale introduces your little ones to a baby beluga who is really on the go! The simple storyline offers a great opportunity for your youngsters to study the action words that describe what the baby whale does during her day. First, read the story through so that your youngsters can enjoy the rhythmic text of the tale. In a follow-up reading, discuss each page in turn, asking youngsters to identify the words that describe the little whale's actions, such as *swim, splash,* and *dive.* Use a black marker to write these words in the center of a large piece of blue bulletin board paper. Next, ask your students to think of additional "doing" words to describe other things that the baby beluga might do during her day. Then add those words to the list. Title the list "What Does a Baby Beluga Do?" To enhance the word list, invite each child to draw a small beluga whale with white chalk or crayon somewhere within the margins of the paper. Later, review the list with your youngsters; then ask them to identify those things that they do during their busy days. They may just discover that their own high and dry doings are similar to Baby Beluga's wet ones!

Baby Beluga Puppet

Art Smarts

The story illustrations of the baby whale could not be any cuter! Invite each child to make a cute beluga bag puppet to use with the song in "Song Performance" at right. To prepare, reproduce the baby beluga patterns on page 197 onto white construction paper for each child. Have the child cut out the pattern pieces and then connect the tail piece to the body piece with a brad where indicated. Direct the child to glue the flipper piece to the beluga's side and then attach a wiggle eye sticker to the head. Ask the child to put his completed whale aside while he decorates a paper bag with a blue sea scene. Have each child sponge-paint one side of his bag with blue paint. When the paint is dry, have him embellish the bag with wave lines made from silver glitter paint. Next, have him cut small fish shapes from construction paper and then glue these to the bag to finish off the marine scene. To complete the bag puppet, help the child apply glue to the back side of his beluga body piece and then glue this section of the whale to the bag. The tail piece will be free to move up and down as the child manipulates his puppet.

Song Performance

Purposeful Play

Once your little whale lovers have learned this song, invite them to sing it together as they use their puppets to demonstrate how a baby beluga can swim, dive, and splash in the deep blue sea!

A Baby Beluga
(sung to the tune of "Did You Ever See a Lassie?")
Did you ever see a baby
Beluga, beluga?
Did you ever see her **swimming**
In the deep blue sea?

Did you ever see a baby
Beluga, beluga?
Did you ever see her **splashing**
In the deep blue sea?

Did you ever see a baby
Beluga, beluga?
Did you ever see him **diving**
In the deep blue sea?

Did you ever see a baby
Beluga, beluga?
Did you ever see him **sleeping**
In the deep blue sea?

Learning Links

Beluga Behavior

Since the words in *Baby Beluga* are actually the lyrics to Raffi's wonderful song, a singing session is a must before your youngsters complete this little beluga unit! Because your youngsters' learning has focused on Baby Beluga's behavior, have them demonstrate what they've discovered by acting out the words to the song as they sing. To give the movement activity a marine theme, give each child two blue crepe paper streamers to use as ocean waves. Next, take your youngsters to a large open space; then invite them to imitate baby whales at play in the waves as they sing along to a recording of Raffi's song.

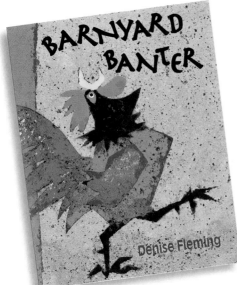

Barnyard Banter

Written and illustrated by Denise Fleming

Animal sounds abound in this dazzling display of boisterous barn-yard animals down on the farm.

Storytime Song

Make an announcement, loud and clear, that storytime is here with a lively song sung to the tune of "Take Me Out to the Ballgame."

Let's go down to the barnyard.
Let's go out to the farm!
We'll hear the animals loud and clear.
The hens and roosters will give us a cheer!
We'll hear hee-haw-haw from the donkeys.
The cows will say, "Moo, moo, moo!"
Come and hear some animal sounds
As I read to you!

(Repeat the song until all the children have joined together.)

Once your young ones have gathered round, read aloud *Barnyard Banter*.

Animal Sound Classification

This barnyard tale stars lots of frolicsome farm critters that are full of spirited sounds. After reading the story aloud, ask your youngsters to name all of the animals in the story as you list the names on chart paper. Have your students classify the animal characters in the story by dividing the list into two groups. Ask volunteers to circle the names of the birds with a red marker and to circle the names of the other animals, including the crickets, with a blue marker. Next, review the story with your youngsters as you turn their focus to the actual sounds that each animal makes. Return to your list, pointing to each name as all of your youngsters make the animal's matching sound as it is described in the story. To wrap up the activity, divide the class into two groups, assigning one of the farm critter sets to each group of youngsters. Point to a bird name on the list; then prompt the bird group to chime in with the proper sound effect. Point to one of the other animal names next, prompting the other animal group to make their matching animal sound. When your youngsters have vocalized for every critter on the list, give students the opportunity to switch groups; then work through the list once more.

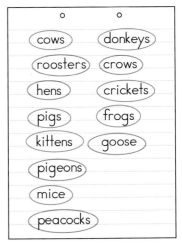

Splatter-Paint Poster

Art Smarts

It's hard to take your eyes off a tale with illustrations as bright and lively as those in this snappy storybook. When your youngsters make these splatter-painted projects, they'll be involved in the first step of creating a similar bright and lively work of art of their own. To set up a center for splatter painting, you will need a large box with sides at least 18 inches high; one 9" x 12" sheet of yellow construction paper for each child; containers of brown, orange, and red paint; and a brush for each color. To begin, ask a child to put on a paint shirt and join you at the center. Direct the child to write her name on the back of her paper; then have her place the paper in the bottom of the large box. Next, ask the child to dip the tip of a brush into her choice of paint and then hold the brush a few inches above the paper inside the box. Have her carefully flick the brush toward the paper to create a splattered effect. Encourage the child to continue the process with the remaining colors of paint. Set each child's project aside to dry before going on to the next activity.

Secret Sound Game

Purposeful Play

The animal sounds in the story make it just the thing for getting your youngsters involved in a choral reading of the tale. Before you reread the story and invite your youngsters to chime in, cut a class supply of one-inch paper squares. Draw a small butterfly on one of the squares; then place all of the squares in a bag. Invite your students to return to the reading circle, telling them that they will help you read the story this time. Tell your students that you want them to read the animal sounds in the story together. Let them know that since the goose doesn't surprise us with its sound until the very end, someone in the group will secretly get to be the goose. Tell your students that each one of them will draw a paper square from the bag. The child who draws the square marked with the butterfly will be the secret goose and will be the only one to make the goose's sound when it appears in the story. Read *Barnyard Banter,* prompting the class to chime in with the animal sound that is written on each page. When you come to the final page of the tale, it will be time for the mystery goose to "honk, honk, honk" the final sound of the story!

Books About Animals

Barnyard Collage

Art Smarts

Now that each little artist has splatter-painted a barnyard background, provide some materials for him to transform his paper into a farmyard collage. Encourage each child to glue small bits of straw, raffia, and torn paper to his splattered background to mimic the story illustrations. Provide birdseed to be glued on as well. Ask each child to draw and color a small version of a farm animal from the story, cut it out, and then glue it to his collage. Staple a sentence strip to the bottom of each child's artwork. Personalize each child's project by writing a sentence on his strip. Use the format shown, programming each child's sentence with the name of the animal in his collage, its location in the story, and the sound that it makes.

The **rooster** in the **barnyard** says, **"Cock-a-doodle-doo!"**

Fish Eyes: A Book You Can Count On

Written and illustrated by Lois Ehlert

Your little minnows will be all eyes as they practice their counting skills with the bright and vibrant fish in this colorful book.

Storytime Song

Lure your youngsters to storytime with this song sung to the tune of "Daisy, Daisy."

Fish eyes, fish eyes,
You'll see some in this book.
Lots of fish eyes—
Come on, let's take a look.
They come in all shapes and sizes.
You're in for some surprises!
So come and see
Some fish with me
As we look at this fish eyes book.

(Repeat the song until all of the children have arrived at the reading area.)

Once your youngsters are in the swim of storytime, read aloud *Fish Eyes.*

Describing Fish Tales

The vivacious fish in this tale will draw your little ones into the story from the very first page. As you read the story aloud, encourage your youngsters to listen carefully to the descriptions of what the fish look like and what the fish do. When you've finished, ask your youngsters to help you list the words in the story that describe what the fish look like, including *green, striped,* and *flashy.* Have them help you list the words that describe fish behavior, including *darting, flipping,* and *jumping.* Next, invite each child to follow the example of the author and imagine what she would look like and what she would do if she were a fish. Program a sheet of paper with the incomplete sentences shown, and then make a class supply. Give one to each child. Direct her to draw and color a picture of the fish in the center of the paper; then have her write one descriptive word to complete the sentence at the top of the page. To complete the sheet, have her write a word with an "ing" ending to finish the sentence at the bottom of the page. Later, give each child an opportunity to share her fish picture and descriptions with the rest of the class.

Art Smarts

Fishy Counting Book

This colorful art project will produce the brightest school of fish your youngsters have ever seen! To create a fish-themed scene that reflects the artwork in the book, give each child a 9" x 12" sheet of dark blue construction paper. Ask each child to cut fish shapes of different sizes and colors from construction paper scraps; then have her glue as many as possible to her blue paper. Next, have the child embellish the eye area of each fish with one colored sticky dot. Have her stick a brightly colored paper reinforcer on each circle label to finish each artistic fish eye as shown. Ask each child to complete her project by counting the fish eyes on her paper. At the bottom of her paper, have her write "I see [number] fish eyes." Bind your students' projects together between construction paper covers to create a book titled "Can You Count Fish Eyes?" Later, invite each child to take a peek at the class book and use each page for counting practice.

I see 5 fish eyes.

Purposeful Play

Big Eye Patterns

If your youngsters are eager for more big-eyed fish, this patterning activity will do the trick. First, cut out a supply of four-inch-long fish shapes from a single color of construction paper. Embellish each fish with a colorful eye as described in "Fishy Counting Book." Create several different eye designs so that you have a variety to use for patterning; then glue some of the fish to tagboard patterning strips. Store the patterning strips and extra fish shapes in a large plastic fishing tackle box. To play, have each child complete each patterning strip from the supply of extra fish shapes in the tackle box.

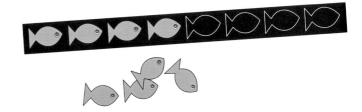

Storybook Café

Fish Cracker Snacks

There's something fishy about this snack…and your youngsters will love it!

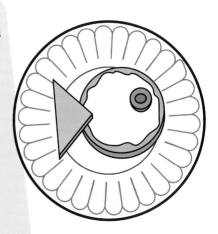

Supplies:
small paper plates   plastic knives

Ingredients:
large round cracker for each child
American cheese slices cut into triangles (1 triangle per child)
spreadable cream cheese
pimento-filled green olives, sliced

To make one fishy cracker snack:
1. Place one large round cracker on a paper plate.
2. Use a plastic knife to spread cream cheese on the cracker.
3. Add a cheese triangle tail to the cracker.
4. Top the cracker with an olive-slice eye.

Going to the Zoo

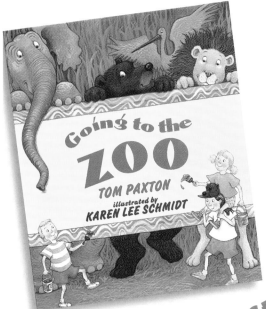

Written by Tom Paxton
Illustrated by Karen Lee Schmidt

Take your little animal lovers on a rhythmic trip to the zoo with this book based on the well-known song by Tom Paxton.

Storytime Song

When you sing this song to the tune of "We Wish You a Merry Christmas," your little ones will want to come right to storytime. But watch out! They may want to stay all day!

Let's read all about a good trip.
Let's read all about a great trip.
Let's read all about a cool trip,
A trip to the zoo!

Let's read all about a neat trip.
Let's read all about a nice trip.
Let's read all about a fine trip,
A trip to the zoo!

(Repeat until all the children have joined together.)

Once your youngsters have gathered together, read aloud *Going to the Zoo.*

Learning Links

Sequential Story Recall

With a literary trip this bouncy and fun, your little ones will find it quite easy to remember the critter characters that they've met along the way. Before you read, copy the animal patterns on page 198 and prepare them for the flannelboard. After reading the book, ask your youngsters to name the animals in the story in any order that they remember them. As each child names an animal, place the corresponding flannelboard figure at the top of the flannelboard. Next, ask a volunteer to find the animal that is the *first* one introduced in the story; then have the child place the elephant on the right side of the board. Continue to ask volunteers to help rearrange the animals on the board, following the sequence from the story. Later, give each child a construction paper copy of the animal pattern page to color and cut out. Have each child glue his animal cutouts to a sentence strip in sequential order.

Me at the Zoo Poster

Now that your little ones have reviewed all of the zoo animals in the story, give them the opportunity to create "zoo-rific" works of art! Provide a class supply of both 9" x 12" and 12" x 18" construction paper in a variety of colors. Have each child select one of each size paper in contrasting colors. Instruct him to center the smaller sheet atop the larger sheet and glue it in place to create a framed canvas. Provide inexpensive pastel crayons and invite him to draw pictures of zoo animals in the frame area, and a picture of her family preparing to go to the zoo in the center area. Have him write, or dictate as you write, a one-sentence description of what his family is doing to prepare to go to the zoo. Post all of your youngsters' artwork on a wall beneath the title "Let's All Go to the Zoo!"

My family will pack a picnic lunch for our zoo trip.

Books About Animals

Purposeful Play

Musical Immitations

Since little ones enjoy learning through creative expression, they'll love getting to know more about the zoo animals in the story through a little bit of creative playacting. Because the text of the book actually uses the words to Tom Paxton's lively animal song, a musical retelling of the tale is a must! Set up a CD or audiotape player in the middle of a large space that provides plenty of room to move. Ask your students to sit and listen while you play your favorite version of "Going to the Zoo." (*Singable Songs for the Very Young* by Raffi contains a version of the song.) Tell your youngsters that you will play the song again while they move around and pantomime the animal actions without making any sounds. Play the song a third time, encouraging your youngsters to repeat their animal antics, this time adding the appropriate animal sounds. What a zoo!

Storybook Café

Cagey Critter Treat

Animal cookies are an all-time favorite, so why not use them to create a crunchy critter snack to munch?

Supplies:
small paper plates

craft sticks

Ingredients:
large box of animal crackers
box of graham crackers

spreadable cream cheese
piece of Twizzlers Pull-n-Peel candy

To make one cagey critter treat:
1. Lay a graham cracker on a paper plate.
2. Spread cream cheese on the cracker with a craft stick.
3. Select an animal cracker; place it on the cream cheese–topped cracker.
4. Lay several strips of candy on top of the cookie-cracker stack to make it look like an animal cage.

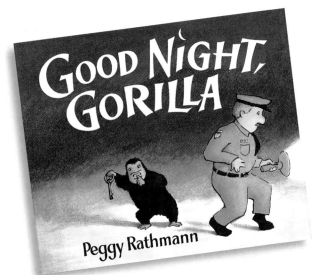

Good Night, Gorilla

Written and illustrated by Peggy Rathmann

Doesn't everyone wonder what the animals in the zoo do when night falls? This sweet story uses hilarious illustrations to propose an improbable, but comical, answer.

Storytime Song

All of your eager readers will be intrigued when you invite them to story-time with this song sung to the tune of "Down by the Station."

> Meet a gorilla
> Living in the zoo. Oh,
> Where does the gorilla go
> When the day is through?
> Does the tired gorilla
> Slip into a bunk bed?
> Oh, I don't know!
> How 'bout you?

(Repeat the song until all of your little ones have joined together.)

Once all of your curious kiddies have joined together, read the story aloud.

Cozy Comparison

This bedtime tale tells us where the zoo animals like to go when they toddle off to bed, but it doesn't tell us why they want to go there. After reading the story to your youngsters, encourage each child to tell you why he thinks the animals did not want to sleep alone in their cages. Divide a sheet of chart paper into two columns. Label one column "Zoo-keeper's Room" and the other column "Our Rooms." Ask your youngsters to recall the things that were in the zookeeper's room that helped make it cozy. List these student-generated ideas in the "Zookeeper's Room" column. Next, ask your youngsters to brainstorm a list of the things that they like to have in their bedrooms at night, such as soft music, a night-light, a favorite plush toy, or even a sibling to share the room. Write these things in the "Our Rooms" column. Finally, have students compare and contrast the things that make them comfortable at bedtime to the things that might have attracted the animals to the keeper's home.

Zookeeper's Room	Our Rooms
night-light	night-light
other animals	stuffed toy
cozy bed	blanket
banana	snack

Art Smarts

Painted Zoo

The nighttime scenes in the story express a wonderful dusky evening quality. Your youngsters can imitate this style when you provide materials for a crayon-resist art project. Prior to the activity, prepare two pans of tempera paint that you've thinned with water. You will need one pan of diluted purple and one pan of diluted blue paint. Test the thinned paint before you use it; when you brush the watered-down paint on a piece of paper, the paint should be transparent. To begin the project, ask each child to draw and color a zoo animal on a 9" x 12" sheet of white construction paper. Be sure that the child applies the crayon very thickly. Next, use a wide brush to apply two bands of the purple paint to the top of the child's paper. Brush very lightly over any crayon-covered areas; do not scrub the crayon with the brush. Cover the rest of the paper with bands of the blue paint to create a dusky effect. Display the completed projects on a bulletin board titled "Good Night, Zoo Animals."

Purposeful Play

Follow the Gorilla Game

When it came to guiding friends to bed, the gorilla was quite a leader. Inform your youngsters that you are going to pretend to be the little gorilla in the story for a game of Follow the Leader. To begin the game, ask your students to stand in scattered positions around the room. Next, walk up to a child and say, "Good night," adding his name to your statement. Prompt the child to respond by saying, "Good night, Gorilla!" as he lines up behind you. Move to a second child and invite her to join you in the line with the same statement and response pattern. Continue this lead-and-follow activity until all of your little ones have joined the line. Play as many additional rounds of the game as desired with a different child volunteer as the leader for each new round. To end the game, ask the final leader to usher each child to his seat where he can say good night and pretend to settle down for a good night's sleep!

Storybook Café

Good Night Goodie

This simple snack is something that the little gorilla in the story might love to have at bedtime.

Supplies:
small paper plates
plastic knife

Ingredients:
graham cracker square for each child
banana slice for each child
jam
colorful candy sprinkles

To make one good night goodie:
1. Place a banana slice pillow near one end of the cracker.
2. Spread jam over the rest of the cracker.
3. Add sprinkles to the jam cover.

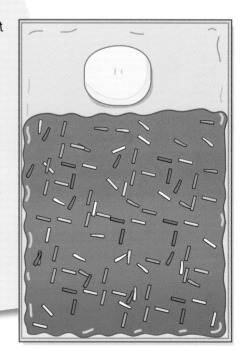

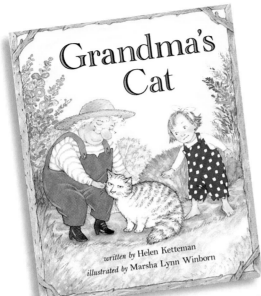

Grandma's Cat

Written by Helen Ketteman
Illustrated by Marsha Lynn Winborn

This tale of a slightly grumpy cat and a friendly little girl will draw children to storytime quicker than you can say "Here, kitty-kitty!"

Storytime Song

Sing this song to the tune of "Mary Had a Little Lamb" to call your little cat lovers to storytime.

Can you make friends with a cat,
With a cat, with a cat?
Can you make friends with a cat?
Let's read this book to see!

Can you be pals with a cat
With a cat, with a cat?
Can you be pals with a cat?
Let's read this book to see!

(Sing the song several times until every child has joined you at the reading area.)

When your youngsters are quiet and ready, read *Grandma's Cat* aloud.

Creating Kind Kitty Rules

Sometimes it's hard for a little one to learn the best way to approach a persnickety kitty! When Grandma teaches her granddaughter the basic rules for a cat-and-little-girl relationship, making friends becomes much easier. After you read the story, ask your youngsters to tell you what the little girl finally does to make friends with her grandma's cat. Next, encourage each child to take a turn sharing her own idea for a rule that assures kind behavior toward cats. Write these student-generated rules on chart paper, if desired. Later, teach your youngsters this traditional nursery rhyme to reinforce the best way to behave with a kitty!

I love little Kitty; her coat is so warm.
And if I don't hurt her, she'll do me no harm.
I'll not pull her tail nor drive her away,
But Kitty and I very gently will play.

1. Pet its head softly.
2. Speak in a quiet voice.
3.

Art Smarts

Cute Cat Carrier

Every youngster will scamper straight home when she proudly carries her completed work in this cute kitty portfolio! To make a portfolio, each child will need a 12" x 18" sheet of colored construction paper, scissors, access to a stapler, crayons, and six pipe cleaner halves. Fold the construction paper in half and then trim the open ends as shown to create the shape of a cat's head. Give each child a trimmed and folded paper; then have her use crayons to draw a cat face on one side. Next, unfold the paper and help each child push pipe cleaner sections through the paper on either side of the cat's nose to make a set of whiskers. To complete the portfolio, refold the paper and staple the edges together along the left and right sides.

Purposeful Play

Positional Placement

Grandma's cat likes to hide *in* the grass, *up* a tree, *on* the stairs, and *behind* a bush. Your youngsters will love looking for a little kitty who likes to hide just like the cat in the story. You will need one plush toy cat for this seek-and-find position-word activity. Direct your youngsters to hide their eyes while seated in their chairs; then place the plush cat *on* a table. Ask each child to open his eyes, remain seated, and quietly scan the room for the toy cat. Encourage a volunteer to tell you exactly where the cat is "hiding," using a complete sentence to describe the location. Write the sentence on a tagboard strip, using a different color of marker to write the position word. Continue the activity in the same way, hiding the cat in different places so that students have the opportunity to use the words *in, up, on, under,* and *behind* in describing the locations. Later, give each child a chance to replace the cat in one of its previous hiding places; then help the child find the sentence strip that describes the kitty cat cache.

Storybook Café

Persnickety Pies

Win over your finicky little ones with these "meow-velous" treats.

Supplies:
ice-cream scoop
clear plastic cup for each child
plastic spoon for each child

Ingredients:
box of graham cracker crumbs
gallon of vanilla ice cream
16 oz. bag chocolate chips
jar of caramel syrup

To make one persnickety pie:
1. Spoon cracker crumbs into cup to cover bottom.
2. Fill cup one-third full of ice cream.
3. Layer cracker crumbs and chocolate chips atop ice cream.
4. Top with caramel syrup.
5. Repeat steps 2–4.

I Went Walking

Written by Sue Williams
Illustrated by Julie Vivas

Join a little girl who goes walking down on the farm and meet all of the friendly animals who decide to tag along.

Storytime Song

Round up your young ones for storytime with this lively song sung to the tune of "For He's a Jolly Good Fellow!"

A little girl went walking.
A little girl went walking.
A little girl went walking
To see what she could see!

And oh, what did she see?
And oh, what did she see?

A cat, a horse, and a red cow;
A duck, a pig, and a yellow dog—
She saw a lot of farm animals,
And that's what she did see!

(Repeat until all the children have joined together.)

Once your students have gathered together, read aloud *I Went Walking.*

Learning Links

Sequential Walk

The tagalong animals in this tale provide a perfect opportunity for your youngsters to work on sequencing skills. Before you read, copy the farm animal patterns on page 199. Color the animals as described in the story; then prepare all of the animals (omitting the lamb) for the flannelboard. After reading the book, ask your students to name the animals in the story. Randomly place each animal figure on the flannelboard as it is named. Next, ask a volunteer to find the animal that is the first one to tag along after the girl in the story. Have the child place the black cat on the right side of the board and say, "I see a black cat looking at me!" Continue to ask volunteers to help rearrange the animals on the board from right to left, following the sequence in the story. To extend the activity, use the animal lineup to teach your youngsters the concept of *first* and *last* and to help them review counting from one to six.

Orderly Farm Scene

After being introduced to the animals in the story, your youngsters will be ready for some expressive yet orderly artwork. Prior to the activity, mask the lamb pattern on page 199; then reproduce the page onto white paper for each child. Set the pages aside for later use. To begin the project, invite each child to draw and color a farm scene on a large sheet of white construction paper. Encourage the child to include a drawing of himself very close to the right edge of his paper. Next, give each child a copy of the pattern page so that he can color each animal to match its description in the story. Direct each child to cut out the animals and glue them to his farm scene in sequential order, placing the first animal (the cat) directly to the left of his self-portrait. When each child has completed this artistic story synopsis, encourage him to take his project home and use it to help retell the story to his family.

Miniature Farm

Transform your block center into a miniature farm to give your little ones opportunities for hands-on retellings of the tale. Place a miniature plastic cat, horse, cow, duck, pig, and dog in the center. As an alternative, make stand-up cardboard figures from the farm animal patterns on page 199. Include several toy people figures, extra farm animals, and any other toy farm accessories that you might have. You can also include several sheets of green, brown, and blue craft foam for youngsters to use for farm field and pond props. Once your center is well stocked with farm supplies, invite pairs of students to use the center together. Encourage each pair of youngsters to use the animal and people figures to retell the story through dramatic play. Later, invite youngsters to create their own farm story scenarios with the props in the center.

Farm Animal Sandwich

Turn ordinary jelly sandwiches into farm-themed treats for snacktime!

Supplies:
paper plates
plastic knives
large farm animal cookie cutters

Ingredients:
2 slices of wheat bread for each child
low-sugar jam

To make one farm animal sandwich:
1. Make a jelly sandwich on a plate.
2. Use a cookie cutter to cut a farm animal shape from the sandwich.
3. Tear the sandwich scraps into small pieces; arrange the scraps on the plate to look like food for the farm animal.

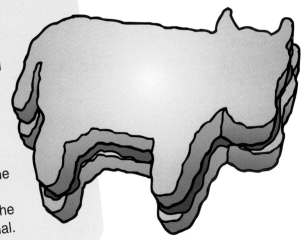

In the Small, Small Pond

Written and illustrated by Denise Fleming

There's action all around in the small, small pond until the weather turns chilly and all the pond animals settle down for the winter.

Storytime Song

Encourage your youngsters to come to storytime by singing this song to the tune of "Old MacDonald."

Let's look in the small, small pond.
Oh, what will we see?
Animals live in the pond.
Oh, what will we see?
Will we see a frog?
Will we see a bird?
In the grass, in the air,
In the water everywhere.
Let's look in the small, small pond.
Oh, what will we see?

Let's look in the small, small pond.
Oh, what will we see?
Animals live in the pond.
Oh, what will we see?
Will we see a bug?
Will we see a fish?
In the grass, in the air,
In the water everywhere.
Let's look in the small, small pond.
Oh, what will we see?

(Repeat the song until all of your little animal lovers have joined together.)

Once your young ones are seated, read the story aloud.

Learning Links

Picture Reading

Although there aren't many words in this lively tale, the illustrations speak volumes! As you read, be sure to allow your youngsters plenty of time to study and discuss each illustration to discover the story being told by the pictures. When you display each double-page illustration, prompt your youngsters to share their ideas by asking, "What's happening in the small, small pond now?" Include in the discussion the identification of the animals that are not named in the text: a frog, dragonflies, turtles, crayfish, ducks, and raccoon. After you've completed the initial reading of the book, you'll be amazed at the amount of information your little ones have gathered from such a small, small story! Later, assign two or three students to represent an individual animal in the story. As you reread the book, give each group of youngsters the opportunity to demonstrate the actions of their animal when it is described in the text.

Critter Collage

Invite each child to create a colorful collage pond and then fill it with water creatures. To begin the project, give each child a 9" x 12" sheet of purple construction paper, a container of starch, and a brush. Also provide pieces of blue and green tissue paper. Ask each child to write his name on his paper, and then lay it name-side down on a large piece of newspaper. Have him brush starch over his construction paper, and then lay tissue pieces over the starch. If some of the tissue is not saturated, have him brush more starch over the dry areas. Direct him to set his work aside until it is dry. Cut several sponges into fish, turtle, and water bug shapes. Provide shallow dishes with small amounts of paint and invite him to fill his pond with sponge-printed creatures, and then use markers to add details such as eyes and legs. Post your youngsters' pond pieces on a large bulletin board backed with blue paper to create a body of water that's teeming with life!

Books About Animals

Purposeful Play

Pond Scope

Stock your water table with plenty of play fish and other toy water creatures to create a small, small pond that's just waiting to be explored. In addition to small plastic fish, bugs, frogs, and turtles, supply your water table with aquarium nets and clear, plastic peanut butter jars with lids. Then enhance your youngsters' play experience by adding easy-to-make pond scopes to your water table exploration center. To make one pond scope, cut off the top and bottom of a pint-size milk carton. Next, cut a 10" x 10" piece of clear plastic wrap; cover one end of the milk carton tightly with the wrap, making sure that the wrap extends well up the sides of the carton. Secure the plastic wrap in two places with rubber bands as shown. To use the pond scope, have each child hold it with two hands, place her eyes close to the open end, and submerge the plastic-covered end in the water. Encourage each child to use this discovery tool to scope out what's in the water; then invite her to use a net to capture some pond critters and put them in a water-filled jar for observation.

Storybook Café

Pond-in-a-Cup

After he's enjoyed the story, each child will want to make a treat that looks just like the small, small pond deep in its winter sleep!

(makes about 6 servings)

Supplies:
small, clear plastic cups   tablespoons   bowls

Ingredients:
large package of Berry Blue Jell-O gelatin, prepared and chilled
package of graham crackers, crushed
green M&M's candies
package of coconut, optional

To make one pond-in-a-cup treat:
1. Place three tablespoons of graham cracker crumb soil in a plastic cup.
2. Add a green M&M's candy frog.
3. Spoon blue gelatin in the cup to represent pond water.
4. If desired, top the gelatin with coconut snowflakes.

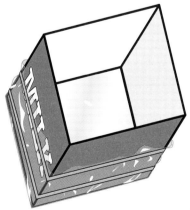

Is This a House for Hermit Crab?

Written by Megan McDonald
Illustrated by S. D. Schindler

Invite your little ones to take a literary stroll along the seashore with a hermit crab who is looking for a home.

Storytime Song

Request each youngster's presence at storytime by singing this song to the tune of "The Itsy-Bitsy Spider."

Let's meet a hermit crab who
Is walking on the shore.
He needs a home with
A hermit crab–size door!
He needs to find a place
That fits him just right.
So the little hermit crab tries on
Every home in sight!

Repeat the song until each child has strolled together; then read aloud *Is This a House for Hermit Crab?*

Learning Links

Homey Story Recall

Hermit Crab tries on many potential houses before he finds the one that is just right. After reading the story to your youngsters, take time to find out what each child recalls about the unsuitable homes in the story. To begin, show the first page of the story to the group and say, "Why did Hermit Crab need a new home? Because he was too big!" Next, show your youngsters the page with the rock illustration and ask, "Is a rock a house for Hermit Crab?" Prompt your youngsters to respond with a sentence that's similar to the words in the story: "No! A rock is too heavy!" Review the picture of each unsuitable house in the story using the question-and-answer process that you've demonstrated. Wrap up the activity by showing your little ones the last page of the book, asking if this last item is a suitable house for Hermit Crab. If your little ones have been listening all along, they'll eagerly answer in the affirmative!

Seashore Scene

Art Smarts

Invite each child to create a seashore scene that looks authentic enough to be the real thing! Provide each child with a 9" x 12" sheet of white construction paper. Help each child fold his paper in half lengthwise; then have him use a wide brush to paint half of the paper blue. When his paper is dry, have each child brush a mixture of white glue and water on the unpainted half. Help each child pour cornmeal over the glue, covering it completely. While he waits for the glue to dry, ask him to draw a small picture of a hermit crab on white construction paper. Have him cut out his crab illustration and glue it near one side of his paper. Encourage him to decorate the blue-painted ocean area of his paper with shell stickers or rubber stamp designs. To complete the creation, give each child a plastic spoon to scrape "scritch-scratch" marks through the corn-meal sand to show where the hermit crab has been!

Sandy Simulation

Purposeful Play

Transform your sand table into an indoor beach complete with a small colony of make-believe hermit crabs. Your little ones will scurry to visit the sandy site to reenact Hermit Crab's house-hunting actions. Stock the sand table with objects from the book, including empty cans, rocks, shells, small sand pails, plastic netting, and a piece of smooth, splinter-free board or driftwood. Make several hermit crab manipulatives for the scene from craft foam. Use the simplified hermit crab shape in the illustrated sample on this page to make a tracer. Trace the pattern onto the foam several times; then cut the crab shapes out. Invite small groups of youngsters to use these foam crabs with the other objects at the sand table to act out Hermit Crab's sequence of seashore discoveries.

Sandy Snacks

Storybook Café

It won't hurt a bit to get a little sand in this snack, especially when the sand is made of crunchy, crushed graham crackers!

Supplies:
craft sticks   small paper plates

Ingredients:
graham cracker for each child
6 finely crushed graham crackers
spreadable cream cheese, tinted with blue food coloring
box of oyster crackers

To make one sandy snack:
1. Use a craft stick to spread blue-tinted cream cheese on a graham cracker.
2. Sprinkle the cream cheese with crushed graham cracker sand.
3. Top the cracker sand with several oyster crackers.

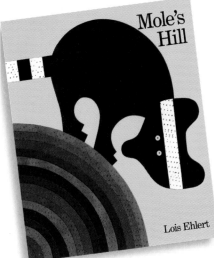

Mole's Hill

Written and illustrated by Lois Ehlert

Who would think that a meek and lowly mole could create a hill full of beautiful flowers? This woodland tale shows how the power of determination can help anyone make a beautiful idea bloom!

Storytime Song

Give your youngsters a hint of the story to come by singing this song to the tune of "My Bonnie Lies Over the Ocean."

The mole in this tale has a notion
To make her hill lovely to see.
She wants her hill to look pretty.
Oh, what can Mole's idea be?
Mole's hill, Mole's hill,
Her hill will be pretty to see, to see.
Mole's hill, Mole's hill,
Oh, what can Mole's idea be?

(Sing the song several times until all of your little ones have joined together.)

When your students are ready, introduce them to *Mole's Hill* with the activity below.

Learning Links

Character Characteristics

This woodsy tale contains wonderful animal characters with definite personality traits. Help your youngsters focus on the animal personalities in the story with this simple character-study activity. Before you begin, create posters by labeling a separate 12" x 18" sheet of construction paper for each woodland creature in the story; then display the sheets on a wall near your reading area. Read the story aloud, pausing when appropriate to discuss the behavior and temperament of the fox, mole, skunk, and raccoon. When you have finished reading and discussing the story, ask your youngsters to brainstorm a list of descriptive words for each animal. Encourage them to think of words to describe both the animal's personality and appearance. Write the student-generated list of words for each creature on its construction paper poster. At the end of the brainstorming session, divide your youngsters into four groups. Assign an animal from the story to each group. Ask each child in a group to draw and color a small picture of the animal and then cut it out and glue it to the group's poster. What a great way to use your youngsters' words and pictures for story character descriptions!

Mole

busy	clever
creative	hardworking
nice	helpful
small	gray

Dandy Descriptive Booklets

The flowery pages of this colorful tale are based on Native American art from the North American woodlands. The bright color combinations and simple flower shapes in the collage illustrations make this style a natural for little artists! To prepare collage materials for your youngsters, trace several flower shapes from Ehlert's book and photocopy the shapes on fluorescent paper in shades of pink, red, yellow, orange, purple, blue, and lime. Provide three 9" x 12" sheets of construction paper for each child: one green, one gray, and one blue. Prior to the activity, cut matching hill shapes from each child's green and gray paper. Have each child glue his green hill shape to his sheet of blue construction paper. Encourage him to cut out a variety of flower shapes; have him glue these to the green hill shape to create his own design. When the glue is dry, have each child lay his gray hill shape on top of his flower-decorated hill and then staple the pieces together along the left side. At the base of each child's gray hill write the words "Mole's hill is…" To finish the project, write each child's dictated words to complete the sentence at the base of the green hill.

Flower Patterns

Now that your youngsters have had some hands-on practice with flower arrangements, they'll be ready to work on a patterning activity. Extend the use of the flower shapes created for "Dandy Descripton Booklets" by using them to make activity cards for independent patterning activities. First, make a fresh supply of brightly colored flower shapes as directed above. Cut out the shapes; then glue flower pieces and centers together to create several different sets of flower designs to use for patterning. Glue several of the flowers onto one end of a tagboard strip to form a pattern. To do this activity, instruct a child to complete each pattern card with a supply of extra flowers.

Fancy Flower Cookies

Frosted flower cookies in a variety of pretty designs are as much fun to look at as they are to eat!

Supplies:
4" x 4" green construction paper squares
craft sticks

Ingredients:
baked, flower-shaped sugar cookies
cookie-decorating sprinkles in several colors
prepared frosting in several colors
M&M's candies

To make one fancy flower cookie:
1. Place cookie on a green paper square.
2. Spread choice of frosting on the cookie with a craft stick.
3. Shake choice of sprinkles over frosting.
4. Place an M&M's candy piece in the center of the flower.

85

Night Gliders

Written by Joanne Ryder
Illustrated by Melissa Bay Mathis

Open your youngsters' eyes to the secret lives of some seldom seen but very special night creatures with this wonderful book.

Storytime Song

Show your youngsters the cover of the book; then, to usher them to storytime, sing this song to the tune of "Twinkle, Twinkle, Little Star."

Guess who glides from tree to tree.
Guess who has bright eyes to see.
Guess who stays awake all night.
Guess who sleeps when it's daylight.
Guess who seems to fly swiftly.
What kind of squirrel can this be?

(Repeat the song until all of your little ones have joined together.)

When your youngsters are seated and ready to learn about these curious squirrels, introduce them to *Night Gliders* with the activity below.

Learning Links

Prior Knowledge Prompt

Before you read the story, find out whether your students know anything about these hard-to-see squirrels. Prior to the activity, enlarge the flying squirrel patterns on page 200 to fit a large sheet of construction paper. Use the enlarged patterns to cut three squirrel shapes from gray construction paper. Title one squirrel cutout "What We Know About Flying Squirrels," title the second "What We Want to Know About Flying Squirrels," and title the third "What We Learned About Flying Squirrels." Post the cutouts on a wall. Show your youngsters the cover of the book once again; then prompt them to share any tidbits of information they might have about the elusive flying squirrel. Record these comments on the first squirrel cutout. Next, ask students what they would like to know about flying squirrels. Record those comments on the second cutout. Then read *Night Gliders* aloud. After discussing the story, ask students to recall what they found out from the book. Write those facts on the third squirrel cutout. Extend your youngsters' interest in learning by placing a few factual books about flying squirrels in a center along with a copy of *Night Gliders*.

What We Learned About Squirrels

They hide nuts.

They only come out at night.

They live in small family groups.

They don't really fly; they glide.

86

Art Smarts

Squirrel Puppets

Introduce your little ones to a crafty project that will make their study of flying squirrels a real hands-on activity. To prepare, make two white construction paper copies of the flying squirrel patterns on page 200 for each child. Provide each child with crayons or colored pencils in several shades of gray; then have him color both squirrel patterns and one tail pattern to create a furry effect. Next, ask each child to cut out his patterns and stack the two squirrel patterns together, colored side out. Help each child staple his squirrel patterns together along the top and side edges to create a hand puppet. Give each child two small wiggle eyes stickers and a tiny pom-pom to stick or glue to one side of his puppet's head, creating a squirrel face; have the child draw a mouth below the squirrel's nose. Direct each child to glue the tail to the lower back edge of his puppet; then have him fold his puppet's paws in toward the center of the body. Invite each child to use his puppet in the "Puppet Poem" activity below.

Books About Animals

Storybook Café

Squirrel Snacks

Invite your youngsters to snack as the squirrels in the story do. They might feel a bit nutty, but they'll love it!

Supplies:
craft sticks

Ingredients:
cream cheese
sesame crackers
shelled sunflower seeds

To make one squirrel snack:
1. Spread cream cheese on a sesame cracker with a craft stick.
2. Top the cream cheese with a sprinkling of sunflower seeds.

Purposeful Play

Puppet Poem

Even though your youngsters may have never seen a night glider in the wild, they can use their puppets to demonstrate what they've learned about the behaviors flying squirrels display. Encourage each child to put on her hand puppet and use it to demonstrate the actions described in the poem below.

Flying squirrels are a curious sight
As they start their day in the dark of night.
Stretching their four paws out so wide,
They leap from a tree and then they glide
Down to the ground where they dash and run
To nibble a nut—to play and have fun!
Soon they'll climb up a tree and then
They'll leap and glide through the sky again.

Pet Show!

Written and illustrated by Ezra Jack Keats

*Every pet wins a prize at this picture book pet show,
even a pet that's too tiny to be seen!*

Storytime Song

Extend an invitation to gather for storytime with this pet show tune sung to
"I'm a Little Teapot."

Let's go to the pet show
   in this book.
Let's open it and
   take a look.
We will find all kinds of
   pets, you'll see!
So come and sit in the
   circle with me!

Who'll be at the pet show
   in this book?
Let's open it and
   take a look.
Will there be a cat or
   dog or flea?
Oh, come to the circle
   and you will see!

(Repeat until all the children have joined together.)

Once your little ones have gathered together, read aloud *Pet Show!*

Learning Links

Pet Show Recall

Calling all youngsters for *Pet Show!* recall! Cut out a class supply of ribbons
from a roll of two-inch-wide blue ribbon. Pin a small safety pin to the top of each
ribbon. After reading the book, play Pet Show Recall. Have your students brainstorm a list of the pets in the story. Write the list on chart paper. Next, ask each
child to name another kind of pet to add to the list. Encourage your students to
say the name of each pet with you as you read the list out loud. Then ask volunteers to help you circle the names of the most common kinds of pets and put a
star next to those that are the most unusual. To wrap up the activity, invite each
child to select an animal from the list; then have her dictate or write a sentence on
a strip of paper to explain why she would like to be the proud owner of this special
kind of pet. Save each child's written work to pair with the art activity on the next
page for a bulletin board titled "Showing Off Our Favorite Pets!" Finally, award a
blue ribbon to each child. When parents ask what the ribbons are for, your little
ones will enjoy showing off their recall skills.

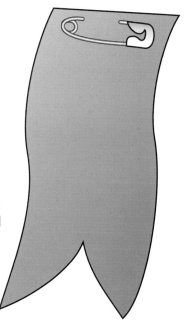

Art Smarts

Chalky Pets

Now that each child has used words to describe a special pet, invite her to highlight her written work with a drawing created in the style of Ezra Jack Keats. Provide each child with a 9" x 12" sheet of construction paper in a dark color of her choice. Have each child use brightly colored chalk to draw and color a picture of her pet. Encourage her to add chalk designs around the pet to create a colorful background. When each child has completed her chalk picture, spray it with a clear acrylic topcoat to prevent smudging. Display each child's pet-themed writing and artwork on a bulletin board titled "Showing Off Our Favorite Pets!"

Purposeful Play

Plush Pet Show

Take advantage of every child's love of dramatic play with a plush pet show! Before the day of the show, cut a class supply of blue ribbons from colored construction paper; add sticker and glitter embellishments if desired. Ask each child to bring his favorite plush animal pet to school to enter in your classroom show. Be sure to provide a supply of extra animals for any child who might need one. To begin the show, direct your youngsters to hold their plush pets as they form a circle. Play some marching music; then invite your little ones to move around the circle, showing their pets as they march. To conclude the pet show, award a prize ribbon to every child as you comment on his pet's special quality. And the pet show winner is… everyone!

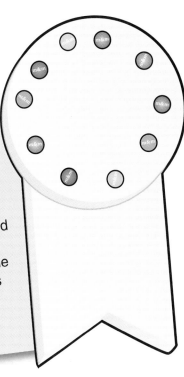

Storybook Café

Blue-Ribbon Cookie

Reward your youngsters' interest in *Pet Show!* with blue-ribbon cookie creations. Purchase prepared sugar cookie dough or mix up a batch from your favorite recipe. Roll out the dough; then cut out a short ribbon shape for each child. Place each dough ribbon shape on a separate piece of foil and give one to each child. Have the child write her name on the foil. Next, have each child cut out a circle shape with a cookie cutter. Assist each child as she places the cookie dough circle on her foil, overlapping the top of the dough ribbon as shown. Encourage each child to decorate her cookie ribbon with M&M's brand mini baking bits. Bake the cookies on a cookie sheet according to recipe directions, cool, and enjoy!

Raccoons and Ripe Corn

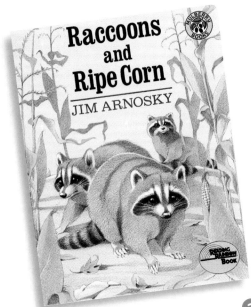

Written and illustrated by Jim Arnosky

Invite your youngsters to accompany a family of raccoons as they make a midnight raid on a field of sweet and savory ripe corn.

Storytime Song

Even though your little ones may have never seen raccoons, this song sung to the tune of "Did You Ever See a Lassie?" will surely make them want to hear a story about some!

Have you ever seen some raccoons,
Some raccoons, some raccoons?
Have you ever seen some raccoons
Eat tasty ripe corn?

They munch it and crunch it.
They crunch it and munch it!
Come listen to the raccoons
Eat tasty ripe corn!

(Repeat until all of your little ones have joined together.)

When your youngsters have joined you, read aloud *Raccoons and Ripe Corn*.

Learning Links
Synonym Sentences

The raccoon characters in this nocturnal tale choose a moonlit night to sneak a supper of sweet corn. After you've read this simple story to your youngsters, ask them to recall the events that lead up to the raccoons' midnight feast. At the top of a piece of chart paper, write "All night long the raccoons **feast**." Next, invite your students to brainstorm a list of synonyms for the verb *feast*, such as *dine, eat, munch, gobble,* and *scarf.* After your youngsters have generated a word list, have each child write the sample sentence at the top of a sheet of white construction paper, leaving out the word *feast* and replacing it with a synonym from the list. Encourage each child to illustrate the sentence on her paper with a crayon drawing of some ravenous raccoons dining on their delicious dinner!

All night long the raccoons munch.

Art Smarts

Bandit Mask

The masked raccoons in the story are appropriately attired for their midnight raid! Provide your youngsters with materials to make raccoon bandit masks, and they'll be ready to reenact the crafty critters' cornfield invasion. Prior to the activity, make a white construction paper copy of the mask patterns on page 201 for each child. Give each child a white paper plate and ask him to color it with several shades of brown crayon. Next, have each child color his mask patterns with black crayon and cut them out. Help each child glue the raccoon face to his paper plate; then staple the ear pieces to the plate above the face. To complete his mask, help each child trim away his paper plate below the raccoon nose and behind the eyes and then glue on a craft stick handle as shown. Have each child write his name on the back of his mask and save it to use with "Raccoon Action" at right.

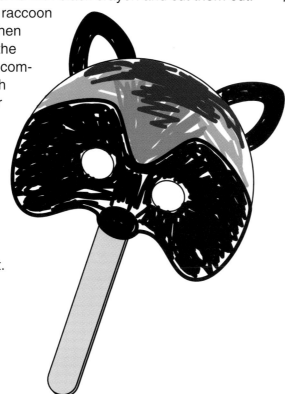

Purposeful Play

Raccoon Action

This energetic animal tale is chock-full of active raccoons, so it's just the thing for reinforcing the concept of action words. To begin, review the story with your students and have them identify the action words that they discover as you read. Write the words on chart paper. Then ask your students to tell you why the raccoons need to do each action in the story and why they make these movements in the dark of night. Next, invite your lively little ones to don the raccoon masks that they made in "Bandit Mask." Then ask them to reenact the active happenings as they occur in the story. Encourage each child to *sneak, walk, climb, pull, peel, feast,* and *hurry* as if she were a wily raccoon! To extend the activity, prompt each child to share a new raccoon-related action word with the group; then have her invite them to act it out along with her.

Storybook Café

Corny Snack

It's finally time to invite your little ones to feast on the vittles that the raccoons enjoy! To serve up a corny snack, you will need enough small frozen ears of corn to provide one for each child. Cook the frozen corn as directed on the package; then keep the ears warm in a Crock-Pot cooker that contains a small amount of water. Set out a choice of seasonings for the corn, such as salt, lemon pepper, Mrs. Dash seasoning, and any other type of packaged seasoning. Also supply a small bowl of melted butter and a pastry brush. Place a warm ear of corn in a plastic bowl for each child. Have the child butter his corn with the pastry brush and then sprinkle his treat with a seasoning of his choice. Don't forget to set out lots of napkins… your little ones will need them after munching such a sloppy but savory snack!

Splash!

Written and illustrated by Ann Jonas

The animal action and splashy artwork in this wet and wild story about a backyard pond will really keep your youngsters' interest afloat!

Storytime Song

Sing this song to the tune of "Home on the Range" as you invite your students to jump right into storytime!

Come splash in the pond
Where the shiny goldfish play.
Let's watch the fish swim
As some critters jump in.
Let's read this pond story today.

Come splash in the pond
Where the shiny goldfish play.
Let's watch the fish swim
As a [turtle] jumps in.
Let's read this pond story today.

(Repeat the second verse three more times, substituting a different animal from the story each time. Use small frog, gray cat, and big dog.)

When all of your students have joined the circle, read aloud *Splash!*

Learning Links

Critter Classification

After reading the story to your little ones, invite them to use the critter characters from the story in a basic classification activity. Prior to the activity, reproduce four sets of the pond animal cards on page 202 onto white construction paper. Color the animals to match their images in the story; then cut the cards apart and prepare them for flannelboard use. (You'll need four goldfish, three frogs, two catfish, a turtle, a dog, and a cat.) To begin, display the turtle, catfish, frog, and goldfish cards in random order in the center of the flannelboard; then tell your youngsters that some of the animals from the story have gotten mixed together in the pond. Next, reread the first page of the story to your youngsters; then ask them to help you rearrange the animal cards on the flannelboard so that the animals that are alike are grouped together. Your youngsters may classify the animals into three (turtle, fish, frogs) or four (turtle, catfish, goldfish, frogs) groups. Next, display the cat and the dog cards. Ask your students if they'd like to place these new animals in the existing groups or if they would like to classify the cat and dog separately. To wrap up the activity, ask volunteers to count the total number of animals in each set.

frog

frog

frog

Splashy Pond Pictures

Art Smarts

Ask each child to study the watery artwork in the book; then invite her to create some splashy art of her own. To begin, give each child a small paper cup. Help her measure and mix one tablespoon of white paint and three tablespoons of water in the cup. Next, have the child write her name on a 9" x 12" sheet of dark blue construction paper and then lay the paper name-side down on several layers of newspaper. Direct the child to put her paint-filled paper cup close to the blue paper, and then use her fingertips to flick the paint out of the cup over the paper to create a splash effect. Provide moist towelettes for cleanup. Set the painted paper aside to dry. To complete the project, ask each child to draw and color her favorite animal from the story on a sheet of white paper and then attach wiggle eyes stickers to the animal. Have the child cut her animal out and glue it to her splashy background. Have students share their pond pictures with family members and retell the story.

Books About Animals

Purposeful Play

Jump Tag

The splashy animal friends in this story and their pond-centered antics are just the thing to inspire a game with lots of jumping fun! Before inviting your youngsters to play, prepare a set of picture tags for the class. Use the pond animal cards on page 202 to reproduce a class supply of frog, fish, and turtle shapes. Cut frog shapes for one third of the class, fish shapes for another third, and turtle shapes for the last third. To play, take your students to a large space and divide them into groups of three. Lay a large plastic hoop on the ground for each group. Give the group one frog, one fish, and one turtle tag; then have each child in the group choose one to tape on his shirt. Ask group members to arrange themselves around their plastic hoop pond. To begin the action call out, "Frogs jump *in* the pond!" prompting each child wearing a frog tag to jump inside his plastic hoop. Then say, "Frogs jump *out* of the pond!" Next, direct the students with fish tags to jump in and out of the hoop; then do the same for the children wearing turtle tags. Ask the youngsters in each group to trade animal tags; then play the game again!

Storybook Café

Fishy Cracker Snacks

Give regular crackers a fishy twist and you'll really make a splash at snacktime!

Supplies:
small paper plates   craft sticks

Ingredients:
round crackers
1 package Goldfish crackers
1 tub spreadable cream cheese tinted with blue food coloring

To make one fishy snack:
1. Lay the cracker on a plate.
2. Spread cream cheese on the cracker with a craft stick.
3. Top cream cheese with Goldfish crackers.

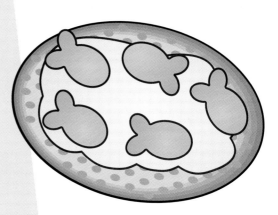

Star of the Circus

Written by Michael and Mary Beth Sampson
Illustrated by Jose Aruego and Ariane Dewey

A cast of uncommonly capable critters takes center stage in this story to answer the question "Can too many stars spoil the circus?"

Storytime Song

Introduce the greatest little circus book on earth with this song sung to the tune of "Are You Sleeping?"

Who's the big star
Of the circus?
Do you know? Do you know?
Could it be a zebra?
Could it be a big bear?
Who's the star, circus star?

Who's the big star
Of the circus?
Do you know? Do you know?
Could it be a giraffe?
Could it be a small mouse?
Who's the star, circus star?

Who's the big star
Of the circus?
Do you know? Do you know?
Could it be an elephant?
Could it be a kangaroo?
Who's the star, circus star?

(Continue to sing the song until your youngsters gather together.)

When your youngsters are seated and ready, read aloud *Star of the Circus.*

Learning Links

Alliterative Alias

All of the amazing animals in this terrific tale want to be the shining star of the circus. If any of the critters did get top billing, there would be a marvelous moniker to put at the top of the circus marquee, since each animal star in the story has a name that is an example of alliteration. As you read the story to your youngsters, ask them to repeat the name of each animal character as it is introduced and tell you what letter the name begins with. Discuss the fact that several of the animal names begin with the same consonant sounds, but not the same letter (Crazy Kangaroo and Jazzy Giraffe). At the end of the story, ask your youngsters to recall the names of the animal characters; then write their names on chart paper. Next, show your students the book's title page illustrations and ask them to help you give each of these animals (rabbit, lion, tiger, leopard, and panther) an alliterative name. Write these new names on the chart paper. Finally, review all of the names on the list with your little ones; then ask each child to author a similar alliterative alias all her own!

Terrifying Tiger	
Radical Rabbit	
Loud Lion	
Perfect Panther	
Lovely Leopard	

Art Smarts

Circus Star Poster

Every circus animal in the story wanted to be the star because of its special skill. Invite each child to put the spotlight on a talented circus animal with this easy art project. To prepare, draw an art starter similar to the one shown. Make a class supply. Review the circus skills from the story with your youngsters; then ask each child to draw and color a circus animal on his paper, positioning the animal on top of the platform on the page. Ask each child to write his circus star's alliterative name on the platform in the space provided. Have him complete the paper by writing or dictating a phrase to complete the sentence at the top. Next, help each child glue his paper to the center of a 12" x 14" sheet of colored construction

paper. Encourage each child to decorate the borders of his construction paper with stenciled or sponge-printed dots and stars to give his creation a circus poster look. Display all of your students' work on a bulletin board titled "We're All Stars of the Circus!"

Purposeful Play

Big Top Action

Books About Animals

Your youngsters will be eager to imitate circus performers as they recite and move to this big top action rhyme.

Could I be a star in the circus? You bet!
Point to self. Nod head "yes."
I could be the most powerful weight lifter yet!
Flex arms like a weight lifter.
I could juggle some balls with the greatest of ease.
Pretend to juggle.
I could swing through the air on a flying trapeze.
Swing arms overhead.
I could walk on a rope way up high in the air.
Pretend to walk a tightrope.
I could do silly tricks like a clown with red hair.
Make a silly face.
I could gallop on horseback with dare-devil style.
Pretend to ride a horse.
And I'd finish my act with a bow and a smile!
Take a bow.

Storybook Café

Circus Star Sandwich

Reward each child with a special snack that will make her feel like a star.

Supplies:
small paper plates
plastic knives
large star-shaped cookie cutter

Ingredients:
2 slices of bread for each child
apricot jam
spreadable cream cheese, tinted
   with yellow food coloring
sugar sprinkles

To make one star sandwich:
1. Use a cookie cutter to cut a large star shape from each slice of bread.
2. Spread apricot jam on one bread star; top with the second bread star.
3. Spread tinted cream cheese on the top bread star.
4. Shake sugar sprinkles on the cream cheese.

Ten Flashing Fireflies

Written by Philemon Sturges
Illustrated by Anna Vojtech

Fireflies flashing in the night are a beautiful, dazzling, wondrous sight! This story spotlights the fascinating firefly—that little insect that captivates both young and old alike.

Storytime Song

Brighten your youngsters' way to storytime with this song sung to the tune of "Twinkle, Twinkle, Little Star."

Fireflies, fireflies, flying high,
Blinking, twinkling in the sky.
Flashing with a little light,

Like a candle in the night.
Fireflies, fireflies, flying high,

Blinking, twinkling in the sky.

Fireflies, fireflies, flying high,
Blinking, twinkling in the sky.
Can you count each little light,

Glowing in the dark, dark night?
Fireflies, fireflies, flying high,
Blinking, twinkling in the sky.

(Repeat until all the children have joined together.)

Once your students are together, read aloud *Ten Flashing Fireflies.*

Learning Links

Identifying Word Endings

You can count on this illuminating tale to introduce your youngsters to the wonders of fireflies. Read the book through once with your youngsters so that they get an uninterrupted feel for the rhyming story. When you've finished, ask your students to recall some of the *-ing* words that the author uses to describe the flashing fireflies in the story, such as *flickering, twinkling,* and *sparkling.* Write your youngsters' suggested words on the board; then refer to the story to identify any additional words that they might have left out. Encourage your students to suggest more *-ing* words to add to the list. Next, use white and yellow chalk to write the listed words in the center of a large sheet of black drawing paper titled "Fantastic Flashing Fireflies." Invite each child to sponge-print a small circle of glow-in-the-dark paint within the area surrounding the word list; then have him use glitter glue to embellish this simple firefly image with a small pair of wings. Later, pull down the shades and turn off the lights so that your youngsters can observe the lovely "glow-bugs" they've created! Give each child an opportunity to use his own words to describe the interesting, illuminated insects.

Fantastic Flashing Fireflies

flickering

twinkling

glowing

glimmering

shining

sparkling

Headlight Headband

Invite each child to let the firefly illustrations in the story inspire a sparkling construction paper headband. Cut a headband strip and a three-inch-diameter circle from black construction paper for each child. Review the artwork in the story with your youngsters, pointing out that the nighttime effect is created by using chalk on dark paper. Provide white, yellow, and orange chalk; then give each child a black circle and ask her to make a firefly image on the circle using the style in the book. Invite her to embellish the image with gold glitter glue. Next, fit a headband strip to each child's head; staple the ends of the strip together to secure. Have each child glue her firefly circle to her headband and embellish the band with gold glitter glue, as shown. Encourage each child to wear her handsome headband in the next activity.

Books About Animals

Firefly Countdown

Invite a group of ten children to wear their fancy firefly headbands as they act out this action poem. Have group members form a line facing the rest of the class. Prompt one child to "fly away" from the line for each stanza of the poem that you recite. When you've finished the first recitation, invite a second group of students to stage Act II!

Ten flashing fireflies twinkling in the air.
One flies away; now nine are there.

Nine flashing fireflies blinking in the air.
One flies away; now eight are there.

Eight flashing fireflies sparkling in the air.
One flies away; now seven are there.

Seven flashing fireflies flickering in the air.
One flies away; now six are there.

Six flashing fireflies glowing in the air.
One flies away; now five are there.

Five flashing fireflies burning in the air.
One flies away; now four are there.

Four flashing fireflies glittering in the air.
One flies away; now three are there.

Three flashing fireflies shining in the air.
One flies away; now two are there.

Two flashing fireflies shimmering in the air.
One flies away; now one is there.

One flashing firefly gleaming in the air.
One flies away; now none are there!

Firefly Cookies

One look at this firefly-inspired treat, and your students will be snacking in a flash!

Supplies:
4" black construction paper circle for each child
plastic knives

Ingredients:
Oreo cookie for each child
yellow mini M&M's candy for each child
small tubes of yellow gel frosting

To make one firefly cookie:
1. Cut the cookie in half; then cut one of the halves in half again.
2. Place the larger half on the black paper circle; then place the two smaller halves above the larger half.
3. Squirt a dot of gel frosting on one end of the larger half.
4. Place a yellow M&M's candy on the frosting dot.
5. Add a gel frosting eye.
6. Use more gel frosting to make lines on the black circle that radiate out from the firefly's light.

Time to Sleep

Written and illustrated by Denise Fleming

Reluctant woodland critters try to postpone their long winter's sleep.

Storytime Song

Extend an invitation to join storytime with this song sung to the tune of "London Bridge."

In the woods it's time to sleep,
Time to sleep, time to sleep.
In the woods it's time to sleep,
But Bear's not sleepy!

Bear just does not want to sleep,
Want to sleep, want to sleep.
Bear just does not want to sleep.
She's not sleepy!

(Sing the song several times until your little ones have joined together.)

When your little ones have joined you, read aloud *Time to Sleep*.

Learning Links

Sequential Lineup

Since the animal acquaintances in the story are presented one by one, take the opportunity to highlight the sequential format of the story when you read it aloud to your youngsters. Before you read, copy the animal patterns on page 203 onto white construction paper. Color the animals, cut them out, and prepare them for the flannelboard. To begin, display all of the animals on the flannelboard in random order. Read the first page of the story; then move the bear figure to the center left of the flannelboard. Ask your youngsters to tell you why they think the bear needs to crawl into her cave to sleep; then prompt a discussion about hibernation. Next, read the second page of the story and ask a volunteer to position the snail flannelboard figure to the right of the bear, saying, "Time to sleep, snail." Continue to ask volunteers to help position each animal in the line after you read its introductory page in the story. As you read the last page of the story, remove an animal from the flannelboard when you come to its "good night" line in the text.

Art Smarts

Colorful Fall Project

After being introduced to the animals in the story, the time will be right for your youngsters to put the critters in a seasonal art project. Prior to the activity, copy the animal patterns on page 203 for each child. Review and discuss the autumn-themed illustrations in *Time to Sleep* with your youngsters. Talk about what colors the illustrator uses to give the pictures a feeling of fall. To begin the project, give each child a 9" x 12" sheet of white construction paper, a small container of starch, and a paintbrush. Also provide torn pieces of red, yellow, orange, and brown tissue paper. Ask each child to lay his construction paper on a large piece of newspaper to make cleanup easier. Have him brush starch all over his paper and then lay tissue paper over the starch to create a design in fall colors. If some of the tissue paper is not saturated with starch, have the child brush more over any dry areas. Set the colorful creation aside to dry. Next, give each child a copy of the animal patterns to color and cut out. Direct him to glue the animals in sequential story order to his tissue paper collage. Encourage each child to take his project home and then use it to retell *Time to Sleep* to his family.

Purposeful Play

Sleepy Time Rhyme

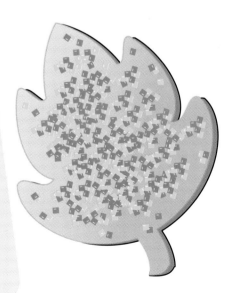

Books About Animals

Teach your youngsters this sleepy time rhyme for some active fun and to reinforce the repetitive language of this bedtime tale's finale.

Good night, Bug. It's time to fly to bed.
Flap arms to fly in place.
Good night, Bear. Lay down your sleepy head.
Close eyes; drop chin to chest.
Good night, Woodchuck. Tuck the covers tight.
Pretend to pull up bedcovers.
Good night, Turtle. Kiss your mom good night!
Make a kissing noise.
Good night, Snail. Set your clock; ding ding!
Pretend to wind a clock.
Good night, everyone. See you in the spring.
Wave goodbye.

Storybook Café

Leafy Treat

Here's a cookie treat that will bring the fall feelings of this woodland tale to snacktime. Invite your youngsters to help you mix up a batch of your favorite sugar cookie dough. Give each child a piece of foil and a portion of cookie dough. Encourage her to mold her dough into the shape of a leaf, inspired by the story illustrations. Next, have her brush a bit of water on top of her cookie and then sprinkle it with red and yellow sugar sprinkles to create a fall effect. Use a permanent marker to write each child's name on her foil. After baking the cookies, invite your youngsters to nibble their leafy treats!

Zoo-Looking

Written by Mem Fox
Illustrated by Candace Whitman

There's lots to look at in this vibrant book about the friendly and colorful creatures in the zoo.

Storytime Song

Your youngsters will run to look at this storytime selection when you tempt them with a song sung to the tune of "If You're Happy and You Know It."

Would you like to do some zoo-looking with me?
Would you like to do some zoo-looking with me?
I would like to ask you to
Look at critters in the zoo.
Would you like to do some zoo-looking with me?

(Repeat until all of your youngsters have joined together.)

When your youngsters are seated, read aloud *Zoo-Looking*.

Zoo Mapmaking

This simple story makes it easy for your little ones to get around the zoo. After you've read the story, invite your youngsters to review the map-themed zoo illustration on the title page spread. Ask volunteers to help you find the tiger, the giraffes, the zoo sign, and the pathways on the map. Next, invite groups of four youngsters to create zoo maps inspired by the geography-themed illustration that they've studied. Provide each group with a large piece of white bulletin board paper that has the word *zoo* written in the center. Also provide crayons and black crepe paper strips. Assign a different zoo animal to each child in a group (a tiger, a giraffe, a penguin, or an elephant). Have each child draw and color her assigned animal in one corner of the white paper. Next, ask group members to arrange crepe paper strips on the paper to create paths around their zoo map, similar to those in the story. Help group members glue the pathway strips in place. To use the zoo maps in a class activity, give every child in each group a small plastic Lego block or Duplo block person. Encourage her to move her figure along the pathways on her map as you give oral directions.

"First, stand your person by the zoo sign. Next, follow a path to the tiger. Now move along the path to the penguin. Then take your person to see the giraffe."

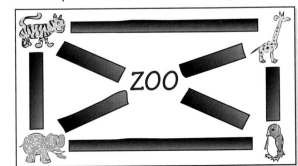

Art Smarts

Wild Puppet Chant

The soft-edged animal art in the book is very appealing, and it's easy for your youngsters to imitate. It's also a great way for each child to personalize a simple stick puppet to use in a story-inspired oral-language activity. To begin, ask each child to select one animal from the story that she would like to see at the zoo. Help each child cut or tear a round, oval, or rectangle body shape from colored tissue paper for the animal she wants to illustrate. Next, assist the child in gluing her tissue paper shape to the center of a paper plate. Help each child cut a head, legs, and a tail from tissue paper; then have her glue it to the animal body on her plate. Have her glue tissue stripes or spots to her animal, if needed. Then glue a craft stick handle to her plate. To wrap up the activity, invite your little zoo-lookers to manipulate their zoo animal puppets as they take part in the circle-time chant below.

Teacher:	Which zoo animal would [child's name] like to see?
Child:	I'd like to see a(n) [animal name] looking at me!

Purposeful Play

Animal Steps

After sitting down to create their works of art, your youngsters will be more than ready for a bit of animal-themed action! Organize a playful activity that is a simplified takeoff on the classic game Mother, May I? First, divide your youngsters into three groups and assign an animal name to each group. Name one group "zebras," the second group "giraffes," and the third group "tigers." Next, take your youngsters to a large open space and ask them to stand in a long row facing you, while you move to the opposite side of the area. To play the game, give each animal-named group instructions to move toward you by calling out directions following this pattern: "I see the [zebras] looking at me. Zebras take [big] steps. One, two, three!" As you continue giving directions, substitute the word *big* with others such as *baby, giant, tiptoe,* and *hopping.*

Put a little extra zing in the game by having your youngsters make and wear the animal-appropriate headbands described in the activity below.

Art Smarts

Crafty Critter Headbands

When your little ones wear these creative critter headbands, they'll really get into the animal antics of your game. First, cut construction paper headband strips and ear shapes for each animal-named group. You'll need orange strips and ears for tigers, yellow strips and ears for giraffes, and white strips and ears for zebras. Give each youngster in each group the appropriate headband strip; then have them embellish their strips with crayon designs. Ask the tiger group and zebra group to color black stripes on their headband strips; have the giraffe group draw brown spots on theirs. Next, hand out the corresponding ear shapes and invite each child to color her ear shapes and glue them to her headband strip. Fit each child's headband to her head, overlapping the ends if necessary. Staple the headband ends together. Now your youngsters are ready to step, hop, and roar into purposeful play!

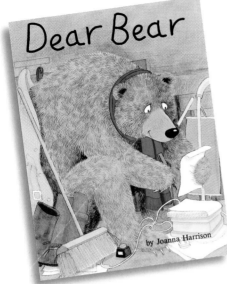

Dear Bear

Written and illustrated by Joanna Harrison

Katie's fears over a bear under the stairs slowly disappear as she communicates with him by letter. Then one day she receives an invitation to tea. Is she brave enough to finally meet the bear?

Storytime Song

Sing this song to the tune of "If You're Happy and You Know It" to signal students to storytime.

Come and hear about a big and scary bear.
Come and hear about a big and scary bear.
There's a big and scary bear that lives under Katie's stair.
Come and hear about a big and scary bear.

(Repeat the song until all of your youngsters have gathered for storytime.)

After all of your students have joined together, read aloud *Dear Bear*.

Learning Links

Emotional Letter Writing

This story makes the perfect springboard for discussing things that your youngsters fear. After a group sharing time, invite each child to prepare this letter. Program a sheet of paper as shown, leaving out the name of the addressee and the sender. Then make a class supply of the letter. Invite each child to illustrate her letter with the object of her fear, whether it is real or imaginary. Address the letter as the child dictates and then send it home along with a parent note explaining the reason for the letter. Also include a summary of the book. Encourage each child to tell her family about the story. Ask her to explain that she wants to give her letter to the object of her fear to see what might happen. Invite youngsters to report their results. Alternatively, you might keep the letters and have volunteers write reassuring responses to them. Post each letter and its response on a classroom display.

Dear Green Monster,
Please go away. Shoo!
Please go away because I'm scared of you.

From,
Samantha

Shadow Puppet

Art Smarts

Katie may have feared the bearlike shadows on the wall, but your students have nothing to fear with these bear shadows. To begin, have each child trace a bear shape. If desired, use the bear pattern on page 198. (Or have him trace or outline a figure of something that he might fear.) Instruct him to color and cut out the shape and then fill in the details of his figure, such as facial features and claws. Help each child glue his cutout to a craft stick. Then invite him to dance and move his stick puppet in front of a light source to create shadows on the wall. Later, encourage youngsters to use their puppets in their dramatic-play activities.

Shadow Posing

Purposeful Play

Shadows can be so scary and so fascinating—at the same time! Encourage youngsters' fascination with shadows with this not-so-scary shadow activity. In advance, make one simple headband with bear ears from white construction paper and three additional headbands from black paper. Divide your class into groups of four; then invite each group, in turn, to play the game. To play, a child assumes the role of bear and wears the white headband. The remaining students wear the black headbands to indicate that they are bear shadows. The shadows stand behind the bear. On a signal, such as a flashlight flicker, the bear strikes a pose. Then each of the shadows imitates the bear's pose. On the next signal, the bear strikes a new pose and the shadows follow suit. After a designated number of turns, appoint a different child to be the bear and repeat the game.

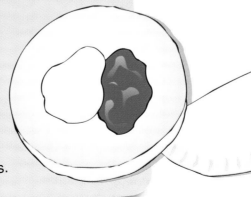

Bear Bites

Storybook Café

Here's an "un-bear-ably" tasty treat for your little cubs to nibble.

Supplies:
circle shape cutter
paper plates
plastic spoons and forks

Ingredients for each child:
slice of bread
cream cheese
jelly

To make one bear bite:
1. Cut out a bread circle.
2. Spoon a dab of cream cheese and jelly onto the center of the circle.
3. Fold the circle in half.
4. Press the edges together with fork tines.
5. Tastes gr-r-reat!

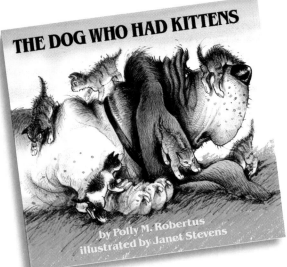

The Dog Who Had Kittens

Written by Polly Robertus
Illustrated by Janet Stevens

Baxter the Basset Hound tenderly cares for a litter of kittens while mama cat takes her breaks.

Storytime Song

Gather youngsters to storytime with this musical invitation sung to the tune of "Ten Little Indians." As you sing, gently stroke a stuffed toy kitten.

Come meet seven of Eloise's kittens
Playing in the basement, hiding in mittens,
Purring in Baxter's ear—he's quite smitten.
Kittens are so cute!

(Repeat the song until all of your caring children have joined together.)

Once students have gathered for storytime, read aloud *The Dog Who Had Kittens*.

Learning Links

Pet Patterns

Reinforce your little ones' problem-solving skills with this pet patterning game. To prepare, copy the cat and dog patterns (page 204) several times onto construction paper to make a supply; then cut out each one. To begin, create a simple pattern with the pet cutouts. Invite each child, in turn, to add to the pattern until all of the cutouts have been used. Then invite a volunteer to start a pattern for the next round. Afterward, put the cutouts in a center for youngsters to use individually or in pairs. For a fine-motor extension, encourage student pairs to convert this game into a pencil-and-paper activity in which they draw pet patterns.

Headband Prop

These headbands are the perfect props to prompt a round of role-playing with your youngsters. Poll your students to discover which animal each one would prefer to be—a dog or a kitten. Then make the corresponding number of construction paper copies of each animal pattern on page 204. Ask each child to color and cut out his pet pattern; then have him glue it onto a 1 1/2-inch-wide strip of brown construction paper to make a headband. Write the child's dictated name for his pet on the headband. Then fit the headband to his head and staple the ends together. During play activities, encourage your kittens and dogs to team up to act out the story. Or pair a kitten and dog together; then have the dog care for his kitten following Baxter's example in the story. Afterward, challenge the kitten to perform caring acts for the dog.

Careful Motor Skills

Remind students of just how gently Baxter cared for the little kittens. Then invite small or large groups to play this gross-motor game of gentle caring acts. To prepare, obtain a large sheet and several stuffed toy kittens. Spread the sheet out in an open area of your room; then have students put the kittens in the center of the sheet. Tell them that the kittens are ready for a nap, but they need to be rocked to sleep. Then have each child hold the edge of the sheet to lift it off the floor. Instruct the children to gently move the sheet to make a rocking motion for the kittens. If a kitten falls off the sheet, have a child retrieve it and gently place it back on. Afterward, tell youngsters that the kittens are ready to wake up and play. Have them shake the sheet in a more vigorous, playful manner while still keeping the kittens aboard. Continue as student interest dictates; then conclude the game by praising youngsters for showing such gentle care for the kittens.

Kitten Cookies

When you serve these special cookies with milk, your little kittens will purr over such a scrumptious treat.

Supplies:
plastic knives
small paper plates

Ingredients for each child:
3" round sugar cookie
vanilla frosting
3 Mini M&M's candies
2 pretzel sticks, broken in half
2 pieces of candy corn

To make one kitten cookie:
1. Spread frosting on the cookie.
2. Add M&M's eyes and nose.
3. Put on pretzel stick whiskers.
4. Add candy corn ears.
5. Mmm...meow!

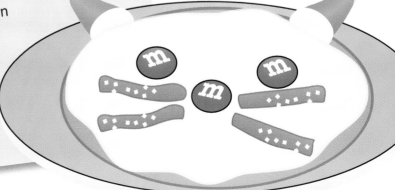

Elbert's Bad Word

Written by Audrey Wood
Illustrated by Audrey and Don Wood

Elbert catches a bad, ugly word covered with dark, bristly hairs. At first, the word slips silently into his mouth. Then—at a most unexpected moment—it leaps out, creating quite a commotion!

Storytime Song

Your young book lovers will eagerly join you with this musical invitation sung to the tune of "For He's a Jolly Good Fellow."

Does Elbert scream out a bad word?
Yes, Elbert screams out a bad word.
Oh, Elbert screams out a bad word
When he hurts his great big toe.

Does Elbert really say *that* word?
Yes, Elbert really says *that* word.
Oh, Elbert really says *that* word.
He's in big trouble, you know!

(Repeat until all the children have joined together.)

Once youngsters have gathered for storytime, read aloud *Elbert's Bad Word*.

Learning Links

Alliterative Alphabet

Use this story as a springboard for creating a class book of strong words. To begin, review the strong words that Elbert uses. Then invite youngsters to generate their own nice, strong words. To do this, have them agree on an alliterative exclamation for each letter of the alphabet. Write an alphabetical list of the exclamations on chart paper. After the list is complete, assign each child a different letter. Write the exclamation for her letter on a sheet of construction paper; then have her illustrate the exclamation. (Ask volunteers to illustrate any leftover letters.) To make a book, alphabetically sequence all the pages and bind them between two construction paper covers. Title the book "Our ABC Book of Nice, Strong Words." During group time, invite each child to read her page to the class; then put the book in your reading center. Refer youngsters to the book whenever they need to use strong words.

jumping jelly beans
kicking kangaroos
leaping lemons
melting milk bottles
nodding noodles

jumping jelly beans

Art Smarts — Painting Madly

Do your youngsters wonder what anger might look like? If so, this painting activity will provide them with a visual image of anger. Working with one small group at a time, remind students of Elbert's anger when he hurts his toe; then ask them to act out the anger he must feel. After a brief period of intense dramatization, send each child to an easel to paint his anger. What might his anger look like? A wild lion? A dark, scary cloud? A swirl of blurry colors? As he works, encourage each child to continue acting out his anger so that he can capture its image in his painting. Afterward, invite students to share their anger paintings with the group.

Purposeful Play — Anger Acting

This dramatic follow-the-leader game will serve as a strong reminder that students can express their anger with appropriate strong words. To begin, display the chart of exclamations from "Alliterative Alphabet" on page 106. Invite a volunteer to choose a letter. Read the corresponding exclamation from the chart; then ask that child to act out and recite the exclamation in an angry manner. Have the rest of the class imitate her actions. On a signal, instruct all the children to freeze. Then invite a new volunteer to select a different letter and play another round of the game. Continue in this fashion until every child has had a turn to choose a letter. Conclude the game by explaining that it's natural and acceptable to feel anger and to use angry words—as long as they are appropriate!

Storybook Café — Elbert's Barbells

Are your little ones feeling weighted down with anger? Then lift their spirits with this lightweight snack.

Supplies:
microwave-safe bowl
microwave
waxed paper
stirring spoon

Ingredients for each child:
2 pieces of banana
pretzel rod
semisweet chocolate chips, melted

Preparation:
1. Put the chocolate chips in the microwave-safe bowl. Microwave them on high for $1\frac{1}{2}$ minutes, stir, and then heat them for 20-second intervals until they melt.
2. Stir the melted chips into a smooth sauce.

To make one barbell:
1. Poke each end of the pretzel rod into a banana piece to make a barbell.
2. Dip each end of the barbell into the chocolate sauce; then set it on a piece of waxed paper.
3. Lift and bite!

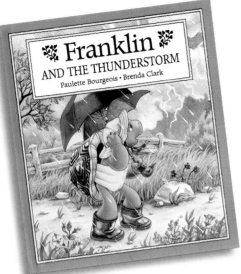

Franklin and the Thunderstorm

Written by Paulette Bourgeois
Illustrated by Brenda Clark

Franklin wants to enjoy his friends, but a storm is coming—and he's afraid of storms! Fortunately, his friends' humorous ideas about thunder and lightning help ease Franklin out of his shell and into a relaxing game of flashlight tag.

Storytime Song

Sing this spirited song to the chorus of "Ain't It Great to Be Crazy" to gather your class for storytime.

> Boom! Boom!
> Who's afraid of the thunder?
> Boom! Boom!
> Who's afraid of the thunder?
> Scared and skittish the whole storm through.
> Boom! Boom!
> Who's afraid of the thunder?

(Repeat the song until all of your students have joined together.)

After youngsters assemble for storytime, read aloud *Franklin and the Thunderstorm.*

Stormy Sounds

You'll find that listening opportunities abound when your class creates this fun thunderstorm. Gather a supply of instruments, such as drums, wood blocks, tambourines, and any others that can be used to make sounds like thunder. Show youngsters how to play the instruments to make different thunder sounds—rolling thunder, a clap of thunder, or a crackle of thunder. Then pass out the same kind of instrument (such as drums) to student volunteers. Designate these students to be thunder makers. Model a hand-clapping, finger-snapping, or knee-slapping rain pattern for the remaining students to imitate. Then, at varying intervals, signal the thunder makers to create rhythmic thunder with their instruments. Repeat the activity, giving different children turns to use different instruments. Each time your class creates a storm, model a different pattern, volume, and/or speed for the storm sounds.

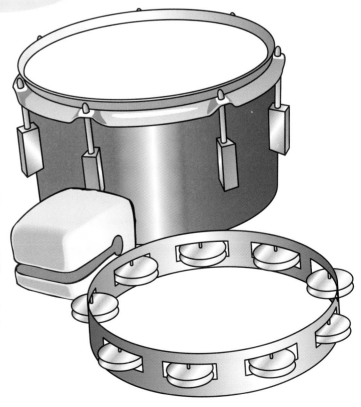

Cloudy Communication

This rainy-day project proves that a storm on the outside can't ruin the fun on the inside! To begin, help each child cut out a cloud shape from white construction paper. Have him randomly mark the cloud with black or gray chalk and then smudge the chalk with his finger to create a dark storm cloud. To make a streak of lightning, have the child draw a zigzag line across the cloud with a silver or gold paint pen. Then have him dictate a few indoor activities that he does on a stormy day. Use a verb + *-ing* phrase to label a separate raindrop cutout for each activity he names. To create a display, title the top of a bulletin board with "It's Storming Outside, But I'm Having Fun..." and the bottom of the board with "...Inside!" Then attach each child's cloud and raindrops to the display.

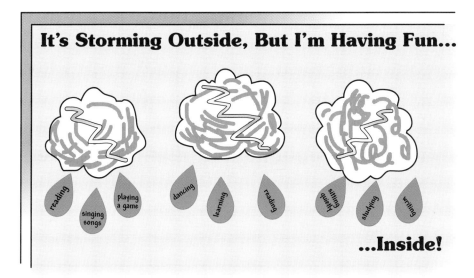

It's Storming Outside, But I'm Having Fun...

reading · singing songs · playing a game · dancing · learning · reading · sitting quietly · studying · writing

...Inside!

Musical Tag

This musical game of flashlight tag is sure to chase away any stormy-day fears. To begin, divide your class into several small groups. Appoint one child in each group to be It; then give each It a flashlight. Assign each group an area in which to move about. Then dim the lights in your classroom. To play, the students in each group dance and move to lively music. Each time you stop the music, It tags a child by shining the flashlight on him. The tagged child positions himself on the floor as if he is a turtle in a shell. Then start the music again and have the remaining students resume their dancing. Continue in this manner until all the children have been tagged. Before playing another round of tag, appoint a different child in each group to be It.

Cloud Cookies

Supplies:
paper plates
plastic knives

Ingredients for each child:
round sugar cookie
whipped topping
2 chocolate chips
licorice lace

To make one cloud cookie:
1. Spread whipped topping on cookie.
2. Put on chocolate chip eyes.
3. Add a licorice smile.

Franklin's Bad Day

Written by Paulette Bourgeois
Illustrated by Brenda Clark

Franklin's sadness turns to frustration and then anger as the day goes by. Finally, his father helps him voice the cause of his glum mood—he misses his friend, Otter.

Storytime Song

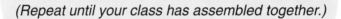

Round youngsters up for storytime with this song sung to the tune of "London Bridge."

Franklin's having one bad day,
One mad day, one sad day.
Have you ever had a day
Just like Franklin's?

(Repeat until your class has assembled together.)

When all your youngsters have joined together, read aloud *Franklin's Bad Day*.

Learning Links

Turtle Telephone Reminder

To Franklin, being able to call or write to Otter is very important. Do your youngsters know the most important phone number of all—their own phone numbers? Use this idea to help teach and reinforce this important number, as well as some other important ones. In advance, send home a copy of the phone number request form (page 205) with each child. When she returns her letter, copy each phone number onto a separate notecard. Then invite the child to create a holder for her special numbers. To make one, the child cuts out a turtle-shell shape from a half sheet of green construction paper. She glues along the bottom edge and partially up the sides of the cutout (but not around the top) and then presses it onto a sheet of construction paper, leaving the top edge open. To complete her turtle, she adds a construction paper head, tail, and legs. After the glue dries, the child punches a hole in all of her cards and in the top of her holder. Then she ties her stack of cards to the holder with yarn. To use, the child finds the card with the desired number and then recites the number as she pretends to call that person. When not in use, have the child store her cards in the turtle holder.

Art Smarts

Stationery Surprise

Turn sadness into smiles with these special letters. In advance, send home a copy of the address request form (page 205). When the forms are returned, help each student prepare a self-addressed envelope and an envelope addressed to her correspondent. Stamp both envelopes. Put a supply of paper in your art center along with an assortment of rubber stamps, stamp pads, dot markers, stickers, and markers. Send each child to the center to create several pages of stationery. On one sheet of stationery, have her write "Please write to me." Have her place her stationery and self-addressed stamped envelope inside her correspondent's envelope and seal it. Lead a parade of little letter carriers to the office to mail their envelopes and get ready for smiles when the replies return.

Please write to me.

Hannah Hall
c/o Ms. Green's Room
Oakview School
High Point, NC 27126

Purposeful Play

Snowbound Imitation

Imaginations will soar as youngsters play these imaginary snow games. Send a small group of children to an open area of your room. Tell them that they are going to play in a pile of imaginary snow. Then suggest some ways in which they can make their play look real. For instance, they can stack imaginary snowballs, build an imaginary snowman, glide on imaginary skis, or even have an imaginary snowball fight. Be sure to encourage the students to create their own imaginary snow activities. You might even challenge them to perform their activities in slow motion, in silence, or in reverse. After a designated time, send another group of youngsters "out" to play in the snow.

Books About Feelings

Storybook Café

Ants 'n' Berries Breakfast

Franklin picks at his food, but this delicious dish will satisfy the appetite of even your most picky little turtles.

(makes eight ¼-cup servings)

Supplies:
large pot
stirring spoon
measuring cups and spoons
hot plate
Styrofoam bowls
plastic spoons

Ingredients:
2 c. dry oatmeal
3½ c. water
¼ tsp. salt
sugar
chocolate chips
blueberries

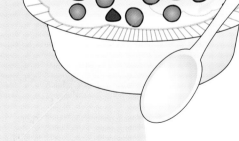

To make one serving of ants 'n' berries breakfast:
1. Boil the water and salt in the pot.
2. Stir in the oats; then cook the mixture over medium heat for about five minutes, stirring often.
3. After the oatmeal cools, spoon a ¼-cup serving into a bowl.
4. Sprinkle a little sugar onto the oatmeal; then top it with chocolate chips (ants) and blueberries. Delicious!

The Giving Tree

Written and illustrated by Shel Silverstein

From its highest branches down to the lowest section of its trunk, a tree demonstrates its devoted love for a little boy. This true spirit of giving without boundaries will tenderly touch readers of all ages.

Storytime Song

Sing this song to the tune of "Do You Know the Muffin Man?" to circle children around for storytime.

Do you know the giving tree,
The giving tree, the giving tree?
Do you know the giving tree?
The tree that's filled with love.

Come and meet the giving tree,
The giving tree, the giving tree.
Come and meet the giving tree,
The tree that's filled with love.

(Repeat the song until all your little ones have assembled for the story.)

After all your youngsters have joined together, read aloud *The Giving Tree.*

Purposeful Planting

Your youngsters will develop a true love for nature with this activity. First, gather a class supply of plastic cups, potting soil, and tree seeds with a short germination period, such as maple seeds. Then take your class on a nature walk to examine the different kinds of trees in your area. (If desired, also have students pick up leaves for "Leaf Prints" on page 113.) After returning to the classroom, prompt students to brainstorm a list of gifts that come from trees, such as shade, fruit, wood, and leaves for autumn play. List their responses on a sheet of paper titled "A tree grows strong and tall to give gifts to one and all." Then photocopy the list for each child. Next, have each child plant a seed in the cup and then water it. Encourage her to nurture her plant until it sprouts into a seedling. Finally, invite the child to give her tree and a copy of the list to a special loved one.

A tree grows strong and tall
to give gifts to one and all.

shade
fruit
wood
leaves to play in
paper   pretty colors

Leaf Prints

Adorn a class giving tree with these colorful leaves. In advance, have youngsters collect a variety of leaves while outdoors. (They might do this during their nature walk in "Purposeful Planting" on page 112). Back in the classroom, provide several fall paint colors, paintbrushes, white construction paper, newspaper, and wooden play dough rollers. To make a leaf, each child paints the vein side of a real leaf. Then she lays the painted side of the leaf on the white paper, covers it with newspaper, and rolls the leaf with the roller to transfer its image onto the paper. After her leaf paintings dry, ask each child to cut out her leaves. Then have her write (or dictate) an act of love on each leaf. Display all of the leaves on a large tree cutout with the title of the book.

Purposeful Play

Happy Heart Game

Rake in some fall fun with this leafy game filled with loving surprises. To prepare, purchase one bag each of Hershey's Kisses and Hershey's Hugs candies. Then cut out two sets of three red construction paper hearts. Label each heart in a set with the numeral 1, 2, or 3. Then take your class outdoors to rake together two leaf piles. (Or you might use a large supply of slightly crumpled paper bag leaf cutouts.) Hide a set of hearts in each pile; then divide your class into two teams. On a signal, send a member from each team to search for the hidden hearts in the leaves. The first child to find all three hearts wins a point for his team. Return the hearts to the leaf pile; then continue play until every team member has had a turn. At the end of the game, total and compare each team's points. Reward the winning team members with candy kisses; then present the other players with candy hugs.

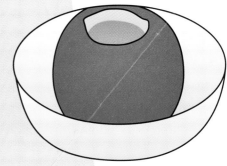

Storybook Café

Apple Treat

Sample one of the giving tree's gifts with this "tree-licious" apple delight.

Supplies:
small knife
measuring cup
measuring spoons
microwave baking dish
microwave oven
spoons
bowls

Ingredients for each child:
large apple
1 tbsp. honey
1 tsp. butter
1 tbsp. brown sugar
cinnamon
¼ c. water

To make one apple treat:
1. Use the knife to core the apple; then stand the apple in the baking dish.
2. Put the honey, butter, sugar, and a dash of cinnamon in the apple hole.
3. Pour the water into the dish. Microwave the apple on high for 2–3 minutes or until it softens.
4. Allow the apple to cool before eating it.

Guess How Much I Love You

Written by Sam McBratney
Illustrated by Anita Jeram

Discover the endless love that Little Nutbrown Hare and Big Nutbrown Hare have for each other in this endearing tale.

Storytime Song

Youngsters will hop straight to storytime with this musical invitation sung to the tune of "If You're Happy and You Know It."

Oh, how Little Nutbrown Hare loves his dad!
Oh, how Little Nutbrown Hare loves his dad!
Guess how much he loves his dad,
And how much he's loved by dad.
Hear how Little Nutbrown Hare loves his dad.

(Repeat the song until all your students have joined together.)

After your class has gathered for storytime, ask your little bunnies to perk up their ears for a tender reading of *Guess How Much I Love You.*

Learning Links

Estimation Jar

Guess how much "love" is in the bunny jar. Youngsters will be hopping to know after they make their own estimations in this activity. To prepare, fill a clear jar with up to 100 heart-shaped candies. Then copy, color, and cut out the bunny pattern on page 206. Tape the cutout and a label printed with "Guess how much love is in my jar" onto the jar as shown. Invite each child to write her name and estimate on a sticky note. After all the guesses are recorded, empty the jar and chorally count the hearts with your class. Ask each child to compare her guess to the actual number. To extend this activity, you might group and count the candy by twos, fives, and tens before dividing it up between your students.

Art Smarts

Bunny Card

Each child will make "some-bunny" feel really special with this unique card. To prepare, enlarge the bunny and text patterns (page 206); then copy a class quantity of the patterns onto construction paper. Next, provide a tray of brown paint and a supply of cotton balls. To make the card, each child cuts out all the patterns; then he uses the cotton to paint the front and back of his bunny cutout. After the paint dries, he glues the text cutout labeled "this much!" onto the bunny's chest. Then the child folds the bunny arms across its chest and glues the remaining text patterns onto the arms. Finally, he glues a cotton ball tail onto the back of the bunny. Encourage each child to present his love bunny to someone he loves.

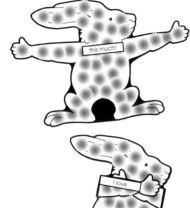

this much!

I love

Purposeful Play

Hop-'n'-Hug Game

Who doesn't like to give and get hugs? Here's a fun musical game in which youngsters can do both! In advance, gather some musical selections with a really hoppin' beat, such as "The Bunny Hop." Then have your class spread out in an open area of your classroom. Invite students to hop and bop as you play the music. Then stop the music and signal each child to give a classmate a gentle hug or handshake. Repeat this activity for as long as "every-bunny's" energy and interest last. But beware—your youngsters just might be hopping and hugging the whole day long!

Storybook Café

Hoppin' Hotcakes

These fancy pancakes are sure to tickle your little ones' "bunny bones."

(makes about 8 pancakes)

Supplies:
quart-sized zippered plastic bags
electric griddle
spatula
nonstick cooking spray
Styrofoam plates
forks
scissors

Ingredients:
1 c. of biscuit mix
½ c. of milk
beaten egg
8 strawberry slivers
chocolate chips
canned whipped topping

Preparation:
1. Pour the biscuit mix, milk, and egg into a zippered bag.
2. Seal the bag; then gently knead the ingredients through the bag to mix the pancake batter. (If desired, add more milk to thin the batter.)

To make one hoppin' hotcake:
1. Coat the griddle with cooking spray; then warm it to medium heat.
2. Snip off a bottom corner of the bag.
3. Squeeze the batter onto the griddle in the shape of a bunny head.
4. Cook the bunny pancake to the desired darkness.
5. After the pancake cools, add chocolate chip eyes, a strawberry nose, and whipped topping whiskers.

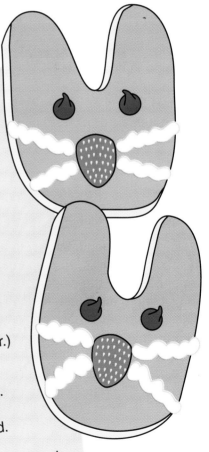

The Happy Hippopotami

Written by Bill Martin Jr.
Illustrated by Betsy Everitt

What's a "hippoholiday"? Find out with these happy hippopotamuses as they enjoy a sunny assortment of holiday activities from dancing the maypole to flying the trapeze.

Storytime Song

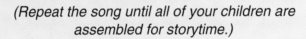

Call youngsters to storytime with this happy "hippo-melody" to the tune of "Ten Little Indians."

Let's join a group of hippopotamuses.
Come climb aboard their hippo picnic buses.
We'll have a day that's hippo marvelous—
A hippo happy holiday!

(Repeat the song until all of your children are assembled for storytime.)

After your class gathers together, read aloud *The Happy Hippopotami*.

Learning Links

Happy Hippo Counting

Here's a tremendous way to help youngsters build their counting skills. To prepare, make ten construction paper copies of the hippo pattern on page 207. Cut out and laminate each pattern; then attach a pocket card to each cutout. Label each pocket with a numeral from 1 to 10. For self-checking purposes, affix a corresponding number of miniature smiley-face stickers to the back of the hippo. Then affix one smiley-face sticker to one end of each of 55 craft sticks. To use, a child inserts the appropriate number of sticks into each hippo's pocket. Then she checks her work by matching the number of sticks to the stickers on the back of the hippo.

Fashionable Hippos

Art Smarts

Give youngsters' imaginations a happy hippo swirl with these stylish hippo fashions. For each child, copy the hippo pattern (page 207) onto white construction paper. Then supply your art center with an assortment of decorative paper, fabric scraps, ribbon, and yarn. Instruct each child to color and cut out his hippo pattern and then use the provided materials to create a unique look for his hippo. Have him dictate a sentence about a fun activity that his stylish hippo might enjoy. Then invite each child to walk an imaginary runway as he shows and tells about his fashionable hippo. Later, display all the hippos and dictated sentences on a bulletin board titled "Happy, Hip Hippos!"

Sandy Measurement

Purposeful Play

Invite students to dig in to some sandy fun with this measurement activity! To prepare, cut a plastic milk jug as shown. Then copy, color, cut out, and laminate the hippo pattern on page 207. Attach the cutout to the milk jug; then place the jug in the sand table along with some cups and scoops. Place a marker, sticky notes, and a chart labeled with "cups" and "scoops" near the table. To use, a student pair visits the sand table for a period of free exploration. Then the children use a cup to fill the jug with sand, counting the number of cups used. They record the results on a sticky note labeled with their names and attach it to the appropriate column on the chart. Then they repeat the procedure, using scoops instead of cups. After each pair has had a turn, compare the results with the class.

Cups	Scoops
16 Amber and Kim	24 Amber and Kim
14 Joey and Alex	33 Joey and Al...

Savory Sand Pails

Storybook Café

No holiday is complete without a special holiday treat. Make these savory sand pails to conclude your happy "hippoholiday" activities.

Supplies:
mixing bowl
large spoon
clear plastic cups
waxed paper
plastic spoons

Ingredients:
2 boxes of instant chocolate pudding
milk
whipped topping
vanilla wafer cookies

Preparation:
1. Mix the pudding according to the directions on the package.
2. Refrigerate the pudding until you are ready to use it for the savory sand pails.

To make one savory sand pail:
1. Scoop a large spoonful of pudding into a plastic cup (the sand pail).
2. To make sand, crush a cookie between a piece of folded waxed paper; then sprinkle the cookie sand over the pudding.
3. Top the sand with another layer of pudding and then a layer of whipped topping.
4. Crush another cookie and add it to the pail.
5. Dig in!

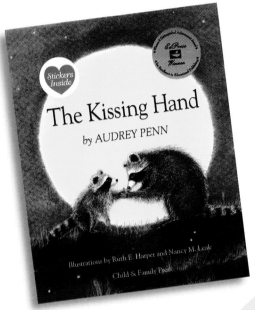

The Kissing Hand

Written by Audrey Penn
Illustrated by Ruth E. Harper and Nancy M. Leak

Facing a new situation can be difficult, even for the strongest of heart. Here's a reassuring story to help ease those pangs of anxiety.

Storytime Song

Gather your class to storytime with this verse sung to the tune of "Jingle Bells."

I am loved.
I am loved.
This is how I know—
I have a special kissing hand
That goes wherever I go!

(Repeat the song several times as children get seated for storytime.)

After all of your youngsters have joined together, ask them to listen for Mrs. Raccoon's wonderful secret as you read aloud *The Kissing Hand*.

Learning Links

Loving Sentences

Watch each youngster's love for a special person blossom with this pretty magnet. For each child, copy six flower petal patterns (page 208) onto one construction paper color and the flower center pattern onto a different color. Then explain that each child will make a special flower for someone that she loves. Have her cut out all of her flower patterns. Then label each petal cutout with the child's dictated response about her loved one. To create a flower, instruct the child to glue the petals around the flower center; then help her attach magnetic tape to the back of her flower. Invite each child to present her flower to her special love. It's flower power!

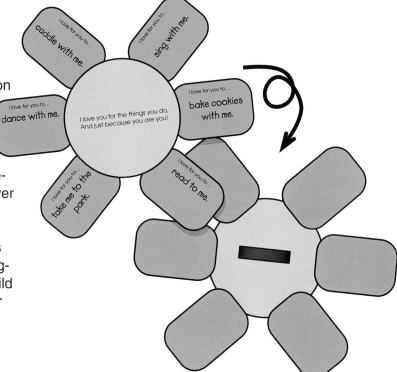

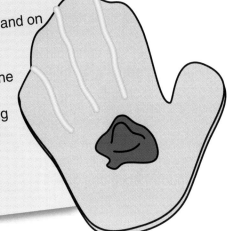

Hearty Hand

Art Smarts

The signs of love are all around with these handy magnets. To prepare, cut out a small sponge heart; then place it with a tray of red paint in your art center. Show students the hand sign for "I love you" on the last page of *The Kissing Hand.* Tell them that this is how some people communicate that very special message to their loved ones. Then invite each child to make a hand sign magnet from the construction paper color of his choice. (You might provide skin-tone colors for this activity.) To begin, the child traces his hand onto his paper. He cuts out his hand outline and then stamps a red heart onto the palm. After the paint dries, attach a magnet sticker to the back of the hand cutout. Next, have the child fold two fingers down to make the hand sign for "I love you." Invite each youngster to give his sign of love to a special person in his life.

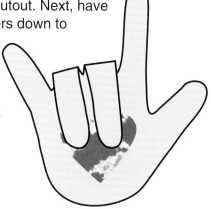

Purposeful Play

Loving Charades

Acts of love come in many different forms. Play this game of charades to prompt youngsters' thoughts about the numerous loving acts that they can do for others. In advance, create a card set in which a different act of love is written on each notecard. To play, spread the cards facedown on a table. Invite a child to select a card; then whisper the card's message into the child's ear. Have her creatively act out the message while her classmates guess the loving act being performed. Then invite the next child to take a turn. Loving acts can be such fun!

clean my room	wash dishes	sing a happy song
share a hug	give away a flower	throw a kiss
help wash the car	share a book	fold clothes

Storybook Café

Kissing Hand Treat

If your youngsters like sweets, they'll *love* these kissing hand treats.

Supplies:
aluminum foil
oven

Ingredients for each child:
¾" slice of refrigerated sugar cookie dough
piece of Hershey's Kisses candy
cake decorating gel

To make one kissing hand treat:
1. Roll the dough into a ball; then form it into a mitten-shaped hand on a piece of foil.
2. Bake the cookie according to the package directions.
3. While the cookie is still hot, place the unwrapped candy in the center of it.
4. After the cookie cools, draw finger lines on it with decorating gel as shown.

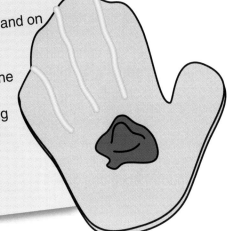

119

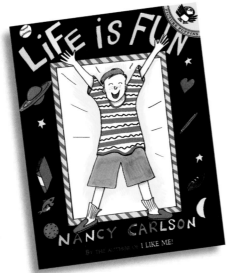

Life Is Fun

Written and illustrated by Nancy Carlson

How can you be happy in this life on earth? Simply follow the playful advice in this warmhearted, whimsical instruction book!

Storytime Song

Chant this cheery verse to the rhythm of "I Caught a Fish" to round up youngsters for storytime. As you recite the last line, show the book to your class.

One, two, three, four, five,
I'm glad to be alive.
Six, seven, eight, nine, ten,
I'm having fun again!
Why is my life such fun?
I follow these rules—every one!

(Repeat the chant until all of your students have joined the group.)

Once your students have gathered, read aloud *Life Is Fun.*

Creating Classroom Rules

Use this book as a springboard for your class to develop its own set of instructions for classroom happiness. To begin, review the seven rules from the book; then ask students to decide which rules might apply to the classroom. List their responses on chart paper, adding any original ideas as well. Write each rule on a separate sheet of construction paper. Ask each student (or student pair) to choose one to illustrate. Bind the illustrated rules between two construction paper covers. Title the book "Simple Instructions for Classroom Happiness." Invite your students to show ownership of the rules by having each child sign his name on the cover. Then place the book in your reading center as a ready reference for classroom happiness.

Be nice to others.

Cooperation Collage

Cooperation is the key word when youngsters create these collages. To prepare, gather a supply of poster board, magazines, scissors, and glue. Divide your class into several small groups; then give each group a sheet of poster board. Remind students of the many ways *Life Is Fun* portrays the main character enjoying life. Then invite them to cut out magazine pictures of people following the instructions given in the book. Have the members of each group create a poster board collage with their cutouts. Afterward, ask each group to share its collage with the class. Invite student comments and observations about the collages. Then display each one in a different area of your classroom to inspire youngsters to look for the fun in each day.

Self-Portrait Charade

Set the stage for a charades-style game with these fun self-portraits. To prepare, enlarge a photo of each child's face onto a half sheet of paper. Then ask each child to color and cut out the copy of her face. Have her glue the cutout near the top of a large sheet of white construction paper and then secretly illustrate the rest of her body doing an activity that she enjoys, such as skating or reading. After all the self-portraits are completed, use them in a game of charades. To play, each child, in turn, pantomimes the activity represented in her self-portrait while her classmates try to guess the activity. If they do not identify the activity after a few guesses, the child shows them her self-portrait. The students continue guessing until they make a correct guess. After the game, display all the pictures in your classroom as a reminder to youngsters that life *is* fun.

Giggly-Jigglies

Snacktime is naturally a fun part of life. Add to the fun with this giggly-jiggly treat.
(makes about 48 pieces)

Supplies:
large bowl
two 9" x 13" baking dishes
spoon
variety of cookie cutters

Ingredients:
four 6 oz. packages of flavored gelatin
5 c. apple juice, boiled

Preparation:
1. Combine the powdered gelatin and hot apple juice in the bowl. Stir until the gelatin is dissolved.
2. Pour the gelatin into the baking dishes.
3. Refrigerate the gelatin for three hours or until it is firm.
4. Dip the bottom of each pan into warm water to loosen the gelatin.

To make one giggly-jiggly:
1. Use the cookie cutters of your choice to cut out two gelatin shapes.
2. Remove the shapes from the pan.
3. Enjoy with a jiggly giggle!

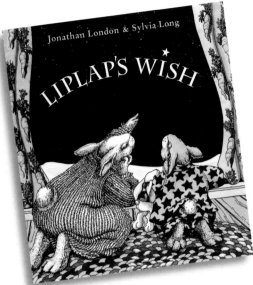

Liplap's Wish

Written by Jonathan London
Illustrated by Sylvia Long

As Liplap plays in the first snow, his heart becomes heavy. He misses his grandma, who didn't live to see this snow. Then he hears an old Rabbit's tale that cheers his heart and brightens his mood.

Storytime Song

Motion children over as you sing a few heartfelt rounds of this song sung to the tune of "Go Tell Aunt Rhody."

Sad little Liplap,
Sad little Liplap,
Sad little Liplap
Misses his dear grandma.

(Continue singing until your students have all joined the group.)

After your little bunnies have gathered together, snuggle up with them for a tender reading of *Liplap's Wish*.

Learning Links

Meaningful Patterns

An abundance of clever patterns adds to the visual delight of this tender tale. Page through the book with students to find the different patterns in the illustrations—carrot and turnip designs on the curtains, Liplap's starry pajamas, and his mother's heart-covered dress. Discuss how each of these patterns might be meaningful to Liplap. Then ask youngsters to think about things that are meaningful to them. After they share their responses, invite each child to create a pattern to represent one or more of those meaningful things. To begin, provide several trays of paint colors and a variety of sponge shapes (or have youngsters cut their own shapes out of dry, pressed sponges). Have the child use up to three sponges to sponge-print a repeating pattern on a large sheet of newsprint. After the paint dries, help her brainstorm a use for her personalized paper. For example, she might use it as a book cover, as wrapping paper, or to make curtains for her dollhouse.

Memory Stars

In this story, Liplap discovers a special way to remember his grandma. He simply wishes upon a star. Use these wishing stars to help your students recall a special memory to brighten sad days. To prepare, make several large tagboard tracers. Ask each child to trace a star onto yellow construction paper. Have him cut out his star and then illustrate it with a happy memory of a person or event. To complete his star, have him outline the edges with glue and then sprinkle gold glitter onto the glue. After the glue dries, invite each child to tell the class about his special memory star. Then have him take his star home. Encourage him to wish upon his star whenever he starts to feel sad and glum.

Secret Wishes

Will a wish come true if you share it? We may never know, but sharing wishes can be lots of fun—especially with this game! To play, a group of children sits in a circle. The first player makes a silent wish on a tagboard star. Then she passes the star and whispers her wish to the next player. That player, in turn, passes the star and repeats the whispered wish to her neighbor. Students continue play in this manner until the star and the wish return to the first player. Ask the first player to repeat the passed-along wish and then to say her original wish. Are they the same, or did the wish change as it was passed along? Repeat the game as student interest dictates, each time appointing a different child to start the round of whispered wishes.

Cocoa and Cake

This tasty treat will give your little bunnies a warm, happy feeling inside.

Supplies:
hot plate
teapot
8.5 oz. foam cups
plastic spoons and forks
small paper plates

Ingredients for each child:
water
1 tbsp. cocoa
1 tbsp. sugar
3 tbsp. nonfat dry milk
pinch salt
slice of (carrot) cake

To make one serving:
1. Heat a pot full of water to almost boiling.
2. Mix the cocoa, sugar, dry milk, and salt in a cup.
3. Fill the cup half full with the water; then carefully stir until the powdered mixture is dissolved.
4. Add water at room temperature to fill the cup to three-quarters full; then stir again.
5. Sip your cocoa as you munch on a slice of cake. It's whisker-wiggling wonderful!

The Little Rabbit Who Wanted Red Wings

Written by Carolyn Sherwin Bailey
Illustrated by Jacqueline Rogers

Be careful what you wish for, Little Rabbit; your wish just might come true! When Little Rabbit's wish for red wings comes true, he discovers that he's happier just being himself.

Storytime Song

Quick as a wink, students will scamper over with this musical invitation sung to the tune of "Pawpaw Patch."

Who's that rabbit with the red wings?
Who's that rabbit with the red wings?
Who's that rabbit with the red wings?
Just Little Rabbit with his wish come true!

(Repeat the song until all of your youngsters have joined together.)

Once students have assembled for storytime, read aloud *The Little Rabbit Who Wanted Red Wings*.

Learning Links

Writing Wishes

A happy person's wish can have a magical effect—even if it doesn't come true! Discuss with students how Little Rabbit just isn't happy with himself. That's why he often wishes to be like others. Explain that when one is not satisfied with himself, even a wish come true can't make him happy. After your discussion, invite each child to create a pair of wishing wings. To begin, help him draw a large wing shape on light-colored construction paper; then have him stack his paper on another sheet of the same color. Instruct the child to cut out the wing shape through both thicknesses. Then have him glue a wing cutout to each end of a craft stick as shown. Ask the child to illustrate one wing with a fun fantasy wish, such as a winged pair of skates. Write his dictation about his wish on the other wing. During group time, invite students to share their wishing wings with the class. Then display all the wings on a cloud-covered background with the title "Wishing on Wings."

I wish I had roller blades with wings. Then I could fly to the moon.

Vince

I wish my bed had a rocket. Then I could fly to the stars.

Theo

Wishing on Wings

Creative Self-Portraits

A rabbit with a bushy tail, a bristly back, and red flippers just wouldn't be a rabbit. Prompt youngsters to imagine how silly Little Rabbit would look with all those different features that he wishes for! Then encourage them to imagine themselves with a few different features, such as those that Little Rabbit wants. Ask each child to illustrate his imaginary self on a large sheet of paper. Then invite him to embellish his picture with an assortment of craft items. Afterward, have each child describe all the different features of his picture to the class.

Wishful Charades

Entice youngsters to try out Little Rabbit's wishing formula with this game of charades. Ask a volunteer in a small group to make a silent wish. Her wish might be serious, such as a wish for a new bike, or it might be silly, such as a wish to have elephant ears. Then have the child whisper her wish into your ear. To play, have the child look into a water-filled dishpan (the wishing pond), turn around three times, and then pantomime her wish. Encourage the other students to try to guess her wish. If necessary, help her act out and voice clues to guide them in identifying the wish. Then invite a different child to make a wish for the next round of play.

Wishing Pond

Invite each little one to make a wish before he dives into this wishing pond.

(makes 4 servings)

Supplies:
large bowl
stirring spoon
pot
hot plate
foam bowls
plastic spoons

Ingredients:
small box of
    Berry-Blue Jell-O gelatin
water
blue decorating gel

To make a wishing pond:
1. Dissolve the gelatin in boiling water and add cold water as directed on the package.
2. Pour a half-cup serving of the gelatin into a foam bowl.
3. Refrigerate for three hours or until the gelatin is firm.
4. Use the blue gel to draw your reflection on the surface of the blue wishing pond.
5. Dive in!

by BERNARD WABER

Lyle and the Birthday Party

Written and illustrated by Bernard Waber

Join Lyle as his jealousy leads him on a hilarious misadventure.

Storytime Song

Invite your youngsters to storytime with this song sung to the tune of "I'm a Little Teapot."

Come sit in our circle.
Come meet Lyle.
He's a jealous
Crocodile.
Come sit down and listen—
You will see
Why Lyle is filled with jealousy!

(Repeat until all of your students have joined together.)

Once your youngsters have gathered, read aloud *Lyle and the Birthday Party.*

Learning Links

Focus on Feelings

Lyle is certainly filled with mean green jealousy! Explain to students that colors are sometimes used to describe feelings. Often, the color green represents jealousy. Invite children to talk about moments when they have experienced the same mean green feeling that Lyle feels. Then have them brainstorm ways that might help them work these feelings out. For example, Lyle finds that helping others makes him forget his jealousy. Afterward, invite students to make these nifty crocodile flip-ups. To make one, the child cuts out a copy of the crocodile patterns on page 209. He colors the crocodile face green. Then he illustrates the inside of the mouth with something that he might do to make his jealous feelings go away. Write the child's dictation in the space provided. Then help him stack the patterns and staple them together at the top. Invite each child to share his flip-up with the class during group time; then have him take it home to share with his family.

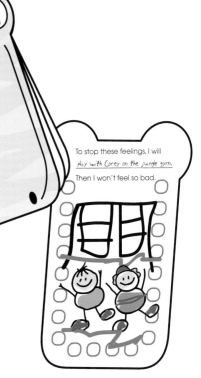

When I feel mean green jealous, I feel both sad and mad.

To stop these feelings, I will play with Corey on the jungle gym. Then I won't feel so bad.

Art Smarts — Croc Visor

When youngsters don these super crocodile visors, they'll be equipped for some "fun-tastic" dramatic-play activities. To make one, the child colors the bottom of a paper plate green. Then she folds one-third of the plate up and staples it to a sentence strip headband as shown. To make crocodile facial features, she draws a mouth and nostrils along the rim of the paper plate snout. For the eyes, the child cuts out white circles to fit inside two plastic soda bottle lids. After she colors the pupils onto each eye circle, she glues each circle into a lid. Then she glues the plastic lid eyes onto the crocodile's head. After the glue dries, fit each child's headband to her head and staple the ends together. Then set your young reptiles loose to create their own crocodilian fun.

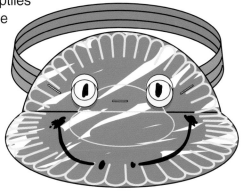

Purposeful Play — Party Center

Lyle's having a party and your youngsters are invited! Set up this party center to give students the opportunity to celebrate Lyle's special anniversary. To make a cake, paint a large whipped topping container with a mixture of brown tempera paint and a few drops of dishwashing liquid. After it dries, invert the container and punch three candle-size holes in the bottom; then push a cake candle into each hole. To make gifts, wrap a few empty boxes and containers in gift wrap. Embellish the gifts with ribbon and bows. If desired, also gather some toy animals and tie a bow onto each one. Then decorate your housekeeping center with colorful streamers and party decorations. Add the cake, gifts, and toy animals to the center along with a supply of party hats and favors. To use, send small groups of children to the center to role-play Lyle's special celebration. Invite each child to wear his "Croc Visor" as he takes on the role of Lyle.

Storybook Café — Crocodile Celebration Cones

Your little helpers will snap up these mouthwatering treats. Mmm. What a yummy reminder of how sweet it is to be helpful! (makes 16 servings)

Supplies:
large bowl
spoon
muffin tins
plastic knives
measuring cup and spoons
oven

Ingredients:
brownie mix for 8" x 8" pan size
eggs, water, oil, and other ingredients in the amounts listed on the brownie mix package
16 flat-bottomed ice-cream cones
frosting
cake sprinkles

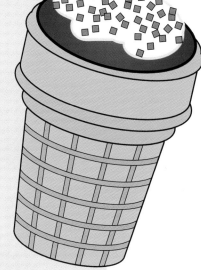

To make crocodile celebration cones:
1. Mix the brownie batter according to the package directions.
2. Stand one ice-cream cone in each cup of a muffin tin.
3. Fill each cone three-quarters full with brownie batter.
4. Set the oven as suggested on the package; then bake the batter-filled cones for 30 minutes.
5. Remove the cones from the oven. Allow them to cool for about 15 minutes.
6. Spread frosting on each brownie cone; then decorate it with sprinkles.

by Barbara M. Joosse   illustrated by Barbara Lavallee

Mama, Do You Love Me?

Written by Barbara M. Joosse
Illustrated by Barbara Lavallee

Explore the Arctic culture with this Inuit mother as she reassures her little one of her unconditional, endless love.

Storytime Song

Sing this song to the tune of "Are You Sleeping?" to affectionately call your little ones to storytime.

My dear children, my dear children,
Gather round, gather round.
Let's read a tender story,
A mother-and-child story.
Come sit down. Come sit down.

(Repeat the song until students are all seated.)

After all your youngsters have joined together, read *Mama, Do You Love Me?*

Defining Vocabulary

Examine the fascinating facets of the Inuit culture with this idea. Refer to the book's glossary to select some things particular to this culture. Then write a simple description for each of your choices on chart paper. Label a separate notecard with the name of each described item; then place the notecards in a bag. To use, a child picks a card from the bag. After you read the card aloud, she finds the illustration in the book that she believes to be the word's match. The class discusses her choice and decides whether or not it is correct. Then you read the definition in the glossary. If the child's choice is incorrect, she locates the correct picture and shares it with the class. Then she attaches the word card to the corresponding description on the chart. After all the cards are displayed, ask each child to illustrate one item from the chart. Later, invite youngsters to share their drawings with the class.

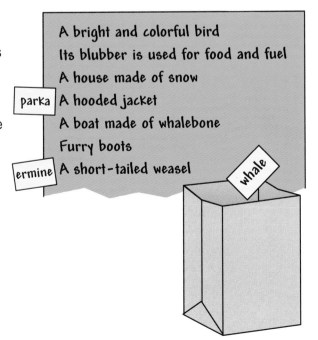

A bright and colorful bird
Its blubber is used for food and fuel
A house made of snow
parka | A hooded jacket
A boat made of whalebone
Furry boots
ermine | A short-tailed weasel

whale

Art Smarts

Parka Pal

Create these adorable parka pals to fill your classroom with love. Provide each child with a white paper plate, a 3" x 12" white construction paper strip, and a sheet of construction paper in his color choice. To make a parka pal, the child draws a face with a heart-shaped mouth on the paper plate; then he fringes and "fluffs" the plate rim so that it resembles a furry coat hood. Next, he glues the white paper strip to the back of the plate to represent the pal's arms. To create mittens, the child traces each of his hands—thumb out and fingers together—onto the construction paper. Then he cuts out the mittens and glues one to each end of the arm strip. After the glue dries, he folds the arms to overlap the mittens over the mouth. To reveal his kiss-blowing pal, the child simply unfolds its arms. *Smack!*

Purposeful Play

Dogsled Races

Books About Feelings

Introduce youngsters to a traditional means of Arctic travel—dogsleds. Show them the picture of the dogsled in the book. Explain that the Inuits once depended on dogs for transportation in the wintry Arctic weather. Then challenge your little ones' gross-motor skills with some mushy, slushy fun! Divide students into pairs. Line the pairs up at one end of an open space outdoors or in the gym. To begin, the first student pair forms a dogsled, wheelbarrow style—one child walks forward on his hands while his partner holds his feet up from behind. (If a child is unable to walk wheelbarrow style, have both partners crawl instead.) On a signal, the lead sled moves forward and the other sleds follow. As the sleds meander around the open space, have the drivers chant "mush" while the dogs respond "slush!" If time allows, switch the roles of dogs and drivers, choose a new lead sled, and begin again.

Storybook Café

Arctic Cream Pie

These delicious ice-cream pies will put a glimmer in youngsters' eyes.

Supplies:
ice-cream scoop
waxed paper

Ingredients for each child:
2 chocolate chip cookies
vanilla ice cream, slightly softened
chocolate sprinkles

To make one Arctic cream pie:
1. Scoop the ice cream onto one cookie; then top it with the other cookie.
2. Gently press the two cookies together to squeeze the ice cream to the edge.
3. Roll the edge of the cookie sandwich in a layer of chocolate sprinkles.
4. Freeze the Arctic cream pie for about 15 minutes before serving.

Mean Soup

Written and illustrated by Betsy Everitt

Horace has a bad day at school. Then he growls and hisses and falls on the floor when he gets home. Fortunately, his mom knows how to help him stir away his anger.

Storytime Song

Invite your little ones to storytime with these verses sung to the tune of "Did You Ever See a Lassie?"

Come and meet a boy named Horace,
Named Horace, named Horace.
Come and meet a boy named Horace.
He's feeling quite mean.

He's had a very bad day,
An angry and mad day.
Come and join us in our circle
To hear of his day.

(Repeat until all the children have joined together.)

Once youngsters have gathered for storytime, read aloud *Mean Soup*.

Learning Links

Dictating Feelings

Horace learns how to stir away his mean anger with the help of his mother's understanding antics. Help youngsters learn how to stir away some of their own angry feelings with this class book. To prepare, make a class supply of the book page pattern on page 210. Then mask the text on the pattern, make two tagboard copies, and cut out the copies to use for book covers. Decorate one cover to resemble a cooking pot and title it "Making Mean Soup!" After sharing the story, review Horace's angry behavior and how his mother helps him stir it away. Invite youngsters to tell about some of their mean, angry moments; then have them brainstorm safe, healthy ways to deal with anger. Afterward, invite each child to cut out her book page and illustrate it with a healthy way in which to "stir away" her anger—perhaps by singing a song, quietly reading a book, or making mean soup. Then write her dictation on her page. Bind the student pages between the book covers. Use the book during group sharing to reinforce appropriate ways to work out anger.

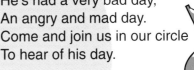

Making MEAN SOUP!

I can stir away my anger by jumping rope a long time...

...or making Mean Soup!

130

Art Smarts

Dough Therapy

Mix up this batch of play dough; then use it to help small student groups knead and pound out their anger in a constructive, creative way. To begin, combine 4 cups of flour, 1 cup of salt, and 1¾ cups of warm water in a large bowl. Mix the ingredients until a soft dough forms. Give an equal portion of the dough to each child; then explain that working with play dough is a good outlet for anger. Invite each child to imagine that he is angry. Have him knead, pound, press, and stretch the dough as energetically as he desires in order to work out his imaginary anger. Afterward, ask him to form a peaceful creation to share with the group.

Purposeful Play

Musical Sing-Along

When youngsters create their own Mean Soup Bands, they'll experience firsthand how music can help them overcome anger. Gather a variety of foil pans, pots and lids, and all sorts of spoons. Then, working with one small group at a time, invite each student to pick a pair of items to use as instruments. Teach your little ones the song below; then invite them to play their instruments as they sing along. After they sing the last line, name one thing that Horace does as he makes Mean Soup, such as growling or banging a spoon on the pot. Then encourage youngsters to perform that action. After a short period of dramatics, repeat the song and name another one of Horace's angry expressions.

Books About Feelings

I Make Mean Soup
(sung to the tune of "Five Little Ducks")

Once in a while when I get mad,
I feel mean and oh-so-bad,
But I don't kick, fall down, or droop.
I get out a pot and make Mean Soup!

Storybook Café

Peaceful Potato Soup

Sometimes a simple serving of real soup can ease the anger right on out. As youngsters enjoy this soothing soup, encourage them to savor its smell and flavor.

(makes 12 half-cup servings)

Supplies:
kitchen knife
vegetable peeler
cutting board
large pot
hot plate
ladle
tablespoon
foam bowls
plastic spoons
one-cup measuring cup

Ingredients:
6 medium potatoes
1 onion
2 tbsp. butter
two 10½ oz. cans of chicken broth
4 c. of water

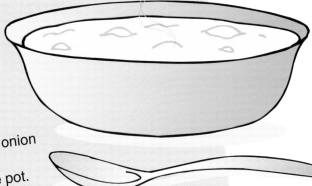

To make peaceful potato soup:
1. Peel and chop the onion and potatoes.
2. Melt the butter in the pot; then sauté the chopped onion in the butter.
3. Add the potatoes, chicken broth, and water to the pot.
4. Bring the soup to a boil; then simmer for 20 minutes or until the potatoes are tender.

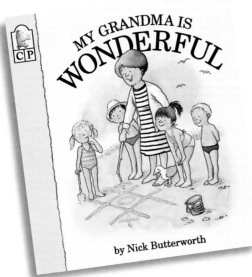

My Grandma Is Wonderful

Written and illustrated by Nick Butterworth

This special grandma shows that she cares about her grandchildren in many loving ways. This charming story is filled with adorable illustrations.

Storytime Song

Spark student interest in storytime with this musical invitation sung to the tune of "Mary Had a Little Lamb."

Grandma can be so much fun,
So much fun, so much fun.
Grandma can be so much fun—
So very special, too!

(Repeat until all of your little ones have joined together.)

When your youngsters have joined you, read aloud *My Grandma Is Wonderful.*

Learning Links

Expressing Caring Thoughts

This caring, thoughtful grandma treated her grandchildren to enormous ice-cream cones. Ask youngsters to name some other caring acts that the grandma showed the children. Then discuss some ways in which they can show others that they care. Afterward, invite each child to create her own enormous ice-cream cone of caring acts. To prepare, make a class supply of the cone pattern (page 211) on brown construction paper. Then, for each child, make several construction paper copies of the ice-cream scoop in different colors. Have each child cut out her cone and scoops. Then ask her to name several things that she might do to show her care for others. Write her dictation for each caring act on a separate scoop cutout. Have her glue her scoops onto her cone to create a multiscoop ice-cream cone. Display all of the cones beneath the title "Here's the Scoop on Caring About Others."

Listen to what others say to you.

Do something nice for someone.

Tell Mom, "I love you!"

Art Smarts
Descriptive Picture Frame

Books About Feelings

With this idea, youngsters can brag about their caring grandmothers (or other elderly friends) and then give their grandmothers something to brag about. To begin, invite youngsters to tell about the many ways their grandmothers show that they care about them. Then give each child a half sheet of white construction paper. Ask him to illustrate his paper with a special picture just for his grandmother. After he completes his picture, help him glue it onto the center of a construction paper color of his choice to create a frame effect. Have him dictate a title for his frame that describes his grandma. Invite him to decorate the frame with an assortment of craft items, such as pom-poms and sequins. If desired, attach two pieces of magnet tape to the back of each child's picture. Then encourage him to give his picture to his grandma along with a huge, loving hug.

Purposeful Play
Memory Game

It's incredible luck (or is it?) that the grandma in this story always has what her grandchildren need right there in her pocketbook! Invite your students to share their comments on this phenomenon; then play this memory pocketbook game with them. To prepare, gather a large purse or bag and five items commonly found in a purse, such as a set of keys, a small package of tissue, a wallet, a comb, and a small mirror. To play, show a small student group the items. Name each item and slip it into the purse. Then remove all but one of the items, again naming each one as you take it out of the purse. Ask youngsters to guess which item is left in the purse. After children guess correctly, invite a volunteer to repack the purse and lead the next round of play. Continue in this manner until each child has had a turn.

My Grandma Is Wonderful

Storybook Café
Fun Cones

These ice-cream cones may not be as enormous as the ones the grandma from the story bought, but they will be enormous fun to eat!

Supplies:
ice-cream scoops
napkins

Ingredients for each child:
ice cream
ice-cream cone
assortment of candy sprinkles

To make one fun cone:
1. Scoop ice cream into a cone.
2. Top the ice cream with your choice of candy sprinkles.
3. Enjoy!

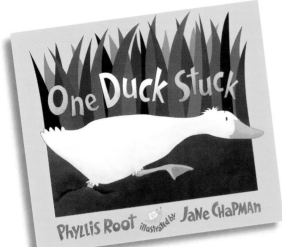

One Duck Stuck

Written by Phyllis Root
Illustrated by Jane Chapman

"Help! Help! Who can help?" *Poor duck is stuck! Count along as his friends work together to help duck out of the muck.*

Storytime Song

Call your students to storytime with this song sung to the tune of "Three Blind Mice."

One duck stuck,
One duck stuck,
Stuck in the muck,
Stuck in the muck.
Come meet the marsh friends who care about the duck.
They all try to help him get out of the muck.
Can his friends help him out or is the duck out of luck?
One duck stuck,
One duck stuck.

(Continue singing the song until your little ducks have gathered together.)

After all of your youngsters have joined together, read aloud *One Duck Stuck.*

Learning Links

Count and Compare Critters

Youngsters won't mind playing in the muck with this fun count and compare activity. To prepare, cut out two large brown construction paper circles to represent muck. Then gather a variety of small toy animals to use as counters. Working with a small group of students, ask one child to count a designated number of animals to put on one circle of muck. Have another child place a different number of counters on the other circle. As a group, count the animals on each circle and compare the quantities. Which circle of muck has fewer animals? Which has more? To extend the activity, invite students to remove from or add to the animal groups to even out the quantities on each circle. Or have youngsters manipulate the counters to solve simple word problems, such as "If two animals get out of this muck, how many will be stuck?"

Art Smarts

Muddy Muck Masterpiece

Discuss with students how the duck must have felt being stuck in that muck. Then invite them to create these related pictures. Provide each child with a large outline of a duck to paint, or enlarge a copy of the duck pattern on page 194. After the paint dries, ask her to cut out her duck and glue it onto a large sheet of green construction paper. Have her sponge-paint brown muck all around the bottom of the duck to give it the appearance of being stuck in muck. While the paint dries, have the child cut out a speech bubble from white construction paper; then write on the cutout her dictation about what the duck might say or think about being stuck. Have her glue the speech bubble onto her picture. During group time, invite youngsters to share their pictures with the class. Then display the pictures beneath the title "[Number of duck pictures] Ducks Stuck!"

Books About Feelings

Purposeful Play

Teamwork Time

Just as the duck's friends worked together to pull him from the muck, your little ducks can learn to accomplish tough tasks through teamwork. Set a task for each child, in turn, such as putting away the blocks or putting together a puzzle. Time the child as he completes the assigned task and record his time on chart paper. Then dump out the blocks or scramble the puzzle and direct several students to help him complete the same task. Time the group and record its time. Once all of your students have participated, invite youngsters to compare and discuss the time recorded for each task. Now that's teamwork!

Storybook Café

Stuck Duck

These little ducks are in luck, for your hungry youngsters won't let them stay stuck. In fact, when each child plucks out her duck, she'll even be happy to clean up the muck!

(makes 16 servings)

Ingredients:
two 3.4-oz. boxes of instant chocolate pudding
4 c. of milk
roll of refrigerator sugar cookie dough

Supplies:
large mixing bowl
stirring spoon
aluminum foil
cookie sheet
oven
plastic bowls
plastic spoons
small duck-shaped cookie cutter

To make one stuck duck:

1. Stir the milk and pudding mix together as directed on the package; then refrigerate the pudding until ready to use.
2. Pat out a slice of cookie dough on a piece of foil. Cut a duck shape from the dough and remove the excess.
3. Put the cookie on a cookie sheet, leaving it on the foil. Bake according to the package directions.
4. After the cookie cools, scoop a ¼-cup serving of pudding into a bowl.
5. Stand the duck cookie in the pudding muck.
6. Help the poor stuck duck out of the muck. Gulp!

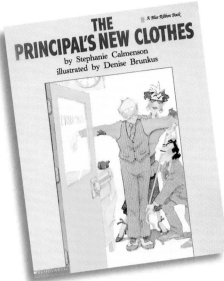

The Principal's New Clothes

Written by Stephanie Calmenson
Illustrated by Denise Brunkus

Meet the vain Mr. Bundy, principal of P. S. 88. He's about to learn that pride can lead to quite an embarrassing moment.

Storytime Song

Youngsters will proudly march over when you sing this invitation to the tune of "Yankee Doodle."

Mr. Bundy is so proud.
He always dresses so cool.
One day he bought a special suit
To show off to his whole school.

"Mr. B, you're looking great.
What fancy clothes you have there!"
But no one really saw his suit.
They saw his underwear!

(Repeat the song until all of your cool kids have joined together.)

Once students have gathered for storytime, read *The Principal's New Clothes*.

Learning Links

Color Word Flips

Put youngsters to work designing the principal's new clothes for this flip book and reinforce color-word skills along the way. To prepare, make a class supply of the book page pattern on page 212. Then instruct each child to color the shirt, tie, and pants on his page as he desires. Have him name the colors used for each article of clothing as you write his dictation on the blank lines. Then invite the child to glue wiggle eyes stickers onto the principal's head and draw facial features to complete his picture. Have him cut out his page, cut the page in half on the bold line, and then punch holes on each page half where indicated. To create a flip book, stack all of the top pages together; then stack the bottom pages. Use metal rings to bind the pages between two tagboard covers. Title the book "The Principal's Colorful Clothes." During group time, invite volunteers to flip the top and bottom pages to create a unique outfit for the principal; then help youngsters read the text for each outfit.

What is the principal wearing today?
A red shirt,
a black tie,
and green pants.

Creative Stitch

Little fingers will stitch up a storm with this fun activity! For each child, edge a 12" x 12" burlap square with masking tape to prevent the fabric from unraveling. Use a permanent marker to draw a simple clothing shape, such as a shirt or pants, on the square. Then invite each child to color the clothing shape with a marker. Afterward, help her thread a length of yarn through a blunt tapestry needle and knot one end of the yarn. Show her how to sew a running stitch along the outline of the shape (as shown). When she reaches the end of her yarn, help her tie it off and rethread her needle. After she sews the complete outline, invite her to embellish her design with craft items, such as large buttons, pompoms, and ribbon. Display each child's clothing creation with the title "Looking 'Sew' Good!"

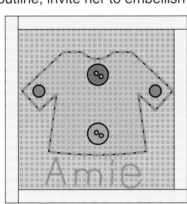

Measurement Bingo

This bingo game is tailor-made for measurement fun. To make a gameboard, have each child draw a full-body self-portrait on large construction paper. Then invite student partners to use a paper-clip chain to measure the length of each other's arms, legs, and body (have students lie on the floor for this measurement). Have each child record the paper-clip total for each measurement on a separate sticky note. Then have him

attach each note to the corresponding part of his self-portrait. Afterward, label a set of bingo caller cards with numerals ranging from the shortest to longest student measurements recorded. To play the game, a caller picks a card and calls out the labeled numeral. If a player has a sticky note with the corresponding numeral on his self-portrait (gameboard), he covers it with a marker. When he covers all of his sticky notes, the player calls out "Bingo!" Continue play in this manner as student interest dictates. Later, send each child home with his self-portrait to share with his family.

Pride Punch

Youngsters will be as proud as punch to make this delectable drink. To begin, explain that when Mr. Bundy's pride spilled over, it affected many people. To demonstrate, draw a tilted cup in the top left corner of a sheet of chart paper. Then draw a large spill coming from the cup (as shown). Label the cup "Mr. Bundy's Pride." Tell students that when a person's pride spills over—like a drink—it can cause a big mess. Then discuss how the principal's pride impacted the characters in the story. Write each character's name inside the spill outline and then write how he or she was affected by Mr. Bundy's pride. What a mess! Assure students that it is good to have pride, but too much can have a negative effect on others. Then invite youngsters to stir up a tasty cup of Pride Punch. To make one serving, a child stirs together a scoop of orange sherbet and a half cup of lemon-lime soda in a plastic cup. After she stirs her punch to the desired consistency, invite her to drink up—but be careful not to spill it!

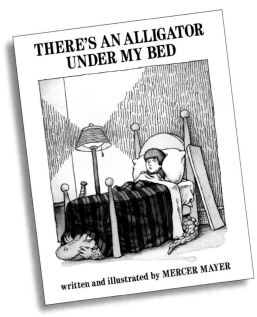

THERE'S AN ALLIGATOR UNDER MY BED

written and illustrated by MERCER MAYER

There's an Alligator Under My Bed

Written and illustrated by Mercer Mayer

A clever young boy lures an alligator into the garage with a trail of healthy eats and delicious treats. But will his dad be able to get into the car in the morning?

Storytime Song

Lure youngsters to storytime with this verse chanted to the rhythm of "Five Little Monkeys Jumping on the Bed."

There's a big alligator under my bed—
Huge eyes and teeth coming out of his head.
Told my mom and dad, and here's what they said,
"We don't see an alligator under your bed!"

(Repeat the chant until all of your students have joined together.)

After your class has assembled for storytime, ask them to listen to *There's an Alligator Under My Bed* to find out how the boy coaxed the alligator into the garage.

Learning Links

Sensory Snack Bag

Give youngsters a sensory surprise with this bag full of alligator bait. To prepare, place an assortment of plastic or real fruits and vegetables in a large bag. Working with one small group at a time, invite students to put on their "Great Gator Headbands" (page 139). Then ask each child, in turn, to close his eyes and reach into the bag to pick out a food item. Challenge him to identify the food without looking at it. After he makes his guess, have him remove the food and show it to the group. Did he guess correctly? At a later time, you might repeat this activity using common objects (such as a block, a paintbrush, and scissors) instead of the food items.

Great Gator Headband

These alligator headbands make great props for students' learning and dramatic-play activities. To make one, each child cuts out a green construction paper copy of the alligator pattern on page 213. Then she cuts on the broken line around each eye and folds the eyes forward so that they stand upright. To create alligator teeth, the child zigzag-cuts one long edge each of two 4" x 1" white paper strips and then she glues a tooth strip along each side of the alligator's snout. Afterward, fit a construction paper strip around each child's head; then attach her alligator cutout to the headband as shown. After she puts on her headband, position the alligator over the top of her head. Then show her how to tilt her head back and forward to snap her gator's mouth open and closed.

Crawl and Collect Relay

Send your hungry reptiles on a food-gathering expedition with this swamp relay. Create two identical obstacle courses with items such as playground cones, plastic hoops, and chairs. Place the same quantity of plastic foods along each course; then collect two small baskets. Divide students into two teams and make half of each team alligators. Ask the alligators to don their "Great Gator Headbands"; then line them up at one end of the team's obstacle course. Make the remaining team members gator baiters. Position them at the opposite end of the course. To play, each alligator crawls along the swamp course. As he moves along, he collects the food in a basket. When he reaches the opposite end, the gator baiter takes the food basket and quickly redistributes the food along the course. Then he passes the basket to the next alligator. After each team completes the course, invite the students to perform a special swamp stomp. Then have the team members switch roles to play again.

Gator Bait

When your little gators snap up this veggie snack, you'll be glad to catch them eating such nutritious munchies. Be sure to invite youngsters to don their Great Gator Headbands (made in the activity above) as they prepare and eat their snacks.

Supplies:
plastic plates

Ingredients:
an assortment of vegetables, such as carrot and celery slices; squash and cucumber slices; and broccoli florets
vegetable dip

To make gator bait:
1. Scoop a dollop of vegetable dip onto a plate.
2. Add vegetable choices.
3. Snap! Snap! Snap!

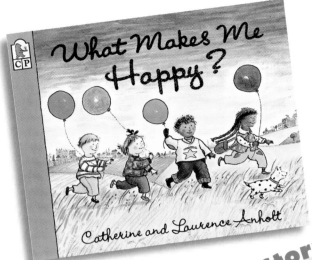

What Makes Me Happy?

Written and illustrated by Catherine and Laurence Anholt

Rhyming text and animated illustrations explore the many moods of childhood. A perfect prompt to help eager young readers share and compare their own moods.

Storytime Song

Set the mood for storytime with an animated version of this song sung to the tune of "Three Blind Mice." As you sing, make a facial expression or gesture to represent each mood mentioned. Then, each time you repeat the song, invite youngsters to imitate your actions.

I feel happy. I feel sad.
I feel jealous. I feel mad.
Come to our circle and find out why
Sometimes I laugh and sometimes I cry.
Sometimes I'm bored and sometimes I'm shy.
I feel happy.

(Repeat the song until all your students have joined the group.)

After your class has gathered together, read aloud *What Makes Me Happy?*

Learning Links

Journal Happy

What makes your youngsters happy? Invite them to make these bright, cheery journals to share the sources of their happiness. To begin, make several eight-inch tagboard circles to use as tracers. Then instruct each child to trace and cut out two yellow construction paper circles and five white construction paper circles. Have her stack and staple the white circles between the yellow ones to create a book; then ask her to draw a large smiley face on the front cover. Help the child title her journal "What Makes Me Happy?" To use, each day invite the child to illustrate a page with something that makes her happy; then write her dictation about each drawing on the page. At the end of the week, hold an author's circle to allow students to showcase their happy little journals with the class.

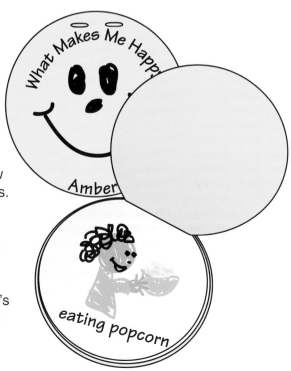

Art Smarts

Expressive Headband

Encourage youngsters to evaluate their own emotional responses with these special headbands. To prepare, gather a class supply of sentence strips and make several three-inch circle tagboard tracers. Then draw on chart paper a simple face to represent each emotion: happiness, sadness, surprise, and anger. Invite each child to trace and cut out four construction paper circles and then draw a face with a different emotion on each circle, referring to the chart as needed. Help her space her circles equally on a sentence strip and glue them in place. Fit the strip to her head to form a headband and staple the ends together. To use, describe a situation that might elicit an emotion represented on the headbands. For example, you might say, "When you walk into your house, all of your friends shout 'Happy Birthday!'" Have each child turn her headband so that the emotion she might feel in that situation faces forward. Each time you repeat the exercise, describe a different situation to elicit a different emotion.

Purposeful Play

Dance and Declare

In the mood to groove? If so, this musical movement game is the perfect activity for a physical *and* emotional workout. To play, students spread out in an open area of your classroom; then they move and dance to a selection of lively, upbeat music. When you stop the music, all the children freeze. Then you ask, "What makes you [happy]?" Appoint several children to respond to the question. Then play the music again and repeat the activity, each time using a different emotion in your question. Now you're groovin'!

Storybook Café

Merry Muffins

This happy little snack is sure to put a smile on every child's face.

Supplies:
plastic knives
paper plates

Ingredients for each child:
English muffin
cream cheese spread
frozen blueberries, thawed

To make one merry muffin:
1. Spread the cream cheese on the English muffin.
2. Use blueberries to make a smiley face.
3. Take a bite and smile!

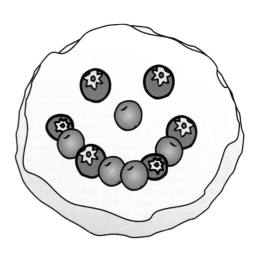

The Bag I'm Taking to Grandma's

Written by Shirley Neitzel
Illustrated by Nancy Winslow Parker

What's a young boy to pack for a trip to Grandma's house? Just what's absolutely necessary: a baseball mitt, toy cars, a space shuttle, wooden animals… Of course, Mom might have something to say about his selections!

Storytime Song

Bid your little ones to pack up and join you by singing this song to the tune of "If You're Happy and You Know It." Hold up the book so youngsters can see its cover.

If you're going to Grandma's house,
What should you take?
If you're going to Grandma's house,
What should you take?
Toy cars, a baseball mitt,
A book to read, or clothes that fit?
If you're going to Grandma's house,
What should you take?

(Repeat the last verse until all your students have gathered for storytime.)

Once your youngsters are settled, read aloud *The Bag I'm Taking to Grandma's.*

Circle-Time Sort

Strengthen students' classification skills with this packing activity. Bring a suitcase to circle time, along with a few articles of clothing, some musical instruments, and some toys. Announce to students that you are taking your own trip to Grandma's house. Ask them to help you sort the items before you pack. Have youngsters survey the collection of items and come up with categories by which to sort. Then pack the sorted items in separate sections of the suitcase. After this group activity, give each child a copy of page 214 for further sorting practice.

Art Smarts

Suitcase Booklet

If your students seem to have a handle on packing, invite them to pack their own bags. In advance, cut a few suitcase shapes from tagboard to use as tracers. Ask each child to trace and cut out a suitcase from a large sheet of white construction paper. (Precut the suitcases for younger children.) Ask each youngster to consider the climate he'd be visiting if he went to visit his grandmother (or another relative). Then have older students draw and label items they need to pack in their suitcases. For younger children, provide magazines and encourage them to cut out and glue on pictures of items they should pack. Compile the completed pages into a class book, with a colored construction paper cover and back cut to match the pages. Share the book at a group time; then add it to your reading center for little ones to enjoy on their own.

Purposeful Play

What To Pack?

This center will get your youngsters sorting and packing—pronto! Gather two sets of pictures (such as those found in travel magazines and brochures)—one that depicts cold climates and one that shows warm climates. Place the two sets of pictures in a center, along with two empty suitcases and a variety of items appropriate to each climate. Invite student pairs to visit this center. Have each child choose one set of pictures and a suitcase. Then have her sort through the items and pack the ones she'd need for a visit to her chosen climate. All packed!

Storybook Café

Pack-Your-Bag Pita

These edible suitcases are packed with nutrition *and* fun!

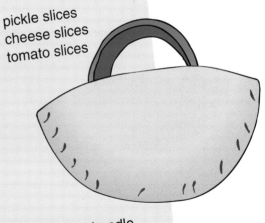

Supplies:
sharp knife (for teacher use)
paper plates
serving spoon

Ingredients:
green pepper
½ pita round per child
tuna salad
shredded lettuce
pickle slices
cheese slices
tomato slices

To prepare the green pepper:
1. Slice the green pepper crosswise. Remove seeds and pith.
2. Cut each slice in half to make suitcase handles.

To make a pack-your-bag pita:
1. Fill a pita half with a large spoonful of tuna salad.
2. Pack your pita with your choice of additional ingredients.
3. Slip a green pepper piece into the opening of the pita to make the bag's handle.
4. Unpack your bag—right into your tummy!

Franklin's New Friend

Written by Paulette Bourgeois
Illustrated by Brenda Clark

Franklin isn't so sure about Moose, but he soon learns that friends can be different and still have fun together!

Storytime Song

Gather your little ones with this musical invitation, sung to the tune of "Pop Goes the Weasel."

Come and meet a great big moose
And a little turtle.
You will see how they make friends
In our reading circle.

Join me now; we'll read a book
About a newfound friendship.
I know you'll want to take a look
In our reading circle.

(Repeat until all your students have joined their friends in the reading area.)

Once your youngsters have gathered in your group area, read aloud *Franklin's New Friend*.

Learning Links

Diverse "Eggs-ploration"

We are all the same inside!

Explore diversity with this "egg-citing" idea! In advance, collect a few different types of eggs, such as a small white egg, a large white egg, and a brown egg. Point out that Franklin does not want to be friends with Moose at first because he seems so different. Then show youngsters the eggs, and discuss the differences in size and color. Gently crack each egg into a separate clear glass bowl. Explain to your students that although the eggs looked different on the outside, they are all the same inside. Guide them to understand that people can also look very different on the outside but be very much alike on the inside, with similar feelings and interests.

Create a visual reminder of this idea with this project. Give each child two same-sized white egg cutouts. Have her decorate one cutout with her choice of art materials, such as markers, glitter, or tissue paper scraps. Then show her how to cut a jagged "crack" across the center of the cutout to divide it into two pieces. On the second egg cutout have her glue a red construction paper heart and then copy this message: "We are all the same inside!" Help her connect the three pieces with a brad on the left side as shown. Encourage youngsters to take these projects home to share with their families and to spark discussions about diversity and friendships.

Friendly Turtles

These terrific turtles will be reminders to little ones that making friends means making an effort to be nice. To make one, have a child paint one side of a white paper plate with brown tempera paint. Have her glue four 1½-inch green construction paper circles to the underside of the plate to resemble the turtle's legs. Then direct her to attach two small wiggle eyes stickers onto a slightly larger green circle and draw a friendly smile to complete the turtle's head. Have her glue the head to one end of a 1" x 4" strip of green paper. Help her accordion-fold the strip before she glues it to the back of the plate to resemble the turtle's neck. Have her add a small green triangle tail to complete her turtle. Display the finished projects on a bulletin board with the title "Stick Out Your Neck for a Friend!"

Piñata Pals

What better way to explore diversity in friendships than to play a childhood game from another culture? This Mexican favorite—*piñata*—is a fun choice! To make a friendship piñata, have each child help a friend paint one of his hands with the paint color of his choice. Have each child make a handprint on a paper grocery bag. Fill the bag with a variety of small treats, making sure the treats can be divided equally among your students. Fold the bag closed; then punch a hole through the folded layers. Thread a strong piece of string through the hole and then use it to suspend the bag from your classroom ceiling.

Before the fun begins, tell students how many treats each of them may collect once the bag is opened. Remind them that a good friend isn't greedy, always shares, and never pushes or shoves. Then have little ones stand back and create a large open area below the piñata. Blindfold one child at a time and give him an opportunity to swing a plastic bat at the bag. Continue until the bag is either broken open or knocked down. Have each child gather the designated number of treats. Further focus on friendship by encouraging each child to share (trade) one of his treats with a friend.

Turtle Cookies

Franklin shares cookies with his new friend, Moose. Encourage each of your youngsters to follow Franklin's example by making two of these cookies and sharing one with a friend.

Ingredients:
small, round sugar cookies
green-tinted frosting
pretzel halves
green M&M's candies

Supplies:
craft sticks
napkins

To make one turtle cookie:
1. Use a craft stick to spread green frosting on a cookie.
2. Use dabs of frosting to attach four pretzel legs.
3. Use a dab of frosting to attach a green M&M's candy for a head.

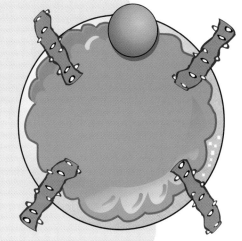

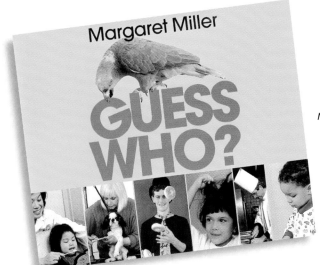

Guess Who?

Written and photo-illustrated by Margaret Miller

Butcher, baker, or candlestick maker? Guess which community helper is hiding behind each page of this fun-filled book!

Storytime Song

Guess who's coming to storytime? It'll be your students when you sing this musical invitation to the tune of "Where Is Thumbkin?"!

Who does this job? Who does that job?
Can you guess? Can you guess?
Let's all read this guessing book
In our reading circle!
Come join me! Come join me!

(Repeat until all your little guessers have gathered in your reading area.)

Once your little ones are settled, read aloud *Guess Who?*

Learning Links

Sort and Graph

What makes a person a community helper? How are they different from other workers? Your youngsters will discover the differences with this graphing activity. In advance, draw a line to divide a large sheet of chart paper into two columns. Label one side "Community Helpers" and the other side "Other Workers." Discuss each worker in Margaret Miller's book; then select a student to illustrate and label an index card for each worker (or do this yourself as younger students watch). Ask a student volunteer to decide which category each card belongs in. Remind students that community helpers work to provide things we all need, such as safety, shelter, food, or health care. Affix the cards to the chart to create a graph. Together, count the cards in each column. Were there more community helpers or other workers in the story?

146

Art Smarts

Poem Pop-Up

You never know who may pop up in this activity! To prepare, duplicate page 215 for each child. Invite each child in a small group to color and then cut out the five community helpers. Have him also cut out the poem box. Then provide each student with three straws and a small Styrofoam cup. Read the poem together; then have each child tape the poem box around the outside of his cup. Have him cut the three straws in half and discard one of the halves. Have him tape one community helper cutout to each remaining straw. Direct each child to push one straw through the bottom of his cup to make a hole. To use the pop-up, a child inserts one community helper straw into the cup so that it is hidden. He recites the poem and gives a clue about the helper. After the other children in the group guess, he pushes the straw up so that the community helper pops up for all to see!

Purposeful Play

Career Choices

Invite youngsters to dress the part of community helpers in your dramatic-play area. Gather a variety of simple clothing items and props that little ones can use to dress as workers from the book, such as aprons, cooking utensils, toy tools, a toy medical kit, a canvas tote bag and a collection of discarded junk mail, and a toy camera. Also include any career hats you have as well as a full-length mirror. Encourage each visitor at the center to dress up and invite playmates to guess her occupation.

Books About People

Storybook Café

Baker's Pretzels

Your youngsters will love taking on the role of baker as they prepare these tasty pretzel treats.

(makes 8)

Supplies:
cookie sheet
knife
pastry brush

Ingredients:
loaf of frozen bread dough, thawed
flour
2 tbsp. butter or margarine, melted
salt

To make baker's pretzels:
1. Slice the dough into eight equal portions.
2. Flour your hands; then roll and stretch each portion of dough into a long strip (about 12 to 18 inches long).
3. Crisscross the strip to form a pretzel shape.
4. Place the pretzels on the cookie sheet and brush with margarine.
5. Sprinkle with salt.
6. Bake at 350 degrees for 25 minutes or until light golden brown.

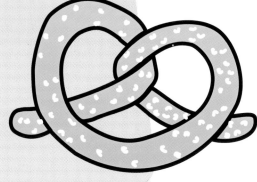

Hazel's Amazing Mother

Written and illustrated by Rosemary Wells

When Hazel takes a wrong turn and ends up in the hands of bullies, who will help her? Her mother is on the far side of town—but you'll be amazed at what Hazel's mother can do!

Storytime Song

Ask students to join you by singing this song to the tune of "Are You Sleeping?"

Where is Hazel?
Where is Hazel?
She is lost.
She is lost.
Who will help find her?
Who will help find her?
Come and see.
Come and see.

Where is Hazel?
Where is Hazel?
She is lost.
She is lost.
Come and join together.
Come and join together.
Read with me.
Read with me.

(Repeat the verses until all your youngsters have gathered together.)

When your students are set for a story, read aloud *Hazel's Amazing Mother.*

Learning Links

Sharing Stories

Do your children have special stories to share about their amazing mothers? After reading the story, invite each child in a small group to sit in your teacher's chair and tell his story to the group. Then ask students to think about all the special things mothers do. Make a list of their ideas on chart paper. Provide older children with colored pencils, crayons, and paper. Have them draw pictures of things their amazing mothers do. Invite them to write words under each picture or dictate as you write. Ask younger students to clip pictures from magazines to represent things their moms do. Have them glue the pictures to pieces of paper; then add their dictation. Gather each child's pictures into a book, add a personalized cover, and staple. Moms will be amazed when they see these projects!

Tonya's Amazing Mother

My mom can ride a bike really fast.

Art Smarts

Pretty As a Picture

These child-drawn portraits of moms are sure to become treasured keepsakes! Ask each child to close her eyes and think about her mother's face. What color is her hair? Is it long or short, curly or straight? What color are her eyes? Does she wear earrings or a necklace? Provide children with large pieces of construction paper and crayons. Ask each child to draw a large picture of her mother's face on a sheet of construction paper.

Prepare a frame for each child's picture. Simply cut the center from another sheet of construction paper in the child's choice of colors (see illustration). Provide a heart-shaped hole puncher and invite each child to take a turn punching heart shapes all over her paper frame. Use strategically placed dots of glue to adhere the frame over the portrait, making sure the corners are secured. Display these masterpieces on a bulletin board in your classroom with the title "Our Amazing Mothers!" After visitors have a chance to admire them, send them home for moms to keep.

Purposeful Play

Amazing Acting

In your dramatic-play center, provide props for acting out the story of *Hazel's Amazing Mother.* You might include a baby carriage, a doll, a soccer ball, a picnic basket, and a blanket. If your young actors and actresses wish, have groups perform the story for neighboring classes.

Storybook Café

Cookie Kisses

Her mother makes sure Hazel doesn't leave home without a kiss! Little ones will enjoy making and eating these kisses. If desired, have each child make one for his mother, too!

(makes 52)

Supplies:
cookie sheets
spatula
table knife

Ingredients:
2 rolls of refrigerated sugar cookie dough
13 oz. bag of Hershey's Kisses candies

To make cookie kisses:
1. Cut each roll of cookie dough into 13 even slices. Then cut each slice in half.
2. Roll a half slice of dough into a ball and place it on a cookie sheet.
3. Bake all cookies at 375 degrees for eight minutes or until lightly browned.
4. Immediately press an unwrapped candy into the center of each cookie.
5. Cool and eat or share with Mom!

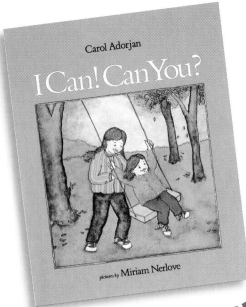

I Can! Can You?

Written by Carol Adorjan
Illustrated by Miriam Nerlove

Older sisters can do so much—but so can little sisters! Share this inspiring look at the flourishing independence of younger siblings.

Storytime Song

Encourage young readers to join you for a story with this song sung to the tune of "I'm a Little Teapot."

Come read about a sister, short and smart.
She uses her brain; she uses her heart!
We're sure to see her try and try again.
Come to the circle as I count to ten.
1, 2, 3, 4, 5, 6, 7, 8, 9, 10

(Sing the verse; then slowly count to ten as youngsters make their way to the reading area.)

When you can see that your youngsters are ready to listen, read aloud *I Can! Can You?*

Learning Links
Buddy Boasting Interview

After sharing the story, ask your little ones to consider what tasks they are able to do. Have kindergarten students pair up; then ask them to interview one another to find out what each child can do. Have each child complete a copy of page 216 by drawing a picture of her buddy performing a task he is proud to be able to do. Help her fill in the blanks to describe the action. Try pairing younger children with older elementary buddies to help them complete this activity.

Invite students to share their completed pages before putting them on display in your classroom. What a wonderful way to boost self-esteem!

Someone I know can ride a pony.

That person is named Maria.

"I Can!" Quilt

Showcase your students' abilities by creating an "I Can!" quilt. Ask each student to think of a new accomplishment from the last few months. Provide each student with a 5" x 5" square of white copy paper and a 6" x 6" square of construction paper. Direct him to draw a picture showing his accomplishment on the white square; then have him write or dictate a sentence telling about it. Have him glue his white paper in the center of his colored paper. Assemble all the squares on a large rectangle of bulletin board paper to form a quilt, adding additional colored squares if necessary. Print the words "I Can!" on any additional squares or on the quilt border. Then display the "I Can!" quilt in a prominent area of your classroom.

4922 Andre

I can say my address!

Mimic Me

Your youngsters will be showing off their many talents in this adaptation of Follow the Leader. To begin, gather students in a circle. Say, "I can touch my toes. Can you?" Encourage students to mimic you as you touch your toes. Then invite the child beside you to name an action and model it for everyone else to copy. Remind her to ask, "Can you?" Bet they can!

"I Can!" Ice Cream

Small groups of youngsters *can* help make this yummy frozen treat, and then they *can* eat it!

(makes 6 servings)

Ingredients:
2 c. whipping cream
⅔ c. sweetened condensed milk
⅔ c. chocolate syrup
⅓ c. mini chocolate chips (optional)

Supplies:
large mixing bowl
hand mixer
rubber spatula
measuring cups
6 small metal juice cans (1 per child)
plastic spoons

To make "I can!" ice cream:
1. Combine cream, milk, and syrup in the mixing bowl. Beat with the hand mixer until stiff peaks form.
2. Fold in mini chocolate chips (if desired).
3. Divide the mixture evenly among the 6 juice cans.
4. Freeze until firm.

Berry Best JUICE

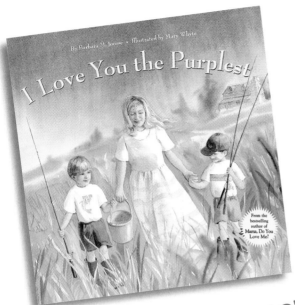

I Love You the Purplest

Written by Barbara M. Joosse
Illustrated by Mary Whyte

"Who do you love best?" each of two brothers secretly asks Mama after a day of competing for her attention. Mama's gentle response is unique to each boy and conveys the strong, unconditional nature of a parent's love.

Storytime Song

Encourage young readers to join you for storytime by singing this song to the tune of "The Muffin Man."

Come hear a story of two young boys,
Two young boys, two young boys.
Come hear a story of two young boys
Whose mama loves them so!

Yes, Mama loves each of her boys,
Each of her boys, each of her boys.
Yes, Mama loves each of her boys,
In a very special way!

(Repeat until all the children have gathered together.)

Once all your students are settled in for a story, read aloud *I Love You the Purplest.*

Learning Links

Counting on Fish

Max, Julian, and Mama enjoy a moonlight fishing trip, and your little ones will enjoy a trip to your math center to play this fishing game. To prepare, make a supply of fish by photocopying the patterns on page 217 onto construction paper. Cut out each fish; then program it with a dot set or a numeral from 1 to 10. Attach a metal paper clip to each fish and then put all the fish in a large plastic tub. Arrange the tub, a prepared magnetic fishing pole, and a container of fish-shaped crackers in your math center. Invite each child who visits this center to use the fishing pole to catch a paper fish. Have him count the dots (or identify the numeral) and then take a matching number of crackers as his fisherman's meal. Or—for more of a challenge—have him catch two fish and compare them to determine which fish shows the greater quantity (or number). Then invite him to count out that many crackers to eat.

Purple Hearts

Mama loves Julian the bluest and Max the reddest. And when she blends her love for her two boys, she loves them both together the purplest. Invite youngsters to blend some red and blue paint to create these purple hearts. At your art center, provide each child with a small foam cup containing some red and blue tempera paint. Have her use a paintbrush to thoroughly mix the two colors together. Then invite her to add small amounts of either color until she achieves a shade of purple she likes. Next, have her paint a large heart on a sheet of white paper. When the paint dries, have her cut out the heart and dictate a love message for you to write on the back. Encourage each child to deliver the special heart to the person she loves the purplest.

Books About People

Purposeful
Play

Sandy Color Sort

Dig into this sand table activity to reinforce color recognition and sorting skills. To begin, cut a supply of worm shapes from various craft foam colors. Then label a separate canister for each worm color. Bury the foam worms in your sand table. Add some sand scoops and rakes to the table; then place the labeled canisters nearby. Invite youngsters who visit this center to dig up the worms, sort them into the canisters by color, and then count how many of each they've found.

As a variation, cut both short and long worms from the foam and encourage students to sort the worms by color *and* length.

Daddy,
I love you
when you read
to me.
Ashley

Storybook
Café

Rice Cake Lake

Youngsters will agree that this lake filled with fishes is really delicious!

Supplies:
small paper plates
plastic knives or craft sticks

Ingredients:
rice cake per child
soft cream cheese, tinted blue
fish-shaped crackers

To make one rice cake lake:
1. Spread blue cream cheese on the rice cake.
2. Put several fish crackers in the cream cheese water.

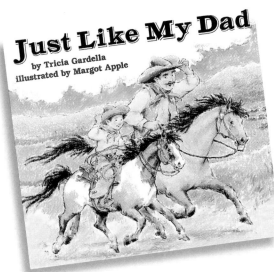

Just Like My Dad

Written by Tricia Gardella
Illustrated by Margot Apple

Saddle your ponies and ride along with a little cowpoke and his dad as they go about their daily routine on the ranch—mending fences, herding cattle, and listening to the old-timers' tales.

Storytime Song

Round up your little cowpokes as you sing these verses to the tune of "Pawpaw Patch."

One little, two little, three little cowpokes,
Four little, five little, six little cowpokes,
Seven little, eight little, nine little cowpokes,
Ten little cowpokes on roundup day!

Saddle your pony, let's ride together!
Saddle your pony, let's ride together!
Saddle your pony, let's ride together!
Ride to the reading circle!

(Repeat the verses until your young cowhands are rounded up in the reading area.)

Once everyone is ready to read, share *Just Like My Dad.*

Learning Links

Dandy Daddy Dictation

The young cowpoke in the story likes working with his dad. Ask your students to share special things they like to do with their dads as you record key words from their responses on a sheet of chart paper. Invite each child to make a special card for his father. Provide him with a 7" x 11" piece of construction paper. Have him fold it in half widthwise and then fold it in half again lengthwise. (It will look like a greeting card and fit in a letter-size envelope.) Have each child decorate the outside of his card with stickers, a drawing, or a sponge-painted design. Then ask him to write a message inside about something special he likes to do with his father. Older students may copy words from the chart, while younger ones can dictate their messages for you to print. Help each child put his card in an envelope, seal it, and add his father's name. Send these love notes home for little ones to share and dads to enjoy!

154

Art Smarts
Marshmallow Printing

Gather round the campfire with some marshmallows, and you've got the makings of an art project! Ask each child the name of her father or other male role model. Using a felt pen, print her father's first name in large letters on a piece of tagboard. (Some children may not know their fathers' first names, so be prepared to write "Daddy" a few times!) Provide the student with a large marshmallow and a pan containing a thin layer of paint. Direct her to dip her marshmallow into the paint and then press it on her paper to make prints along the first letter. Continue, one letter at a time, until the name is printed in marshmallow paint! (When finished printing, have students dispose of their marshmallows in the trash.)

Purposeful Play
Round Up Role Play

During outdoor play, encourage some of the children to role-play cowboys and cowgirls and some to be cattle. Have the cowboys and cowgirls herd the cattle into different areas of the playground. After the round-up, have children switch roles and start the heart-healthy play all over again!

Storybook Café
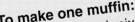

Cowpoke Corn Muffins

After a long day on the range, your cowpokes will enjoy hot corn muffins smothered in jam! Make a muffin for Dad, too!

Supplies:
muffin tin
muffin tin liners
disposable bowls
plastic spoons
measuring spoons

Ingredients for each child:
$\frac{1}{2}$ tsp. sugar
2 tsp. cornmeal
2 tbsp. biscuit mix
1 tbsp. milk
4 tsp. Egg Beaters
jam

To make one muffin:
1. Measure and mix the first five ingredients in a bowl.
2. Spoon the batter into a liner set inside a muffin tin.
3. If you're making a muffin for your dad too, repeat Steps 1 and 2.
4. Bake all the muffins at 375° for 12 to 15 minutes.
5. Spread with jam and chow down!

Loudmouth George and the New Neighbors

Written and illustrated by Nancy Carlson

George is sure he doesn't want to be friends with the new family of pigs next door. Or is he?

Storytime Song

Invite little ones to join you by singing these verses to the tune of "Ten Little Indians."

Loudmouth George has brand-new neighbors.
Loudmouth George has brand-new neighbors.
Loudmouth George has brand-new neighbors
Living right next door!

Come find out what George will do.
Come find out what George will do.
Come find out what George will do
In our reading circle!

(Repeat until all your students have joined together.)

When your students are quiet and ready to hear the story, read aloud *Loudmouth George and the New Neighbors.*

Cool Mud Experiment

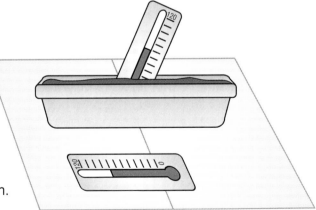

Louanne gets a bad rap when it comes to being a pig. George thinks she is dirty before he even meets her! Actually, pigs keep beds of straw cleaner than horses or cows do. Pigs *do* like to wallow in the mud; that's probably the reason George thinks pigs are dirty animals. But for a pig, wallowing in mud isn't dirty—it's cool! Explain that pigs know that lying in mud will keep them cool in the hot sun. Prove this idea by mixing up a batch of ooey-gooey mud in a large foil pan. Next, lay two thermometers side by side on a warm sidewalk. After students confirm that both thermometers show the same degree of temperature, nestle one into the mud. Leave the other thermometer on the sidewalk. After a few minutes, check the mud-covered thermometer. Youngsters will be pleased to find that the temperature reading has been lowered by the mud. Those pigs! They're not only clean—they're smart too!

Neighborly Class Book

Your little ones will enjoy creating and reading this eye-popping book full of neighborly introductions. Encourage each child to draw a self-portrait on a copy of page 218 and then attach a pair of large wiggle eyes stickers in place. Ask each child to write her name on the blank line. Punch holes along the left margin and put the pages in a three-ring binder titled "Classroom Neighbors All Around." Share the completed book with your group; then tell students that the order of the pages will be changed each day. Youngsters will be sure to pick up this book every day to discover who their new neighbors are!

Class Book Page
Use with "Neighborly Class Book" on page 157.

Hello! My name is _Katie_
How are you today?
Turn the page and you'll find out
Who my neighbor is today!

Books About People

Rolling Introductions

George's friends, Harriet and Ralph, go right over to meet his new neighbors. Encourage your children to practice introducing themselves by playing a game of Hello! Sit in a circle with a small group of children. Have one child roll a ball across the circle to another child in the group and say, "Hello! My name is [child's name]. How are you today?" Ask the child receiving the ball to respond, "I'm fine! My name is [child's name]." Continue the game by having the child who received the ball become the roller and introduce himself as he rolls the ball to another child.

Sprinkled Circles

George can't resist playing in the sprinkler with his friends, and your little ones won't be able to resist this snack made with sure-to-make-you-smile sprinkles!

Supplies:
plastic knives or craft sticks
napkins

Ingredients:
round, buttery crackers (3 per child)
soft cream cheese
sprinkles

To make sprinkled circles:
1. Spread cream cheese on a cracker.
2. Add sprinkles.
3. Eat and repeat!

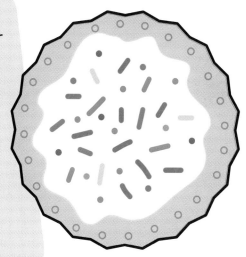

Officer Buckle and Gloria

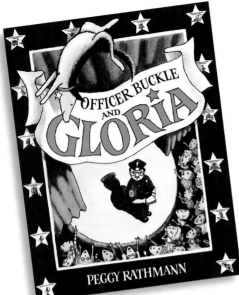

Written and illustrated by Peggy Rathmann

We all know that a police officer is a community helper, but in this book there's a crazy canine that's doing an important job too!

Storytime Song

Call your young reading hounds to storytime with this song sung to the tune of "Old MacDonald."

> Officer Buckle had a dog
> And Gloria was her name.
>
> With a bark, bark here
> And a bark, bark there.
> Here a bark, there a bark,
> Everywhere a bark, bark!
>
> Come meet her during storytime.
> You'll be glad you came!

(Repeat until all youngsters have gathered together.)

Once everyone is settled in to hear a story, read aloud *Officer Buckle and Gloria.*

Learning Links

Safety Stars

Take a tip from Officer Buckle and make these safety stars to remind little ones about school safety. In advance, cut out a class supply of large construction paper stars. Then divide your class into groups. Ask each group to think of tips for a particular area of school safety, such as playground safety, classroom safety, or bus safety. Ask each child to illustrate and write or dictate one tip from the group's brainstormed list. Display the finished safety stars in your classroom or the hallway. Then follow the stars to safety!

Emma

Hold scissors with the pointy side down.

Learning Links

Problem Solving Pooch

Put your young detectives to work on the case of the missing dog! Prior to this activity, hide a stuffed dog somewhere on your playground. Then create a set of clues, leading detectives from one place to another, including a final clue that will lead them to the dog's location. Hide the clue cards in the appropriate locations. Compose a letter from Officer Buckle explaining that Gloria is missing and that he needs their help. Include the first clue card with the letter. Then set your little detectives on the trail. Imagine how proud they'll be when they crack this case!

Dear Boys and Girls,

Help! Gloria is missing! Can you help me find her? Here is a clue to help you.

Officer Buckle

Books About People

Look under the slide.

Purposeful Play

Safety Charades

Are your students as good at acting out safety tips as Gloria? Find out with a game of Safety Charades. Whisper a safety tip from the story into a youngster's ear; then have her act it out for the class. Can they guess the tip?

Storybook Café

Doggie Bones

Your little ones will love sharing these crunchy treats!

(makes approximately 20 small bones)

Supplies:
large mixing bowl
cookie sheet
large spoon
measuring cups
measuring spoons

Ingredients:
1$\frac{1}{2}$ c. flour
$\frac{1}{3}$ c. milk
$\frac{1}{3}$ c. beef bouillon or chicken broth
1 tsp. salt
2 tbsp. butter (softened)
2 tsp. baking powder

To make doggie bones:
1. Mix all ingredients to form a dough.
2. Place the dough on a lightly floured surface and knead the dough several times.
3. Shape a portion of the dough into a bone shape.
4. Place the doggie bone on a cookie sheet.
5. Bake at 400° for 20 to 25 minutes or until browned.

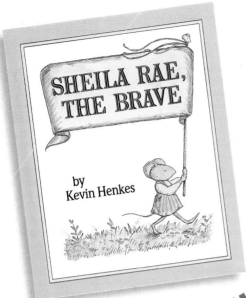

Sheila Rae, the Brave

Written and illustrated by Kevin Henkes

Sheila Rae is a fearless mouse who looks out for her little sister, Louise. But it's Louise who comes to the rescue when Sheila Rae takes her fearlessness too far.

Storytime Song

Invite students to storytime with this song sung to the tune of "Five Little Ducks."

One little mouse
Named Sheila Rae,
She was brave, both night and day!
Sheila Rae, she had no fear,
Till she got lost—oh, dear! Oh, dear!

Come and read
This story now.
A sister helped—you'll find out how.
In this story we will hear
Of Sheila Rae, who has no fear!

(Repeat the verses until all your little mice have gathered for storytime.)

When youngsters are seated, read aloud *Sheila Rae, the Brave.*

Learning Links

Think Safety

Although Sheila Rae was a brave little mouse, she also made some unsafe choices. After sharing the story, provide a copy of page 219 for each student. Direct each child to color and cut out the pictures along the bottom edge. Have her determine whether each action is safe or unsafe and glue the picture in the appropriate column. Ask each student to use the back of her paper to draw a picture of Sheila Rae and Louise doing something brave *and safe* together.

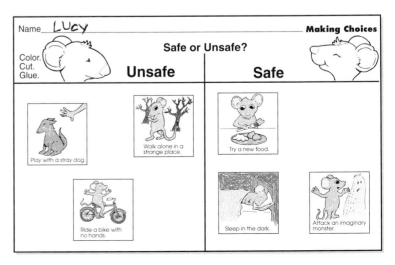

Bravery Badge

Your youngsters are sure to feel more courageous when they're wearing these Bravery Badges. Provide each child with a small paper plate labeled as shown. Ask him to draw himself doing something brave or difficult, such as jumping off the diving board at the pool or eating a new food. Use tape or a safety pin to attach each badge to its badge maker. Invite little ones to wear their badges to boost their bravery throughout the day.

Bravery Badge

Nice Mice

Be brave! Invite your little ones to try their hands at making these sock mice. Direct each child to stuff a white baby sock with cotton balls or polyester fiber-fill to within about two inches of the cuff. Twist a white pipe cleaner around the opening to close it; then have the child wrap the free end of the pipe cleaner around and around the remaining cuff, leaving the loose end of the pipe cleaner to form the tail. Provide each child with a small piece of white or pink felt and have her cut out two round ears. Help her glue the ears in place using fabric glue. Have her use a black marker to draw two eyes, a nose, and whiskers. If desired, reread the story and invite youngsters to act out Sheila's part with their completed mice.

Cheesecake Delights

These yummy treats are perfect for little mice—they're cheesy and they're easy!

(makes 24)

Supplies:
large mixing bowl
hand mixer
large spoon
measuring cups and spoons
foil baking cups
muffin tins
plastic spoons

Ingredients:
four 8-oz. packages cream
   cheese, softened
4 eggs
1 c. sugar
4 tsp. vanilla
24 vanilla wafers
21-oz. can cherry, blueberry,
   or strawberry pie filling

To make cheesecake delights:
1. Combine cream cheese, eggs, sugar, and vanilla. Beat with hand mixer for five minutes or until smooth.
2. Place baking cups in muffin tins.
3. Place a vanilla wafer in the bottom of each cup.
4. Divide cheesecake mixture evenly between cups.
5. Bake at 375° for 15 minutes.
6. Cool. Top each snack with a spoonful of pie filling.

by KAREN ACKERMAN

illustrated by STEPHEN GAMMELL

Song and Dance Man

Written by Karen Ackerman
Illustrated by Stephen Gammell

When Grandpa does his vaudeville act for his grandchildren in the attic, it's a show they'll never forget!

Storytime Song

Hold up a copy of *Song and Dance Man.* Then invite little ones to storytime with this song sung to the tune of "This Old Man."

This old man, he could tap,
He could tap wearing a cap!
With a tip-tap, paddywhack,
Come on over here.
Watch him dance and give a cheer!

This old man, he could sing,
He told jokes and everything!
With a tip-tap, paddywhack,
Come on over here.
Hear his jokes and give a cheer!

(Repeat the verses until all your students have tip-tapped into your reading area.)

Once all your youngsters are gathered together, read aloud *Song and Dance Man.*

Learning Links

Different Dress-Up Discoveries

Put problem-solving skills in the spotlight with this fun activity! For each child, duplicate page 220 onto white construction paper. Instruct each student to color and then cut out the song and dance man and all his clothing. (Precut the pieces for younger students.) Then challenge her to find at least eight different ways to dress him for his vaudeville show. After students have discovered eight combinations, have each child glue her favorite outfit onto Grandpa. Display the completed characters on a black bulletin board with a yellow spotlight.

Art Smarts

Performance Poster

If youngsters want others to view their vaudeville show, they'll need to make posters to advertise. Provide each student in a small group with a sheet of construction paper. Show youngsters a model poster you've made, pointing out the picture of the performer and words that tell about the act. Then ask older students to draw pictures of themselves performing their vaudeville acts. Write each child's dictation as he describes his act. For younger students, take an instant photo of each child wearing his costume. Glue the photo to his construction paper and add his dictation about his act. Display the completed posters near your classroom vaudeville stage.

Purposeful Play

Song and Dance Dress Up

You may not be able to visit a real vaudeville stage, but you can have one in your own classroom! Bring in an old trunk (or a cardboard box decorated to resemble one) and fill it with a variety of men's hats, ties, vests, and shoes, as well as some dancing canes (check your local party-supply store). Invite little ones to dress up and make up dances or songs for their own vaudeville acts. Be sure to have a full-length mirror available where your young dancers and singers can check out their performances. Then set aside a time when children may (if they wish) perform their acts for classmates.

Storybook Café

Dancing Man Cookies

Students will be tap dancing over these delicious cookies!

(makes 12–15 large cookies)

Supplies:
rolling pin
gingerbread man cookie cutters
plastic knives
oven
cookie sheet

Ingredients:
flour
1 roll refrigerated sugar cookie dough
frosting
assorted decorating goodies, such as sprinkles, M&M's brand mini baking bits, mini chocolate chips, and shredded coconut
black string licorice

To make dancing man cookies:
1. Preheat oven to 350°.
2. Roll out cookie dough on floured surface.
3. Press cookie cutter into dough. Place cookies on cookie sheet.
4. Bake cookies according to package directions.
5. Allow to cool; then frost.
6. Decorate as desired.
7. Press a three-inch length of string licorice onto one of the cookie man's hands to make a cane.

Stellaluna

Written and illustrated by Janell Cannon

"Flap" through the pages of this adventure, and you'll meet a little bat who learns that being friends doesn't always mean being alike.

Storytime Song

Call little ones to storytime with this enchanting song about Stellaluna, sung to the tune of "Are You Sleeping?"

Stellaluna,
Stellaluna,
The friendly bat,
The friendly bat.
Come and hear her story
In our reading circle,
Friends, friends, friends,
Friends, friends, friends.

(Repeat until all your little bats have flapped into your reading area.)

Once your youngsters are gathered in your group area, read aloud *Stellaluna*.

Learning Links: Friendship Sentences

Like Stellaluna and her bird friends, friends can be very different. Explore this concept with this "puzzling" activity. In advance, draw a line down the center of a sheet of white copy paper and program it as shown. Photocopy the programmed sheet to make a class supply. Also photocopy a large supply of your students' school photos and cut them apart. Set these materials on a table, along with sheets of construction paper.

My friend likes ISKREM. I like PIZZA.

Have each child prepare a friendship puzzle. First, have her find a copy of her own photo and the photo of a classmate. Direct her to glue her classmate's photo to the top left side of her programmed sheet and her own photo to the top right. Then have her write or dictate an ending for each sentence and add illustrations. Have her glue her paper onto a larger sheet of construction paper. Laminate all the completed pictures; then cut each one into four or five large pieces. Place each child's puzzle in a separate zippered plastic bag. Send each puzzle home to be reassembled and to spark a family discussion about friendship.

Hang in There Card

Friends will go batty over these sweet gifts! To prepare, use an X-acto knife to cut a very simple bat shape from the center of a plastic lid. Then have each child paint a tree trunk on one side of a 12" x 18" sheet of white construction paper, adding a long branch that stretches across the page (as shown). When the paint is dry, have the child position the plastic lid (flat against the paper) so that the bat's head on the cutout is facing down and the bat's bottom is almost touching the branch. Direct her to use a sponge dipped in black paint to fill in the cut-out. Have her lift the lid and repeat the process to create another bat. After the paint dries, have her draw legs for each bat so the bats appear to hang from the branch. Then have each child write on her picture "I like hanging out with you!" Invite each child to present her finished picture to a good friend.

I like hanging out with you!

Books About People

Purposeful Play

Batty Game

Here's a new twist on an old favorite—the game Duck, Duck, Goose. Gather your class into a circle. Select one child to be the bat. Have him walk around the outside of the circle, tapping each child on the head and saying "bird" until he decides to choose a new bat. The new bat jumps up and flies (chases) after the original bat, trying to tag him. If he is tagged, the old bat climbs into the nest (the center of the circle), until a new bat is tagged. Now, *that's* a game to flap your wings about!

Storybook Café

Bat Bite Cupcakes

Grab a friend and work together to make these tasty treats!

Supplies:
small paper plates
craft sticks

Ingredients:
unfrosted cupcake per child
chocolate frosting
mini M&M's candies
candy corn
chocolate-covered cookies (such as Keebler Grasshoppers), cut into quarters

To make one bat bite cupcake:
1. Use a craft stick to spread chocolate frosting onto a cupcake.
2. Add two M&M's candies for eyes.
3. Add two pieces of candy corn for fangs.
4. Add two cookie quarters for ears.

Together

Written by George Ella Lyon
Illustrated by Vera Rosenberry

When friends work together, they can do nearly anything!

Storytime Song

Invite your students to storytime by singing this song to the tune of "If You're Happy and You Know It."

If you'd like to read together,
Come sit down.
If you'd like to read together,
Come sit down.
If you'd like to read *Together*
'Bout a friendship built forever,
If you'd like to read together,
Come sit down.

(Repeat the song until all your youngsters are joined together.)

Once everyone is settled in for storytime, read *Together* aloud.

Friendly Sentences

Learning Links

Create a visual reminder of all the wonderful things friends can do together when you make Friendship Wheels. In advance, photocopy page 221 for each child. Have a child cut out both patterns, including the opening on the top wheel indicated by the dotted lines. Ask her to complete each sentence on the bottom wheel and to add an illustration to the space above it. Have her color the friends on the top wheel. Then have her use a brad to join the two patterns as shown. Just spin the wheel to see the fun friends can have—together!

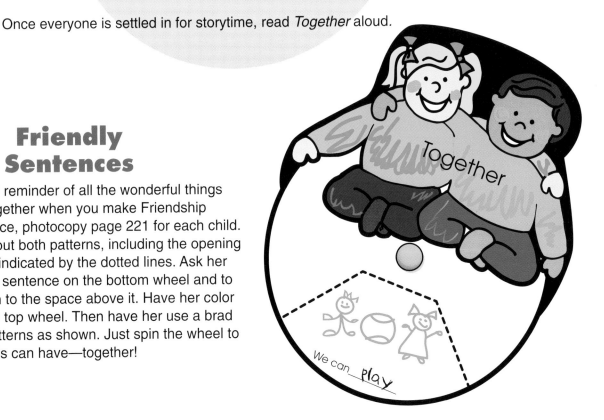

We can play

Art Smarts

Good Buddy Garland

Togetherness and friendship go hand in hand, as you can easily demonstrate with this good-friends garland. In advance, accordion-fold a 6" x 18" strip of white construction paper three times to make four sections. Trace a very simple person shape (as shown) on the folded paper; then cut along your outline, being careful not to cut the edges of the arms. Unfold the paper to reveal a string of four friends. Repeat this procedure until you have one paper friend for each child in your class. Place the strings of friends in your art center, along with a supply of crayons that include various skin tones.

Invite friends to visit your art center in pairs. Have each child in the pair color a paper friend to resemble her partner, carefully choosing crayons to match her friend's skin, hair, eyes, and clothing. After every child has decorated a paper friend, use clear tape to attach the strings of four friends into one long chain. Display the chain on a bulletin board with the title "Hand In Hand, Friends Go Together."

Purposeful Play

Together Time

The friends in *Together* show that it takes two to do many things! Bring home the importance of cooperation by providing some games that need to be played by more than one person. Set up a center with games such as Go Fish, Concentration, and tic-tac-toe. Invite pairs of children to visit this center to play—together, of course!

Storybook Café

Friendship Salad

It takes a whole lot of togetherness to make this salad a success! In advance, send home a note to parents (similar to the one shown). Then get ready for some cooperative cooking!

Supplies:
plastic knives
plastic spoons
disposable bowls
large bowl
large spoon

Ingredients:
fresh fruit provided by students

To make friendship salad:
1. Have each child wash and/or peel his piece of fruit.
2. Have each child use a plastic knife to cut his fruit into small slices or pieces.
3. Place all the cut fruit into a large bowl.
4. Scoop the fruit into individual bowls.

Dear Family:
We will be celebrating the true spirit of friendship by creating a Friendship Salad on _____. Please have your child bring a piece of his or her favorite fruit to share that day.
(date)
Thank you!

The Adventures of Taxi Dog

Written by Debra and Sal Barracca
Illustrated by Mark Buehner

A homeless dog finds love and adventure with a taxi driver named Jim. Join Maxi and Jim as they travel the city of New York picking up interesting people to ride in their cab.

Storytime Song

Your little ones will be ready to ride with Maxi when you call them to storytime with this song sung to the tune of "My Bonnie Lies Over the Ocean."

Oh, look at that dog in the taxi,
Sitting there with his friend Jim.
They drive all around the big city.
People pay just to ride with them.

Riding, riding, in the big city all day-a-a!
Riding, riding, around in the taxi for pay.

So everyone gather together,
And hear all about these two friends,
Riding uptown and downtown,
The taxi dog Maxi and Jim!

(Repeat until your little pups settle down for storytime.)

After your youngsters have gathered around, read *The Adventures of Taxi Dog.*

Learning Links

On-the-Go Graphing

The illustrations in this book depict a city bustling with travelers. This graphing activity will illustrate how many different ways your children have traveled. Prepare a graph by drawing three large inter-secting circles on a sheet of tagboard. Label one circle with a picture of a taxi, one with a bicycle, and one with an airplane. Make a copy of each students' school picture. Revisit the illustrations that show different means of travel, such as by taxi, by bicycle, or by airplane. Then pose the following question to your students: Have you traveled by bike, by taxi, or by airplane? Show students the graph; then discuss that the intersection of circles stands for people who have traveled by two or more of the modes of travel. Ask each child to answer the question by gluing her photo in one of the seven parts of the graph. When each child has participated, discuss the results.

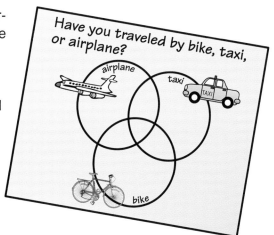

168

Goofy Glasses

Maxi the taxi dog sure likes to joke around! Your students will too when they make these silly glasses just like Maxi's. For each child, provide an inexpensive pair of children's sunglasses (available at party stores) with the lenses removed. Cut three ½" x 2" strips of fake fur for each child. To make a class supply of noses, cut out one egg cup from a cardboard egg carton for each nose, leaving a tab for gluing as shown. To make a pair of silly glasses, a child uses an emery board to roughen the plastic frames, then uses thick craft glue to glue a fake fur eyebrow over each eye. Then he glues the egg cup nose to the nosepiece of the glasses. Finally, he glues a fake fur mustache to the bottom of the egg cup. Allow the glue to dry thoroughly before wearing.

Taxi Time

Turn your dramatic-play area into a Maxi-and-me taxi. Set up four chairs in two rows of two. Make a sturdy steering wheel and a stoplight from heavy cardboard. Have your little ones help you paint these props using tempera paints. Place the steering wheel on the driver's chair and tape the stoplight to a nearby wall. Add a few other props, such as a map of your city, a newspaper, and a toy dog with a red bandana tied around its neck. Finish your taxi by posting a sign that reads "Maxi's Taxi." Then encourage youngsters to take turns cruising the city streets of their imaginations.

Maxi's Delicious Dog Bones and Dip

Every dog loves a bone, but when they are dunked in this dip, they're delicious!

Supplies:
craft sticks
small paper bowls
tablespoon

Ingredients for each child:
1 tbsp. softened cream cheese
1 tbsp. honey
2 large pretzel rods

To make one dog bone with dip:
1. Measure cream cheese and honey into a bowl.
2. Stir the mixture with a craft stick until it is smooth.
3. Dip pretzel bones into dip.
4. Delicious!

169

Curious George and the Pizza

Adapted from the Curious George film series
Edited by Margret Rey and Alan J. Shalleck

Your young readers are sure to cheer the world's most mischievous monkey, who gets into hot water and saves the day during a visit to Tony's pizza parlor.

Storytime Song

Invite youngsters to join you by singing this song to the tune of "I've Been Working on the Railroad."

Tony's serving up the pizza
All the livelong day!
Tony's serving up the pizza
Just to pass the time away.
Do you see a monkey jumping
Up on the counter so high?
Do you see the dough a-flyin'
Up, up to the sky?
Oh, Curious George! Oh, Curious George!
You're in trouble—yessirree!
Oh, Curious George! Oh, Curious George!
You're a tricky monkey!

After all of your youngsters have joined together, read aloud *Curious George and the Pizza*.

Learning Links

Counting Relay

Serve up some counting practice with this number relay. For every six students, color a large paper plate to resemble a cheese pizza. Cut each pizza into six slices; then glue a different number of red circles (pepperoni rounds) onto each slice. For each slice, label a small paper plate with a numeral that matches its number of pepperoni rounds. Store each pizza and its numbered plates in a separate zippered bag.

To play, divide your class into teams of six. Place each pizza and a spatula at one end of an open area. Line up the teams at the opposite end; then give each student a numbered plate for his team's pizza. At your signal, have the first child in each line run to his pizza and serve himself the slice that matches the numeral on his plate. Then have him run back to the end of his line. When the last member of each team serves his pizza and reaches the end of his line, invite the team to cheer, "Hip, hip, hooray! We've got P-I-Z-Z-A!"

Art Smarts

Crayon Dough Magnet

These refrigerator magnets will keep youngsters' minds on pizza all day and all night! In advance, mix together two cups of flour and one cup of salt with enough water to make dough. For each child, place a small portion of the dough on a piece of waxed paper. Have the student shape the dough into a pizza crust. Then have her gently press a layer each of red, yellow, and brown crayon shavings into the crust to represent the sauce and toppings. Bake each pizza in a toaster oven at 250° for about five minutes, or until the crayon is partially melted on the crust. Then air-dry the pizzas for several days. After the pizzas are completely dry, attach a magnet to the back of each.

Purposeful Play

Count on Pizza

Reinforce color or number skills with this small-group game. Collect a stack of sturdy paper or foam plates and a supply of items such as colored cubes or counters. Appoint one child to be Tony, the pizza man. Seat the other players, or customers, at a table. Place a basket containing the items nearby. To play, have Tony circle the table with an empty plate to represent a pizza. In turn, have each customer give her order by reciting, "Tony, Tony, Tony, freeze! Bring me a pizza with [color or number] toppings, please." Direct Tony to stop behind that customer to take her order. Then have him top the pizza with the appropriate number or color of items. After Tony serves the pizza to the customer, give him a new plate and continue the game. Play until each customer is served; then let another child take on the role of Tony.

Storybook Café

Breakfast Pizza

This pizza is the perfect early morning treat, but it's tasty enough to be an anytime eat!

Supplies:
paper plates
toaster oven

Ingredients for each child:
English muffin half
grated cheese
cooked sausage or bacon, crumbled

To make one breakfast pizza:
1. Sprinkle cheese onto muffin half.
2. Top with meat.
3. Heat in toaster oven at 350° until cheese melts.

Farmer Duck

Written by Martin Waddell
Illustrated by Helen Oxenbury

While the lazy farmer lies in bed eating bonbons, his poor duck has to do all the work. It's just not fair! So, the cow, the sheep, and the hens take care of their overworked friend by "taking care" of the farmer in a hilarious act of revolution.

Storytime Song

Invite your ducklings to learn all about the hardworking Farmer Duck by singing this song to the tune of "The Farmer in the Dell."

The farmer sleeps all day.
The farmer sleeps all day.
Who will cook, and clean, and hoe
If the farmer sleeps all day?

Come meet Farmer Duck.
Come meet Farmer Duck.
He works so hard his friends all say,
"Let's help Farmer Duck."

(Repeat until your little ones have waddled to your reading area.)

Once your youngsters have gathered together, read aloud *Farmer Duck*.

Learning Links

Comprehending Conversation

Familiarize your little ducklings with how conversation is written and punctuated with these dialogue-rich booklets. Program the top of four pages with "'How goes the work?' asked the farmer." Program the bottom of each page with a different one of the following:

"Quack!" said the duck.
"Moo!" said the cow.
"Baa!" said the sheep.
"Cluck!" said the hens.

Make a class supply of all four pages. Staple the pages into booklets and give one to each child. Have her draw and color the corresponding animal(s) on each page. Use the booklets to teach your little ones about written conversation, pointing out the use of quotation marks, question marks, exclamation marks, and periods in the text. Afterward, encourage students to add new pages to their booklets by dictating or writing dialogue for other farm animals, then adding illustrations.

Contrast Painting

How does color affect mood? The two sets of end pages in this book offer an interesting contrast in color and mood. Point this out to your students as an introduction to the following painting exploration. Set up two sides of an easel (or two separate work tables) with two very different combinations of colors. On one side, place jars of dreary colors, such as gray, brown, black, and moss green. On the other side, place jars of cheerful colors, such as spring green, sky blue, red, and bright yellow. Assign pairs of students to paint farm scenes. After all of your students have painted, hang the dreary pictures on half of a classroom wall and the cheerful pictures on the other half. Compare and contrast the pictures, discussing how the two groups of pictures differ. Focus on feelings, asking students how the pictures make them feel and how they felt as they were painting the pictures.

Chore Charade

Expand your little ones' knowledge of what a farmer does with a game of Farmer Duck charades. Reread the book, stopping to discuss all of the different tasks done by Farmer Duck. Write down each task on a separate slip of paper. Place all of the slips of paper into a bag and have each child, in turn, draw one. Take her aside and quietly read to her the task she has drawn. Have her act out the task for the class and let class members guess what work she is doing.

Fantastic Farm Mix

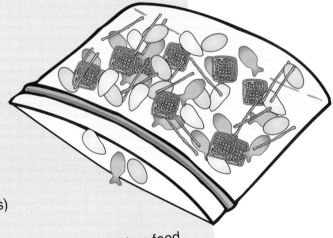

Here's a farm snack that's just right for any season!

Supplies:
zippered sandwich bags
small scoops
tongs

Ingredients (in separate containers):
Corn Pops (pig feed)
Chex cereal (puppy chow)
Goldfish crackers (kitten kibble)
shelled sunflower seeds (chicken feed)
chow mein noodles (hay for horses, sheep, and cows)

To make a serving of fantastic farm mix:
1. Put one scoop each of pig feed, puppy chow, kitten kibble, and chicken feed in the bag.
2. Use tongs to add hay to the bag.
3. Zip and shake bag to mix ingredients.
4. Pig out!

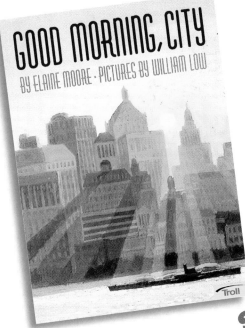

Good Morning, City

Written by Elaine Moore
Illustrated by William Low

Take a peek into the happenings of this busy city as the silvery light of morning floods the sky.

Storytime Song

Call your students to storytime with this song sung to the tune of "Itsy-Bitsy Spider."

The workers in the city work all through the night.
Bakers and grocers work until it's light.
Big trucks work to clean the city streets,
While ships glide up the river at a creep.

Here comes the sun to start a brand-new day.
The city is busy, with cars along the way.
Grown-ups go to work and children go to school.
Good morning, city. How do you do?

(Repeat until your early birds alight in your reading area.)

After your youngsters have gathered around, read aloud *Good Morning, City.*

Learning Links

Sunny Experiment

Your students may be wondering how night turns to day. Try this experiment to illustrate the movement of the sun. Revisit the book, guiding students to notice the progression of light from night to day in the illustrations. Explain that as the earth spins, the light of the sun shines on different parts of the earth. Then head outside to track the sun's movement during your school day. Prepare a mock sundial by inserting a pencil into a margarine tub filled with play dough. Locate a spot near your classroom that receives sun all day. Lay a length of white bulletin board paper on the ground; then place the sundial in the center of the paper. Each hour, visit the sundial, mark where the shadow falls on the paper, and label the mark with the time. At the end of the day, you'll have a visual record of the movement of the sun. Bring the paper inside and tape it to a classroom wall. Invite children to add drawings of what they're doing at each time of day. Good day, children!

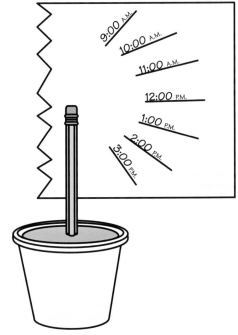

Art Smarts

City Silhouette

Point out the luminous colors in this book to inspire your little ones to create their own cityscapes. In advance, draw several different sizes of city silhouette stencils on tagboard and cut them out. To make a cityscape, a child places a silhouette on a sheet of paper. She uses a purple, blue, orange, pink, red, or yellow oil pastel to outline the border of the stencil, being careful not to smudge the pastel. Next, she removes the stencil, wraps her index finger in tissue paper, and gently smudges the outline outward, feathering it away from the border. She repeats the process as desired, using a different color for each silhouette to create a city filled with sunlight. *(Hint: Use a clean tissue for each color used.)*

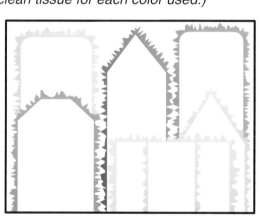

Purposeful Play

Memory Match

Critical-thinking skills are matched with career awareness in this memory game that focuses on the community helpers depicted in *Good Morning, City.* Prepare a set of game cards by duplicating, coloring, laminating, and cutting apart the job cards on page 222. To play, a small group of students lays the cards facedown on a table. In turn, each player turns over two cards. If the cards match the community helper to his job tools, the player may take the cards and then have another turn. If the cards do not match, they are returned to the table facedown and play passes to the next person. Play continues until all the cards have been matched. Good job!

baker

Storybook Café

Sunrise Shakes

Rise and shine! Your students will be feeling sunny when they taste one of these delicious shakes.

Supplies:
blender
small plastic cups
measuring spoons
measuring cups

Ingredients for each child:
1 c. of orange juice
2 tbsp. of powdered milk
2 tbsp. of powdered sugar
1 tsp. of vanilla
5 ice cubes
$\frac{1}{4}$ cherry

To make one sunrise shake:
1. Put all the ingredients (except for the cherry) into the blender.
2. Blend on high for 30 seconds.
3. Pour into the cup.
4. Top with cherry quarter.

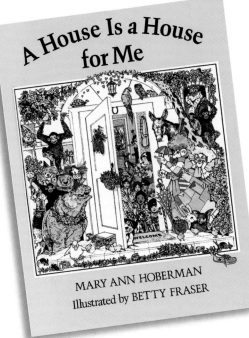

A House Is a House for Me

Written by Mary Ann Hoberman
Illustrated by Betty Fraser

From a pod for a pea to a glove for a hand, all kinds of places serve as houses. Detailed illustrations and whimsical rhymes will engage your young readers and provide an excellent springboard for talking about homes.

Storytime Song

Invite students to storytime by singing the following song to the tune of "Twinkle, Twinkle, Little Star."

A house is a house, oh, can't you see?
A house is a house for you and me.
It could be a hive for a buzzing bee
Or a pod for a little green pea.
A house is a house, oh, can't you see?
Come join our circle and read with me!

(Repeat the song until all of your students have joined together.)

Once your youngsters have all gathered together, read aloud *A House Is a House for Me.*

Learning Links

Comprehension Connection

Use this homey story to strengthen your students' reading comprehension skills. Begin by asking the class to recall the many houses mentioned in the book and the occupants of each. List student responses on the board. Then assign a house and its occupant to each child. Provide each youngster with two index cards. Have her draw the house on one card and its occupant on the other. Under her house drawing, have the student write or dictate "A _____ is a house for a…," filling in the blank with the name of her assigned house. On the other card, have her label her house's occupant.

Collect the completed cards to use in this matching game. Lay the cards faceup on a table. Direct the first player to choose a house card and then find its matching occupant card. If correct, let the student take another turn. Make this game more challenging by setting a time limit for finding a match.

A hive is a house for a…

bee.

Art Smarts

Homey Thoughts

Build a community of delightful dwellings with this fun-to-do activity. For each student, cut out two house shapes from white paper. On one house, cut out one small window flap as shown, cutting the sides and bottom only so that the window can be opened and shut. Attach the other house shape behind this cut-out. As a class, brainstorm other objects that could be considered houses, such as a strawberry as a house for a seed or a dough-nut as a house for a hole. List student responses on the board. Then give each student one of the house shapes made earlier. Below the window, have the student write or dictate "A _____ is a house for a _____," filling in the blanks with one of her ideas. Direct her to lift the window flap and illustrate the idea inside. Then invite the student to decorate the rest of the house with a door, bricks, shutters, or other homey touches. Be sure to display the finished projects at student eye level for easy window watching!

A peel is a house for a banana.

Purposeful Play

Block Building

Call out your pint-size construction crew for this hands-on building center! Place a number of different-size blocks at a center, along with a collection of plastic tools, such as hammers, screwdrivers, saws, and nails (available at many discount stores). If possible, include a few hard hats or plastic base-ball helmets too. After pairing students, encourage each twosome to plan and build a house using the materials pro-vided. Then stand back and watch as students' imaginations and teamwork skills keep building and building!

Storybook Café

Gingerbread Houses

A house for you and a house for me. Gingerbread houses are quite tasty!

Supplies:
paper plates
small rinsed milk cartons
large craft sticks
small cups

Ingredients:
4 tubs of prepared vanilla frosting
2 large boxes of graham crackers
O-shaped cereal
candies for decorating

To make one gingerbread house:
1. Spread frosting on the plate. Gently press the carton on the frosting to secure it to the plate.
2. Spread frosting on the carton's sides. Place graham cracker walls on each side.
3. Spread frosting on the top of the carton. Break crackers in half and attach them to the top as the roof.
4. Spread frosting on the walls and roof. Personalize the house by decorating it with cereal pieces and candy.

Miss Bindergarten
Gets Ready for Kindergarten

Written by Joseph Slate
Illustrated by Ashley Wolff

Travel through the alphabet as Miss Bindergarten and her students get ready to start a brand-new year!

Storytime Song

Get your little ones in the reading mood with this alphabetical invitation to storytime, sung to the tune of "If You're Happy and You Know It."

If your name starts with *A*, come sit down!
If your name starts with *B*, come sit down!
If your name starts with *C, D, E, F, G, H, I,*
If your name starts this way, come sit down!

If your name starts with *J*, come sit down!
If your name starts with *K*, come sit down!
If your name starts with *L, M, N, O,* or *P, Q,*
If your name starts this way, come sit down!

If your name starts with *R*, come sit down!
If your name starts with *S*, come sit down!
If your name starts with *T, U, V, W, X, Y, Z,*
If your name starts this way, come sit down!

Once all of your students have joined together, read aloud *Miss Bindergarten Gets Ready for Kindergarten.*

Beginning Sound Bag

Practicing beginning sounds is as easy as A, B, C, with this fun activity! In a large paper bag, place an object, photo, or picture card to match each letter of the alphabet. With the class, examine the last page in the book, which pictures Miss Bindergarten's new students in alphabetical order. Then select one child to pick an object from the bag and determine which of Miss Bindergarten's students it must belong to (for example, an <u>a</u>pple belongs to <u>A</u>dam <u>A</u>lligator; a <u>b</u>ow belongs to <u>B</u>renda <u>B</u>eaver, etc.). After each student has drawn an object from the bag, have him illustrate the item and its matching book character on a sheet of art paper. Bind the finished pages in alphabetical order to make a class book for your classroom library or writing center.

Art Smarts

Letter Magnet

Beginning letter fun is attractive with this fun-to-do activity. In advance, trace and cut out a letter from heavy tagboard for each student. Provide a variety of art materials, such as crayons, markers, paper scraps, glue, yarn, foil, glitter, and wiggle eyes stickers. Encourage each child to use the materials to transform his cutout into an animal whose name begins with that letter (for example, a cat for the letter *C,* a dog for the letter *D,* etc.). After the student has written his name on the letter, attach an adhesive magnet to the back of it.

Purposeful Play

ABC Bag

Pack your bag—we're off to school! Begin a rollicking rhyming game by having students sit in a large circle. Explain that you need everyone's help to pack a bag to get ready for school. However, everything that goes into the bag must be packed in alphabetical order. Start by reciting this simple rap:

Let's pack a bag to go to school
Because we know that school is cool!
We'll start this game with A, *you see,*
And name new things all the way to Z!

Then say, "In my bag I'll pack [an apple]." Encourage the first child in the circle to repeat the phrase, filling in the blank with something that begins with *B.* Continue around the circle until you've covered the entire alphabet. All packed!

Storybook Café

School Bus Cookies

Your little ones sure "wheel" love these tasty school bus treats!

Supplies:
small paper plates
craft sticks

Ingredients:
box of graham crackers
can of vanilla frosting, tinted with yellow food coloring
bag of Oreo cookies

To make one cookie:
1. Place one whole graham cracker on a plate.
2. Break off one small rectangle from another graham cracker. Then break this rectangle in half. Put one of the two pieces on the end of the whole graham cracker to make a bus shape.
3. Spread frosting on the crackers.
4. Break another small cracker rectangle in half. Stick both pieces to the bus to make windows.
5. Twist apart one Oreo cookie. Place each half on the bus as a wheel.

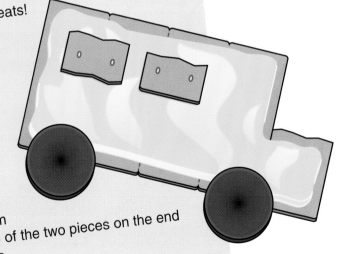

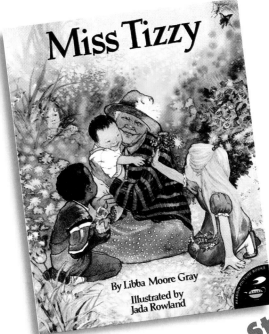

Miss Tizzy

Written by Libba Moore Gray
Illustrated by Jada Rowland

The children in the neighborhood love their grown-up friend, Miss Tizzy. Together they bake cookies, sing, dance, and laugh. And when Miss Tizzy takes ill, the children know just what to do to make their friend feel loved.

Storytime Song

Set the mood for this cozy story by laying a blanket or quilt on the floor near your reading area and adding a bouquet of fresh or artificial wildflowers. Then invite your students to storytime by singing the following verses to the tune of "Pop Goes the Weasel."

All around the neighborhood
The children are a-running
To the pink house down the street.
Come meet Miss Tizzy!

Miss Tizzy is the children's best friend.
She's always lots of fun.
This wonderful lady makes every day great.
Come meet Miss Tizzy!

(Repeat until all of your youngsters have joined the circle.)

When everyone has joined together, read aloud *Miss Tizzy*.

Learning Links

Observing Seed Sprouts

Invite your students to learn about seeds after reading about Miss Tizzy and her lovely garden. Assist your youngsters in making their own window gardens. Have each child stuff a paper towel inside a small plastic jar or a clear plastic cup. Direct the student to push six cress seeds or three lima beans between the side of the container and the paper towel. Then have him lightly water the paper towel. Place the containers on a windowsill and wait for the seeds to sprout, watering them as needed. As a class, observe and record the progress of the seeds each day. When the sprouts have grown several inches tall, remove the plants from the window and send them home for children to plant in their own yards. Miss Tizzy would be proud!

Tizzy Tambourine

Join in Miss Tizzy's weekly Wednesday parades by making these creative tambourines. Have each child paint the bottoms of two small paper plates with watercolors. When the paint is dry, secure the rims of the plates together with several paper clips. Then help the student use a hole puncher to punch holes through the rims. Remove the paper clips and thread a length of yarn through the holes as shown. Thread a jingle bell onto the yarn and secure it with a knot. Invite your youngsters to tap their tambourines as they march around your classroom just like the little ones in Miss Tizzy's parades.

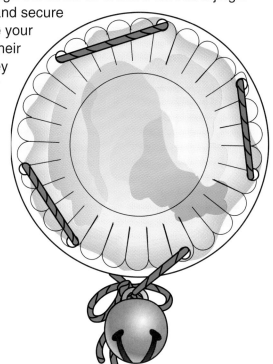

Puppet Place

Send imaginations soaring by transforming your dramatic-play area into a puppet theater. Make a theater by cutting a large window in one side of a tall appliance box. Cut out a door in the back of the box. Then invite a group of students to paint the box. When the paint is dry, place the box in your center along with a collection of puppets. At your art center, let the children create their own simple puppets using materials such as paper bags, glue, scissors, construction paper, wiggle eyes stickers, yarn, small paper plates, and craft sticks. Encore!

Miss Tizzy's Hat

Your little ones are sure to tip their hats to this yummy hat-shaped treat!

Supplies:
small paper plates
craft sticks

Ingredients:
prepackaged sugar cookies
mini muffin
strawberry-flavored cream cheese
purple candy sprinkles

To make one treat:
1. Frost the cookie with cream cheese.
2. Stick the muffin upside down on the center of the cookie and frost it.
3. Decorate the cookie hat with candy sprinkles.

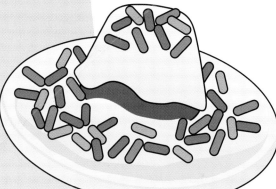

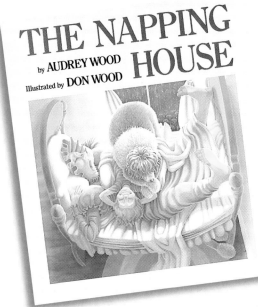

The Napping House

Written by Audrey Wood
Illustrated by Don Wood

This delightful story features a cast of sleepy characters who are simply trying to get a little shut-eye. Young readers will be so enchanted by the marvelous oil paintings and cumulative rhyme that they will ask to hear this story again and again!

Storytime Song

Call your students to storytime by singing this song to the tune of "Hickory, Dickory, Dock."

Everyone's sleeping, you see.
They're awakened by a flea.
The mouse jumps up
And awakes the pup.
Come read the story with me!

Everyone's sleeping, you see.
They're awakened by a flea.
The child is awake,
For goodness' sake!
Come read the story with me!

(Repeat until all of your youngsters have joined together.)

Once everyone is ready, invite them to visit *The Napping House* with you!

Learning Links

Restful Reading Party

Encourage your little readers to snuggle up with a good book by holding a naptime slumber party. Send invitations home with students asking them to bring sleeping bags or favorite blankets to school along with several picture books. For a fun twist, encourage students to also wear their favorite pajamas or bring stuffed animals that they sometimes nap with. On the day of the party, move classroom furniture to the sides of the room. Then invite students to spread out their blankets and bags, and let the reading begin! Encourage youngsters to read both independently and with partners. Take a break from reading to serve some slumber party snacks. While students munch on their fun fare, share a favorite story or two.

You're invited to a Naptime Slumber Party!

Manipulative Math

Wake up students' math skills! Provide each student with a copy of page 223. Direct her to color and cut out the bed and character cards. Then use the manipulatives for these activities:

- Practice counting skills by ringing an alarm clock a given number of times. Ask each student to place the corresponding number of sleepers on the bed.
- Review numeral recognition by showing students a numeral card. Instruct each child to place the corresponding number of sleepers on the bed.
- Strengthen operational skills by sharing story problems about the characters. Have students use the manipulatives to solve the problems. Extend the activity by inviting each youngster to create his own word problem for a partner or cooperative group to solve.

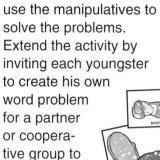

snoozing cat

dreaming child

snoring granny

Naptime Number Game

Books About Places

Your little ones are sure to love this delightful dozing game. Begin by using masking tape to make four large rectangles (beds) on the floor in different areas of the classroom. Number the beds 1–4.

Choose one student to be the wakeful flea and sit him in the center of the room. Tie a scarf loosely around his eyes so he cannot see his classmates, the nappers. At your signal, have the nappers quietly scatter to the different beds as the flea recites this rhyme:

> *Go to bed, you sleepyheads!*
> *Go to bed and slumber.*
> *I am a little wakeful flea,*
> *And I'm going to call a number!*

Once all students are sitting or standing in a bed, ask your flea to announce a bed number. All nappers in that bed are out. Repeat these steps until there is only one remaining napper. Invite her to be the wakeful flea; then play another round.

Storybook Café

Skinny Sleeper Sandwich

Even the sleepiest slumberer is sure to wake up for these sensational sandwiches!

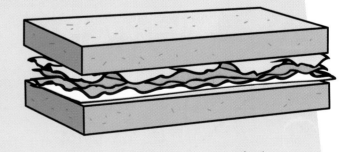

Supplies:
paper plates

Ingredients:
In advance, cut all ingredients into ½" strips.
½ lb. each sliced ham and turkey
½ lb. each sliced Swiss and Muenster cheese
lettuce
loaf of whole wheat bread

To make the sandwiches:
1. Give each student a paper plate, two strips of bread, and one strip each of the other ingredients.
2. Direct each child to place one strip of bread in the center of his plate as the bed.
3. Reread *The Napping House*. As each character climbs onto the bed, instruct each youngster to add an ingredient to his sandwich.
4. When you reach the flea, have each child add the second slice of bread to his sandwich. Invite students to eat their sandwiches as you finish the story.

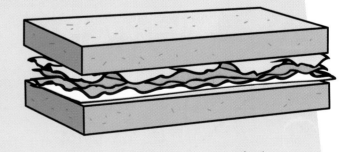

Walter the Baker

Written and illustrated by Eric Carle

When a cat-and-mouse chase ends in spilt milk, Walter the Baker is forced to make his rolls with water instead. The result is a bread so hard that the angry Duke bans Walter from the kingdom unless he can create a special roll in just 24 hours.

Storytime Song

Walter the Baker has quite a challenge before him. Call your children to storytime to find out what happens with this song, sung to the tune of "The Itsy-Bitsy Spider."

Walter the Baker bakes delicious rolls.
The Duke and the Duchess, oh, they love them so!
But then one day the rolls are bad; the Duke is very mad.
He banishes Walter from the town; now Walter's very sad.

Come and join our circle and soon you will know
How Walter changed the Duke's mind with just one piece of
 dough.
He pulled it and pushed it and twisted it around.
Now Walter the Baker makes pretzels for the town.

(Repeat until your budding bakers have all joined together.)

After all of your youngsters are seated, read aloud
Walter the Baker.

Sorting Graph

After reading this tale aloud, roll into an activity that focuses on sorting and graphing skills. In advance, gather at least three different types of pretzels. Give each child a copy of a simple bar graph like the one shown and an assortment of pretzels and crayons. Encourage the child to sort and then graph his pretzels. To extend the activity, have each student record his results on a large class graph. Then, as the children munch on their manipulatives, discuss what the graph reveals.

Art Smarts

Tiny Twists Wreath

The Duke and Duchess would have been pleased to have been presented with one of these petite pretzel wreaths! Have each child glue the sides of eight small pretzel twists together so that they form a circle. When the glue is dry, have her glue another layer of pretzels on top of this circle, positioning the centers of these twists over the connecting sides of the bottom pretzels. When the glue is completely dry, show the student how to weave a length of raffia or ribbon through the holes and tie the ends into a bow.

Purposeful Play

Play Dough

Like Walter in Eric Carle's tale, your little ones will enjoy making their own unique rolls. Enlist the help of your little bakers in preparing a batch of dough. Place eight cups of flour and four cups of salt in your sensory table. Invite students to use their hands to mix the ingredients together. Then add enough water to create a pliable dough. Encourage students to push, pull, twist, and roll the dough to create their own unique rolls. Bake the rolls at 300° for one to 1½ hours (depending on the thickness of each roll). When the rolls have cooled, use them to create a bakery display in the dramatic-play area. *Caution: These rolls are for play only. They are not edible.*

Storybook Café

Perfect Pretzels

Step aside, Walter! Your little chefs will be ready to open up their own bakery after making these sweet, buttery pretzels.

Supplies:
small paper plates
toaster oven

Ingredients for each child:
2 refrigerated biscuits
 ("Texas-style" works best)
cinnamon sugar
spray butter

To make one perfect pretzel:
1. Roll and pull each biscuit into a long, skinny snake. Connect the two biscuits to make one extra long snake.
2. Twist the biscuit snake into a pretzel shape.
3. Bake the pretzel at 400° for 10–12 minutes or until golden brown.
4. Spray the baked pretzel with butter.
5. Sprinkle cinnamon sugar on the pretzel. Then eat!

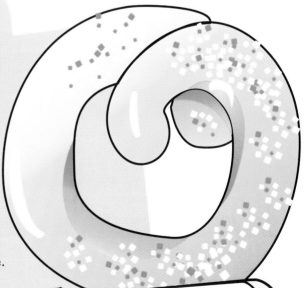

Handsign Cards

Use with "Making Handsigns" on page 28 and "Handy Fingerpainting" on page 29.

Aa	**Bb**	**Cc**	**Dd**	**Ee**
Ff	**Gg**	**Hh**	**Ii**	**Jj**
	Kk	**Ll**	**Mm**	

Use with "Making Handsigns" on page 28 and "Handy Fingerpainting" on page 29.

Nn	Oo	Pp	Qq	Rr
Ss	Tt	Uu	Vv	Ww
Xx	Yy	Zz		

Duck Head and Foot Patterns
Use with "Just Ducky" on page 31.

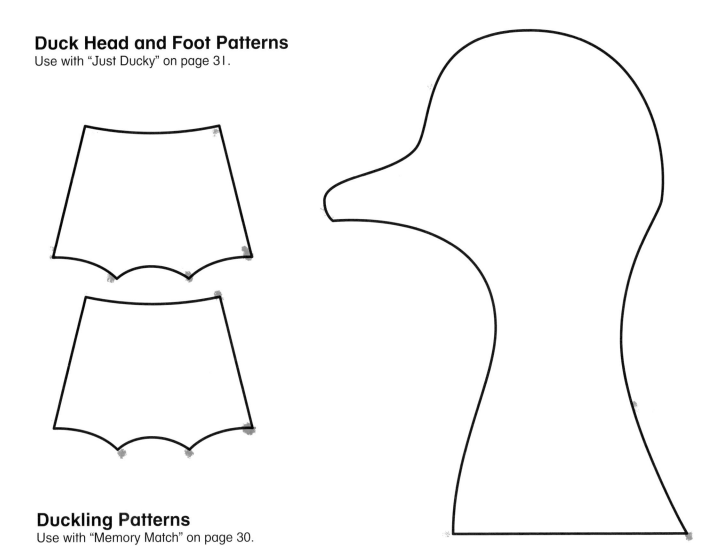

Duckling Patterns
Use with "Memory Match" on page 30.

front	back	in	out
hot	cold	happy	sad
scared	brave	old	young
wet	dry	awake	asleep

Three-in-a-Row Bingo

	Smile!	

Use with "Lunchtime Color Words" on page 42.

Lunch for

Mouse

orange carrot

yellow corn

green peas

blue blueberries

red apple

pink watermelon

Naptime!

Mouse Patterns
Use with "Lunchtime Color Words" on page 42 and "Mouse Print Count" on page 43.

Hand Pattern
Use with "Handy Color Identification" on page 48.

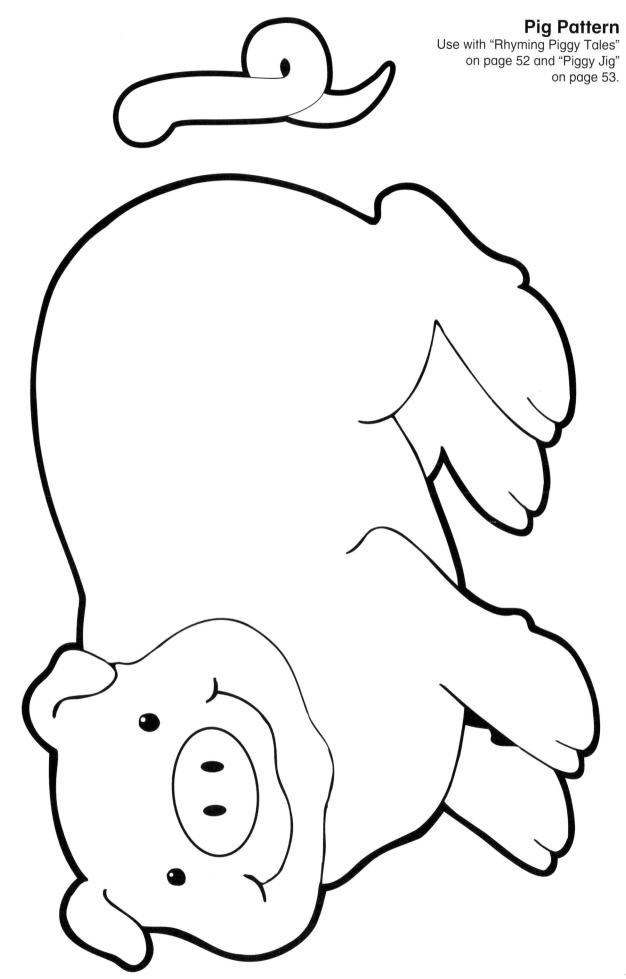

Animal Patterns
Use with "Rhyme Time" on page 60.
Use the duck pattern with "Muddy Muck Masterpiece" on page 135.

duck

pig

trout

goat

cow

hen

lamb

goose

Bear Pattern

Use with "Rhyming Class Book" on page 62.

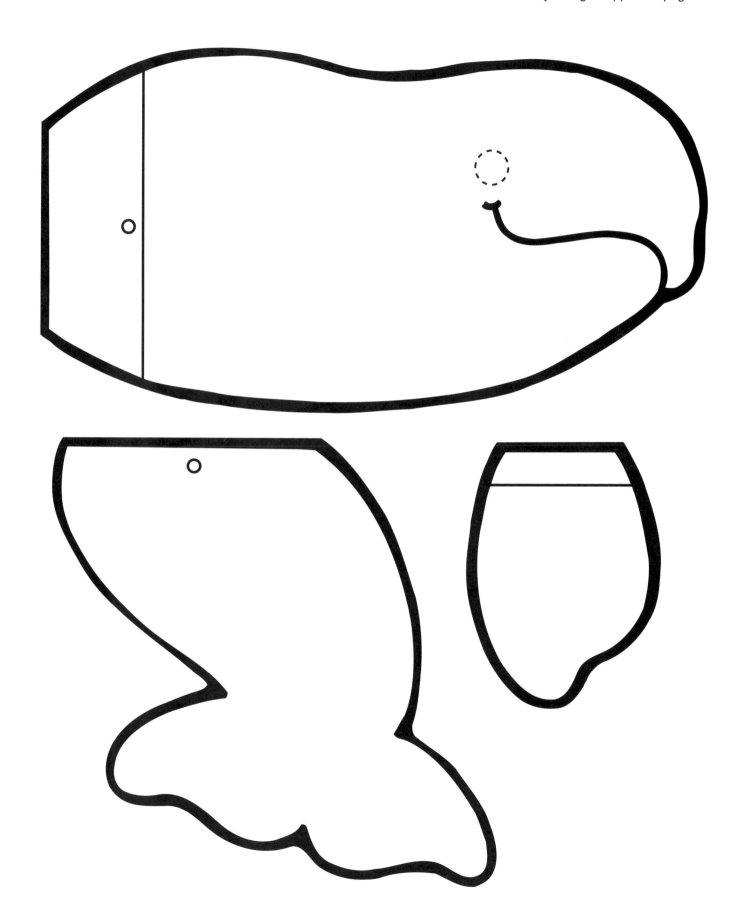

Animal Patterns

Use with "Sequential Story Recall" on page 72.
Use the bear pattern with "Shadow Puppet" on page 103.

Flying Squirrel Patterns

Use with "Prior Knowledge Prompt" on page 86 and "Squirrel Puppets" on page 87.

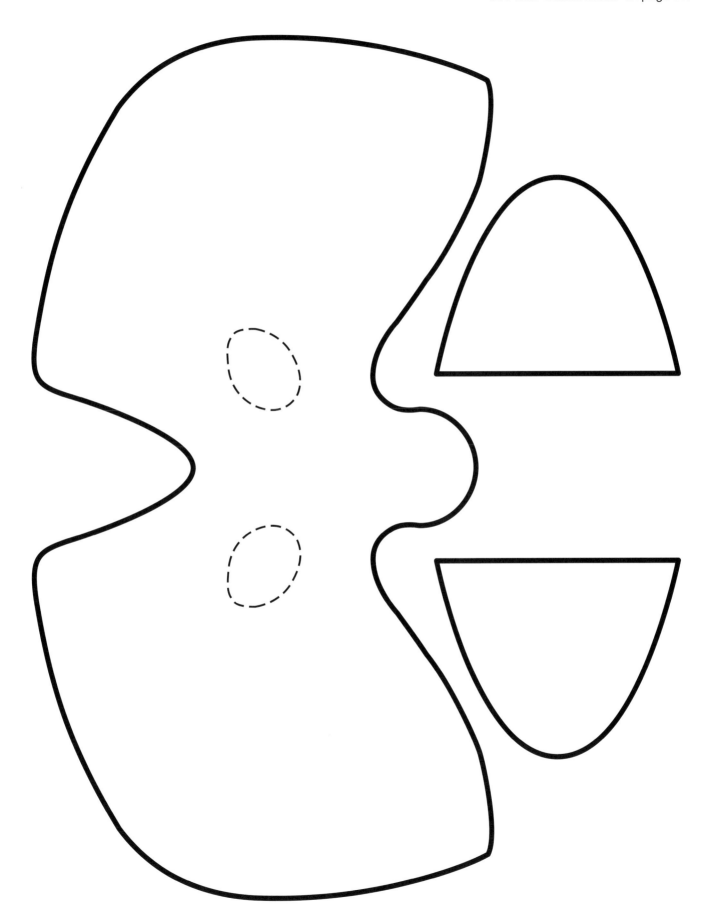

Pond Animal Cards

Use with "Critter Classification" on page 92 and "Jump Tag" on page 93.

turtle

goldfish

catfish

frog

cat

dog

Woodland Animal Patterns

Use with "Sequential Line Up" on page 98 and "Colorful Fall Project" on page 99.

bear

skunk

woodchuck

snail

ladybug

turtle

Cat and Dog Patterns

Use with "Pet Patterns" on page 104 and "Headband Prop" on page 105.

Dear Parent,

    We are all working very hard to learn important phone numbers: our home numbers, parents' work numbers, or numbers of close relatives or neighbors. To make sure your child is learning the correct phone numbers, please complete this form and return it as soon as possible. Thank you for your help!

Person or Place

Phone Number

_____

_____

_____

©The Education Center, Inc. • *Literature for Little Learners* • TEC60786

Dear Parent,

    Our class has been reading *Franklin's Bad Day* by Paulette Bourgeois. In the story, Franklin writes to a friend who has moved away. He includes several self-addressed stamped envelopes so that his friend may write back. We are planning an activity to follow Franklin's example. Please help your child decide on a person to whom he or she will write (this might be a relative or a friend). Provide the information below for that person. Then return this form by _____ with two postage stamps. Thanks for your help!

(date)

Name _____

Street _____

City _____

State _____ Zip _____

©The Education Center, Inc. • *Literature for Little Learners* • TEC60786

Bunny and Text Patterns
Use with "Estimation Jar" on page 114
and "Bunny Card" on page 115.

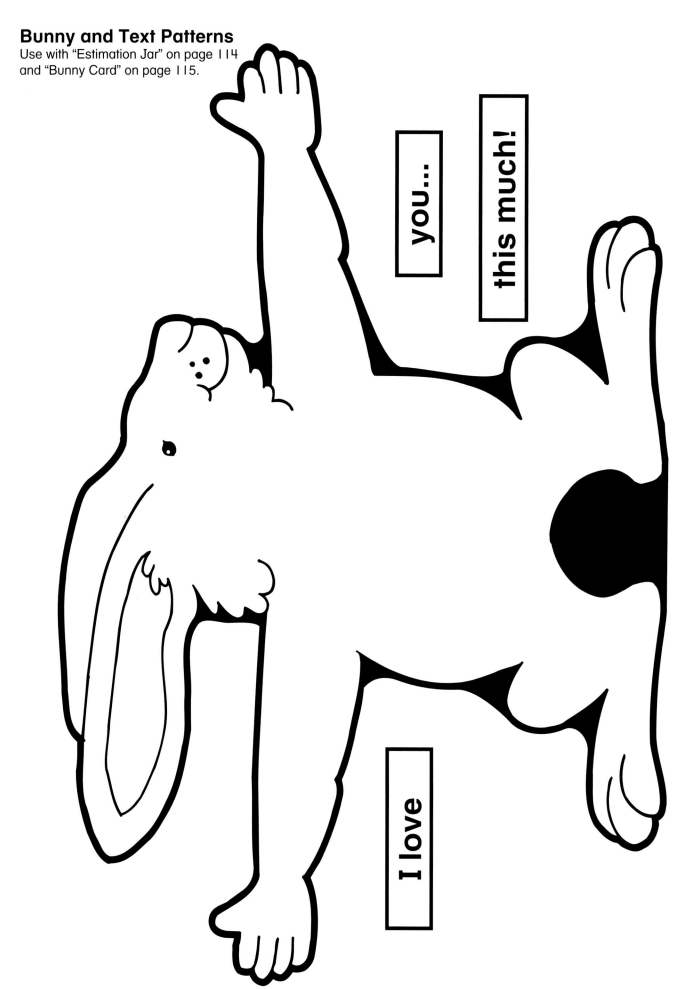

you...

this much!

I love

Hippo Pattern

Use with "Happy Hippo Counting" on page 116 and "Fashionable Hippos" and "Sandy Measurement" on page 117.

Flower Patterns

Use with "Loving Sentences" on page 118.

petals

center

I love for you to...

I love you for the things you do,
And just because you are you!

I love for you to...

I love for you to...

I love for you to...

I love for you to...

I love for you to...

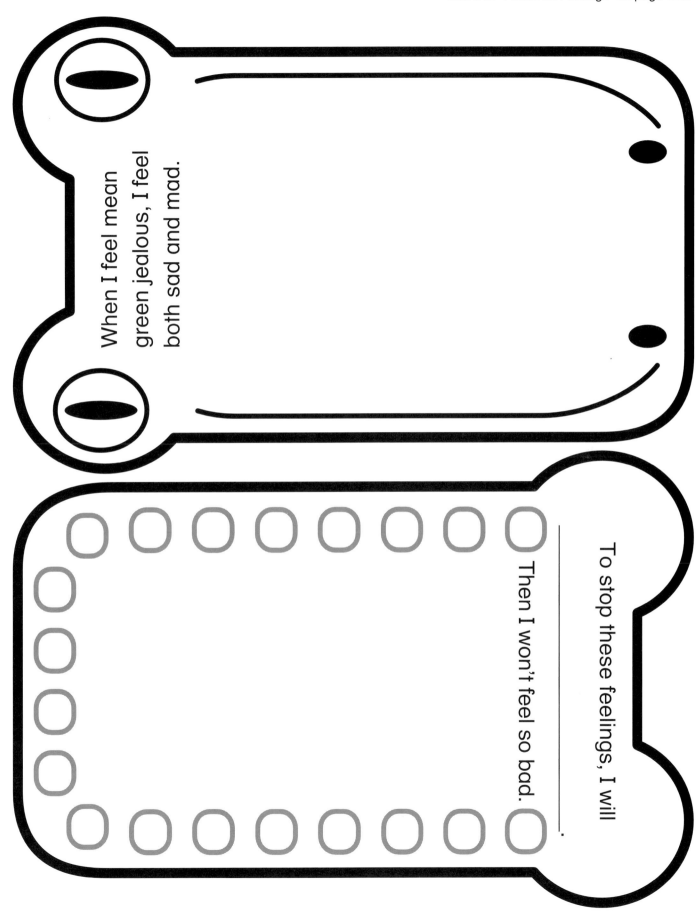

When I feel mean green jealous, I feel both sad and mad.

To stop these feelings, I will

Then I won't feel so bad.

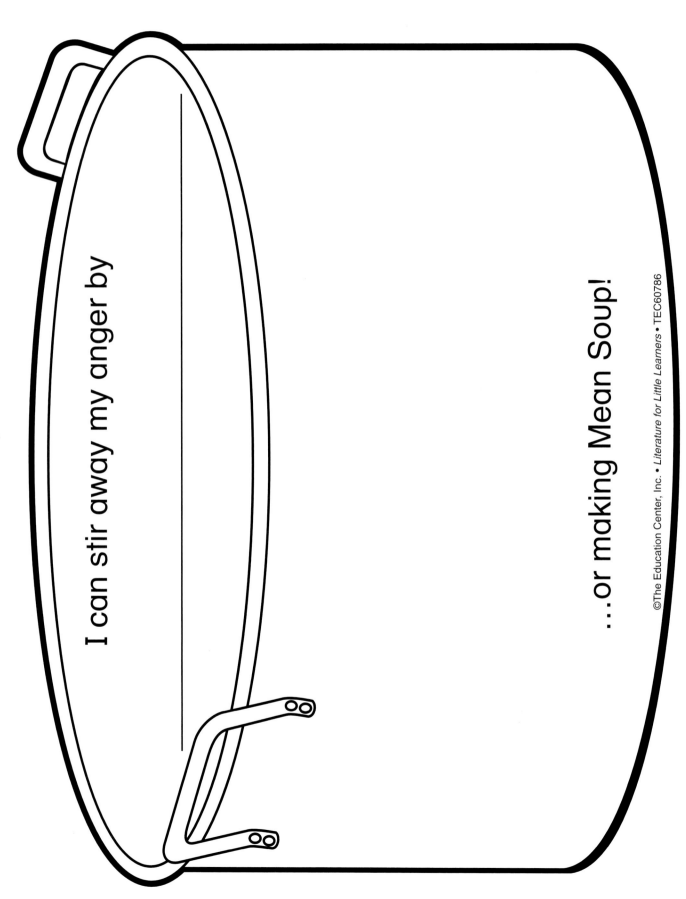

I can stir away my anger by

...or making Mean Soup!

Book Page Pattern
Use with "Color Word Flips" on page 136.

What is the principal wearing today?

- A _____ shirt,

  a _____ tie,

cut here

- and _____ pants.

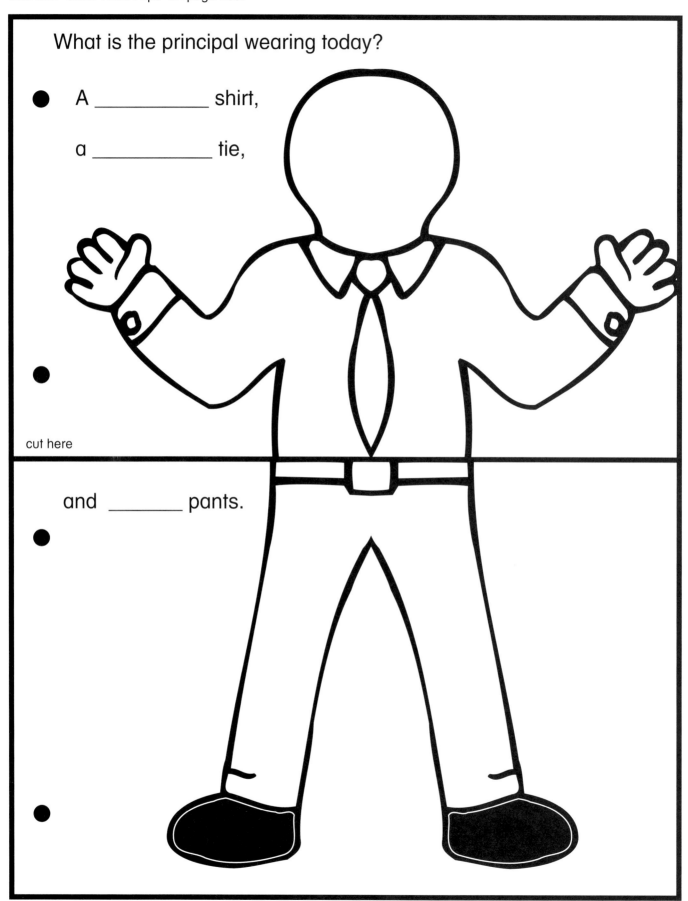

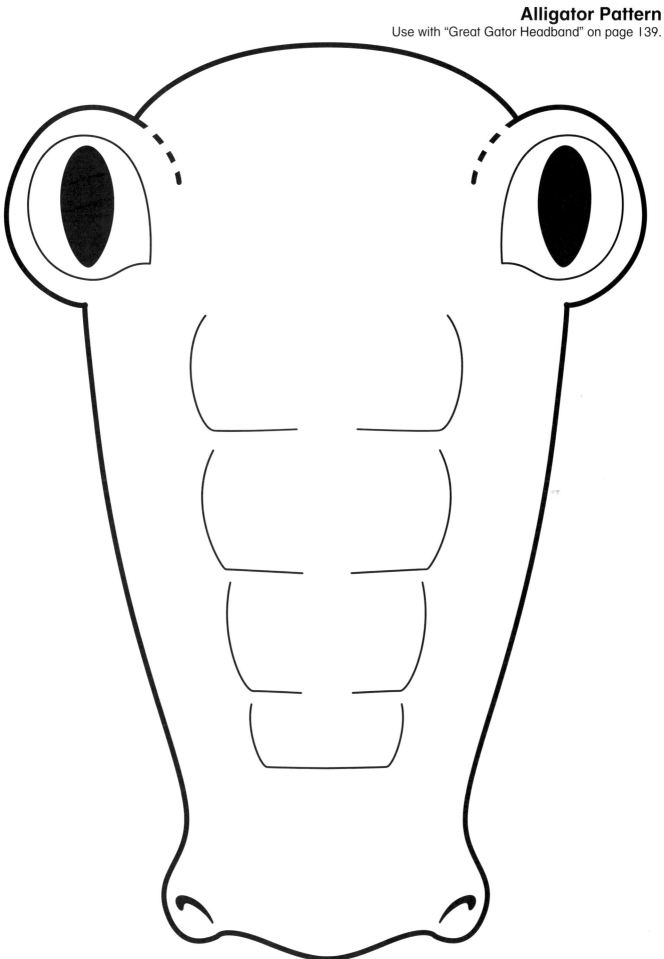

Name _____

Suitcase Sorting

 Color.

 Cut.

Glue.

Clothes	Toys	Other

©The Education Center, Inc. • *Literature for Little Learners* • TEC60786

Note to the teacher: Use with "Circle-Time Sort" on page 142.

carpenter   doctor   police officer   baker   letter carrier

Poem
Use with "Poem Pop-Up" on page 147.

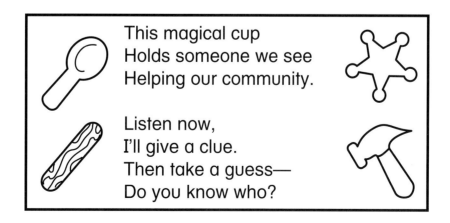

This magical cup
Holds someone we see
Helping our community.

Listen now,
I'll give a clue.
Then take a guess—
Do you know who?

Buddy Pattern
Use with "Buddy Boasting Interview" on page 150.

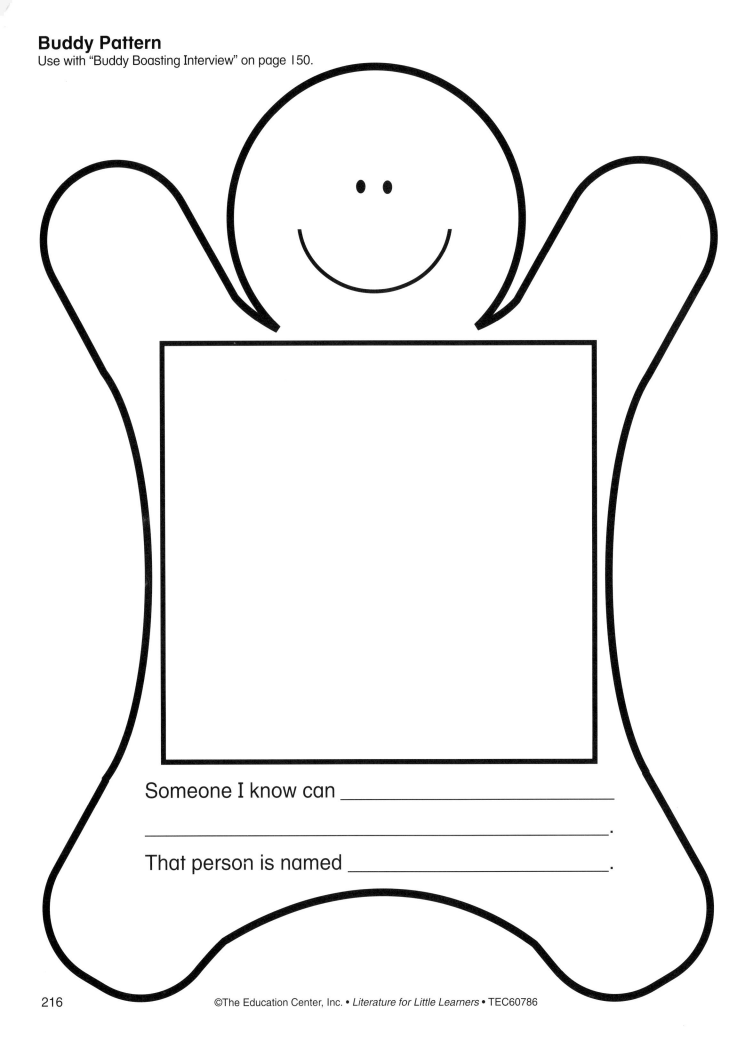

Someone I know can _____

_____.

That person is named _____.

©The Education Center, Inc. • *Literature for Little Learners* • TEC60786

Hello! My name is _____.

How are you today?

Turn the page and you'll find out

Who my neighbor is today!

Making Choices

Safe or Unsafe?

Color.

✂ Cut.

Glue.

Unsafe

Safe

Play with a stray dog.

Sleep in the dark.

Try a new food.

Ride a bike with no hands.

Attack an imaginary monster.

Walk alone in a strange place.

Note to the teacher: Use with "Think Safety" on page 160.

Grandpa Pattern and Clothing

Use with "Different Dress-Up Discoveries" on page 162.

©The Education Center, Inc. • *Literature for Little Learners* • TEC60786

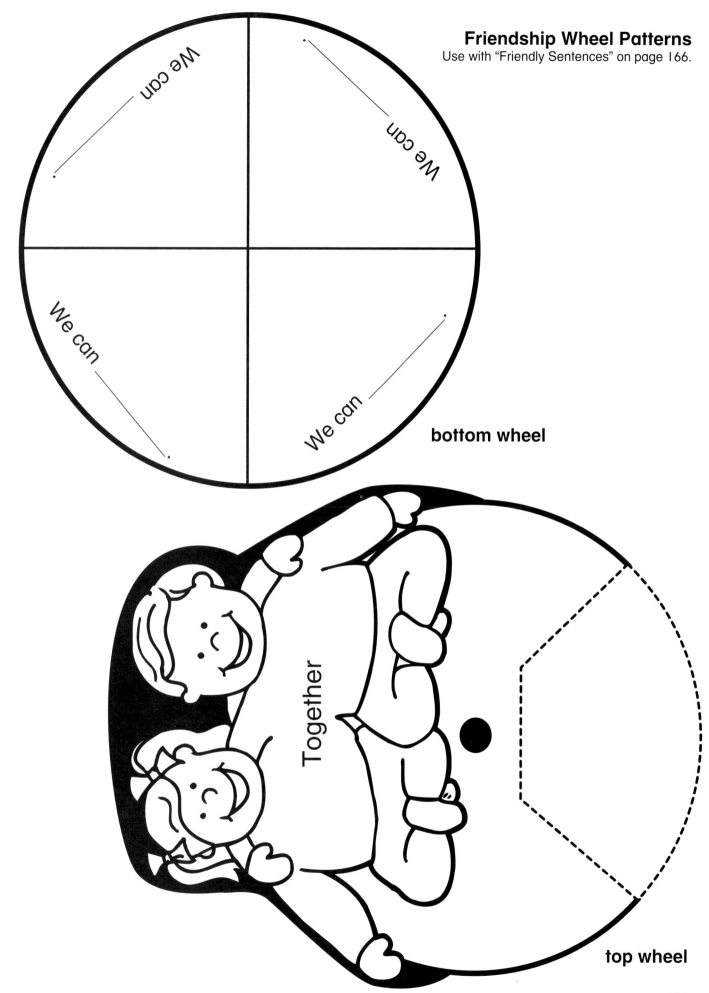

We can

We can

We can

We can

bottom wheel

Together

top wheel

Job Cards

Use with "Memory Match" on page 175.

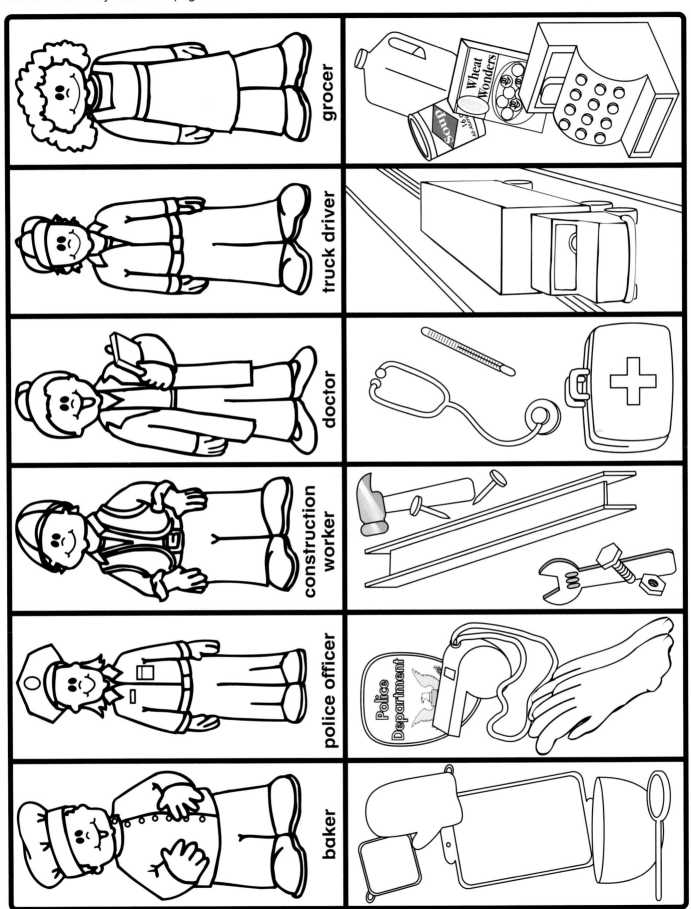

grocer

truck driver

doctor

construction worker

police officer

baker

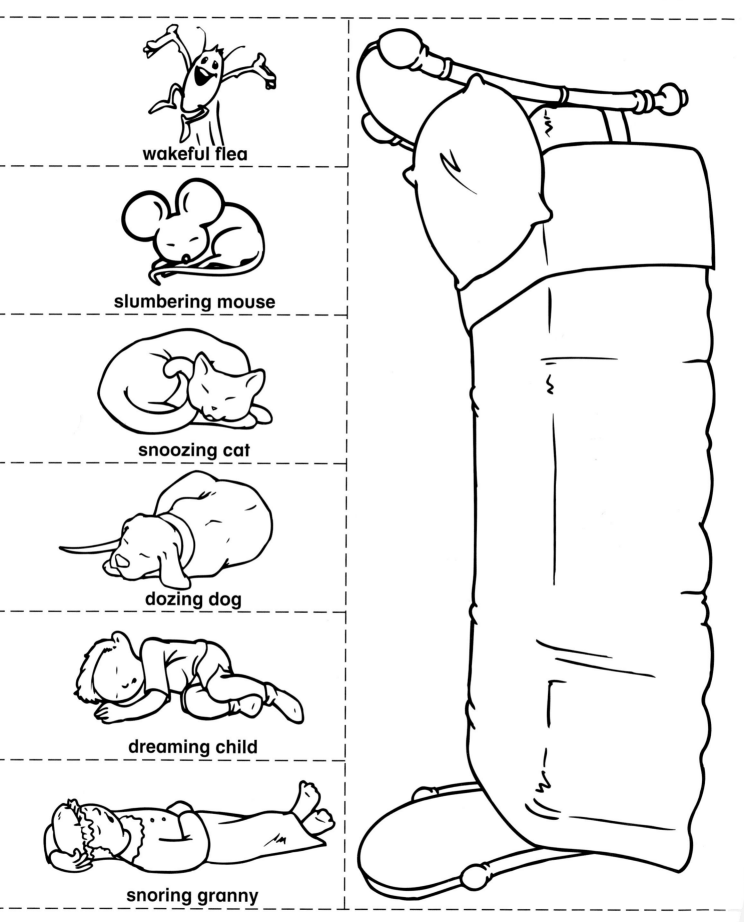

wakeful flea

slumbering mouse

snoozing cat

dozing dog

dreaming child

snoring granny

Literature
for Little Learners

Managing Editor: Cindy Daoust
Editor at Large: Diane Badden
Editors: Becky Andrews, Ada Goren, Kim T. Griswell, Mackie Rhodes, Allison E. Ward
Contributing Writers: Joe Appleton, Sue DeRiso, Lucia Kemp Henry, Lisa Kelly, Lori Kent, Suzanne Moore, Mary Nethery, Kathleen Padilla
Copy Editors: Tazmen Carlisle, Amy Kirtley-Hill, Karen L. Mayworth, Kristy Parton, Debbie Shoffner, Cathy Edwards Simrell
Cover Artist: Rebecca Saunders
Art Coordinator: Rebecca Saunders
Artists: Pam Crane, Theresa Lewis Goode, Clevell Harris, Ivy L. Koonce, Clint Moore, Greg D. Rieves, Rebecca Saunders, Barry Slate, Stuart Smith, Donna K. Teal
The Mailbox® Books.com: Jennifer Tipton Bennett (DESIGNER/ARTIST); Karen White (INTERNET COORDINATOR); Paul Fleetwood, Xiaoyun Wu (SYSTEMS)

President, The Mailbox Book Company™: Joseph C. Bucci
Director of Book Planning and Development: Chris Poindexter
Curriculum Director: Karen P. Shelton
Book Development Managers: Cayce Guiliano, Elizabeth H. Lindsay, Thad McLaurin
Editorial Planning: Kimberley Bruck (MANAGER); Debra Liverman, Sharon Murphy, Susan Walker (TEAM LEADERS)
Editorial and Freelance Management: Karen A. Brudnak; Sarah Hamblet, Hope Rodgers (EDITORIAL ASSISTANTS)
Editorial Production: Lisa K. Pitts (TRAFFIC MANAGER); Lynette Dickerson (TYPE SYSTEMS); Mark Rainey (TYPESETTER)
Librarian: Dorothy C. McKinney

©2003 by THE EDUCATION CENTER, INC.
All rights reserved.
ISBN# 1-56234-576-1

Manufactured in the United States
10 9 8 7 6 5 4 3 2